Kitchen Garden Cooking
with kids

Kitchen Garden Cooking with Kids

Stephanie Alexander with Anna Dollard

Photography by Simon Griffiths

LANTERN
an imprint of
PENGUIN BOOKS

LANTERN

Published by the Penguin Group
Penguin Group (Australia)
250 Camberwell Road, Camberwell, Victoria 3124, Australia
(a division of Pearson Australia Group Pty Ltd)
Penguin Group (USA) Inc.
375 Hudson Street, New York, New York 10014, USA
Penguin Group (Canada)
90 Eglinton Avenue East, Suite 700, Toronto ON M4P 2Y3, Canada
(a division of Pearson Penguin Canada Inc.)
Penguin Books Ltd
80 Strand, London WC2R 0RL, England
Penguin Ireland
25 St Stephen's Green, Dublin 2, Ireland
(a division of Penguin Books Ltd)
Penguin Books India Pvt Ltd
11 Community Centre, Panchsheel Park, New Delhi – 110 017, India
Penguin Group (NZ)
Cnr Airborne and Rosedale Roads, Albany, Auckland, New Zealand
(a division of Pearson New Zealand Ltd)
Penguin Books (South Africa) (Pty) Ltd
24 Sturdee Avenue, Rosebank, Johannesburg 2196, South Africa

Penguin Books Ltd, Registered Offices: 80 Strand, London WC2R 0RL, England

First published by Penguin Group (Australia), 2006

1 3 5 7 9 10 8 6 4 2

Text copyright © Stephanie Alexander and Anna Dollard 2006
Recipes copyright © Stephanie Alexander 2006
Illustrations copyright © Simon Griffiths 2006

The moral right of the author has been asserted

Designed by Tony Palmer © Penguin Group (Australia)
Front cover photograph by Simon Griffiths, back cover photographs by Simon Griffiths and others (see below)
All internal photographs by Simon Griffiths except for those on pages i, 3 (right), 5 (top and bottom), 9 (bottom), 14 (all), 21 (all), 22, 29 (top right, centre,
bottom right, top left), 30, 34 (top right, bottom left), 39 (centre, bottom right, bottom left), 45 (top, right, bottom), 52 (left), 57, 60 (all), 65 (bottom right,
top left), 66 (all); these are by or have been provided by Stephanie Alexander, Kirsty Argyle, Peta Christensen, Anna Dollard, Peta Heine, Liz Moore,
Heidi Sanghvi, Karen Yann and others, as part of the documentation of the Kitchen Garden program

Typeset in 10.5 Berkeley Old Style Book by Post Pre-press Group, Brisbane, Queensland
Colour reproduction by Splitting Image, Clayton, Victoria
Printed and bound in Singapore by Imago Productions

National Library of Australia
Cataloguing-in-Publication data:

Alexander, Stephanie, 1940–.
Kitchen garden cooking with kids: the story of a kitchen garden for kids and the recipes they cooked with the food they grew.

Includes index.
ISBN-13: 978 1 920989 49 1.
ISBN-10: 1 920989 49 8.

1. Kitchen gardens. 2. Vegetable gardening. 3. Cookery (Vegetables). 4. Cookery – Juvenile literature.
I. Dollard, Anna, 1965–. II. Griffiths, Simon (Simon John). III. Title.

635.0484

www.penguin.com.au

Contents

Introduction

What is a kitchen garden? A kitchen garden is a garden created to provide edible, aromatic and beautiful resources for a kitchen. This book tells the story of one garden established in a particular place at a particular time. It does not provide a complete or precise blueprint for making other school gardens. What I do hope is that this story will provide inspiration, motivation and perhaps the underpinnings of a broad philosophy for the teachers, principals and parents setting out to establish kitchen gardens in their own schools, community sites and even private homes.

Just as each kitchen garden is different, each kitchen garden teacher will design their classes accordingly. Six such teachers have participated in the program at Collingwood College at various stages and each has brought with them their own vision of how best to organise the classes. Much of the practical information presented in the following chapters is a synthesis of these individual contributions.

While it is impossible for any one kitchen garden, and therefore kitchen garden class, to be seen as a template for another, we have worked with children in non-classroom settings now for five years and we know what they respond to and like doing, and the sorts of things that help them learn. Scattered throughout these pages are class plans, ideas for activities and games, and basic-equipment lists – information that other schools will be able to use as a starting point for their own class planning.

This is a book about a garden, but it is not a gardening book. You won't find specific information here on, say, the parts of a plant. But it is very much a cookbook, one with plenty of information on seasonal availability of garden produce and recipes that describe how to turn produce into dishes that children will love to cook as well as eat. In all, the book contains around 120 recipes, grouped into thirty-two menus – one for almost every week of the school year. The recipes have been written to be read and cooked by children. All have been tried and tested at Collingwood College, and are equally suitable for children cooking at home with adult supervision.

The cooking program at Collingwood College has never underestimated what children can achieve and what kind of food they will enjoy eating. I have worked as a kitchen volunteer at Collingwood College almost every week for five years. During that time I have watched with delight as small hands have chopped, mixed, rolled, stuffed, shaped and baked an impressive array of ingredients, including produce grown by the children in the garden. And every week, as I have looked at the children arrange their lovely dishes with such pride and care, it has made me sad to realise that so few parents, teachers and policymakers get to see and appreciate what young children are capable of when it comes to the preparation and enjoyment of good food.

Many, many people and organisations have been involved with the Kitchen Garden at Collingwood College, and each has brought with them enormous insight, energy, skills and enthusiasm.

My former personal assistant and co-author Anna Dollard has been there from the beginning. There would be no Kitchen Garden at Collingwood College were it not for Anna. She has been

Anna Dollard and Stephanie Alexander in the Kitchen Garden at Collingwood College

far more than my right-hand person. She has challenged, she has researched, she has refined submissions, she has listened, she has collated and recorded, she has carted manure, she has provided the thermos and, most importantly of all, she has believed in the project from the very first day and has been a loving friend throughout this enormous adventure.

There are a number of other people, and one important organisation, whose contributions have been of such significance that it is hard to imagine how the project could have come together without them. They are: community garden activist Basil Natoli; principal Frances Laurino; vice-principal Stanley Pamieta; school-teachers Mary-Ann De Carlo, Ken Watson and Kevin Conroy; garden and kitchen teachers at Collingwood College, Peta Christensen, Liz Moore, Heidi Sanghvi, Peta Heine, Karen Yann and Desley Insall; parent and architect Freda Thornton; gardener Shane Quinn; mother, volunteer and major donor Barbara Heine; the not-for-profit organisation Cultivating Community; and the tirelessly committed volunteer team. The contributions of these people and many, many others are outlined in the following chapters.

But from the beginning the children have been at the heart of the program, and their enthusiastic responses have determined the program's direction more forcefully than anything else. The children have given us the strength and motivation to overcome the numerous obstacles we have faced along the way, including the perennial threat of funding shortfalls and the ongoing quest for more resources.

MY IDEA SEEMED SIMPLE. I wanted to get children gardening and cooking in order to teach them about the joys and benefits of freshly grown food. To do this, I needed to find a primary school with the following attributes: one, a bit of spare land to grow some fruit and vegetables; two, an innovative principal with a shared concern for the eating habits of young children, a commitment to the practice of community involvement and a willingness to contemplate the educational relevance of this hands-on approach.

I set this down as my departure point. Typically, I ignored all the reasons why such an idea would be difficult to achieve: Who would fund, build and manage the garden? How would this program fit in with the rest of the curriculum? Would there even be time in the curriculum for gardening classes? And if so, who would teach these classes?

My starting point was nothing more than a belief that the idea could work, along with the refrain 'Just do it!'

This is the story of how we 'just did it', of how my simple idea was transformed with the help of many talented and passionate people into a vigorous reality – the Kitchen Garden at Collingwood College, in the inner-city Melbourne suburb of Collingwood.

Beginnings

Inspirations

Early on

When I was a small child, it was my mother's father who cared for our garden – the first garden I remember. His passion was growing dahlias, but he also tended the few fruit trees we had growing in our suburban backyard. I remember a photo of myself aged around six, holding a peach in a rather stagey way, as I stood beneath a laden tree. By the time I was nine, the family had moved to a seaside town on a large bush block, and my maternal grandparents had both died. My father's father came to live with us, and he and my mother plotted and planned and planted an enormous garden of herbs and fruit trees and duck enclosures and leafy crops of potatoes, sweetcorn and cottage flowers. My father cared for the cows (two) and built the caravan park that was to provide the family income. In the evenings we had music and books, discussion and argument and, of course, the lovely food cooked by my mother, which we ate sitting at the large round table made by my father.

This idyllic picture took place before 1956, the year television arrived. It wasn't all idyllic of course. My brothers were asthmatics, my father was often depressed, Grandpa was a radical revolutionary and my mother sometimes displayed a gloomy, pessimistic view of the future. Nevertheless, when we came together over dinner, we usually set aside our woes to enjoy one another's company and my mother's wonderful food. It has always been the food that I remember.

Food was the first colour in my life, followed by the colours of the garden. Certainly it was the taste, but so much more as well. It was the conviviality, the invitation to be together with my mother and share in the kitchen doings, the passing-on of her kitchen wisdom, the closeness sometimes missing in our day-to-day exchanges, the satisfaction of achievement, the gathering of family, the sense that if all else was sinking, there would still be the food.

Dad made our family table. It was a round table of silky oak, rather Art Deco in style, I now realise, with its circular top and central cylindrical trunk. Where the trunk met the tabletop, Dad had inserted a circle of smoky glass, with a small light to illuminate the glass from below. For parties, my mother arranged dainty strewings of love-in-the-mist, blue salvia, pink phlox and other cottage flowers on the glass, and the petals would glow translucently in the reflected light. 'Why don't you grow proper flowers?' I asked accusingly and hurtfully. By 'proper flowers' I meant the showy roses I admired in other people's gardens, an early example of a failing to understand personal style. My mother always preferred the slightly retiring, overlooked or elusive, as opposed to the dramatic or flamboyant. She was like that herself. I think I have inherited this.

Grandpa starred at our rare family gatherings. He was one of nine children and when my great-uncles assembled, there was much riotous conversation as these grand old men with their magnificent heads of white hair and brilliantly blue eyes began to reminisce about Gippsland in the old days – about bushfires, farming disasters, courting exploits, snake stories, and the musical evenings that had been the family entertainment when they were young. Invariably, there would be disagreements and usually a few songs, sung in still-strong tenor voices, including some hymns from their days at the Poowong Methodist church.

And the wonderful food just kept on coming: beef casseroles or meat loaf; heaped bowls of home-grown vegetables or vegetables from the newly discovered Italian greengrocer; Polish dishes or Austrian dishes; dishes inspired by Mum's attendance at an early class of Elizabeth Chong, probably Melbourne's first teacher of Chinese cookery; or a searing curry after a trip to Sri Lanka. Mum's curiosity knew no bounds and she was game to try anything at all and substitute if an unusual ingredient could not be found locally.

Several lifetimes later, in reality fifty years on, almost everything has changed. The great-uncles and Grandpa and Mum and Dad have all gone. The next generation of family is widely scattered. The table, surprisingly, still exists – in Darwin – still highly valued, if a little warped by tropical heat. But the memories of all that went on around that shared table will never be lost.

I have written of my childhood and the culinary skill of my mother before. It is important to mention it again in telling this particular story because I know how important my early food experiences were in setting me on my path – my more than thirty years' work in restaurants, every day consumed with the desire to offer pleasure and lovely flavours to others. But growing up around a table with three generations present also contributed to my understanding of the world in a broader sense, allowing me to challenge and be challenged, forcing me to develop my own ideas, opening my eyes to the realisation that there is always more than one way to proceed.

Over the years, I have had the pleasure of working with many young people: apprentices, waiters, kitchen hands and young cooks. It has come as a very pleasant and unexpected bonus of my work to realise the influence I have had on them. I have tried to use this influence responsibly, to be positive and encouraging, always allowing my enthusiasms, knowledge and passions to be freely communicated. Nevertheless, there were times when I could not help but be astonished at how little some of my trainees and recruits knew about gardens in particular, and the growing world in general. Many did not understand simple notions, such as the fact that fruit follows flowers. They had only a vague understanding of the seasons, and many of them had limited experience of different foods. And these were people who were planning a career in the food world!

During my professional career, the food scene in Melbourne has been transformed out of all recognition in terms of the availability of ingredients. This has impacted on restaurants and on travelled and affluent middle-class families, but for others, the preparation and cooking of simple fresh food has become, conversely, something of a mystery.

Alongside the expanding array of fresh food on offer, there has been an upsurge in the availability of packaged and pre-prepared food. Our daily food rituals have changed beyond recognition. Many adults live alone. Single-parent families are more common. In many families, both parents work very long hours and food preparation is seen as a chore or is dispensed with altogether in favour of eating out or taking-out. Cafe society has boomed. The family table has taken a battering. Far fewer families eat together on a regular basis and it is not uncommon for children to eat on their own in front of a television set, where the only advice they receive regarding food choices is from the manufacturers of convenience foods.

It is the fate of the children that concerns me. Statistics show that more than one-quarter of our children are overweight. Few children eat the number of serves of fruit and vegetables recommended for optimum health. Many children are leading more and

< Stephanie exploring her first garden

< David and Beau work with Stephanie in the kitchen

> Freshly picked herbs

> Our first garden teacher, Peta Christensen

more sedentary lives. The intake of snacks featuring high levels of fat, sugar and salt is widespread and crosses all socioeconomic boundaries. Education about food choices has almost entirely disappeared from school curricula and in too many homes nobody is offering positive examples of healthy eating. Over the past twenty years, various state and federal campaigns have sought to address these problems. But while these initiatives have raised awareness among health professionals, little else has been achieved. Obesity levels continue to increase. We are warned there is a public health crisis looming, with rates of diabetes, heart disease and cancer expected to rise.

And yet, with all these horror statistics, what seems to be missing is any thinking outside the square. Nobody is talking about the absence of love and enjoyment in the preparation of food, let alone the ability to care for oneself by preparing simple, healthy dishes.

Tables and pyramids, 'good' foods and 'bad' foods, guidelines to canteen managers and discussions centred on 'health' and 'nutrition' have all failed to make changes in the food habits of our children. For the past fifteen years or so, I have been involved in think tanks, symposiums, public forums, conferences, and festivals, and at each of these events the same questions have surfaced: Is there an Australian cuisine? What is the food of the future? But what has not been understood by those asking the questions is that unless we can influence children, unless we involve children in pleasurable food activities from an early age, we are just going to have more of the same, and, in fact, we will start to have less of what we have now.

Hence the Kitchen Garden at Collingwood College. It exists as a pilot project that offers children pleasurable experiences in growing, harvesting, preparing and sharing food, which will equip them with practical and necessary life skills, provide knowledge that will make them more discerning consumers and hopefully lead to broader and more enjoyable food lives. Along the way the project also encourages cooperative effort, awakens understanding of landcare and water management, provides considerable boosts to self-esteem and offers opportunity for physical activity.

Further afield

This book is being written in late 2005. It is not accidental that in 2005, chef and food activist Jamie Oliver achieved nationwide media attention in Britain and later in Australia for his efforts to improve the school dinners being served to British children, as shown in the television series *Jamie's School Dinners*. He identified similar problems in British children to those I have referred to in Australian children, although it seems possible that the situation is worse there than it is here. In Australia, we have the advantage of widespread ethnic diversity, with one in three Australians born elsewhere or with a parent born elsewhere, which means a large proportion of our children are exposed to rich and varied food traditions. At Collingwood College, for example, from the very first week in the kitchen, it was noticeable that the Chinese and Vietnamese kids loved eating green leafy vegetables and fruit, and their behaviour exerted a subtle peer pressure on their classmates.

Another important influence has been the work of Californian restaurateur, food writer and food activist Alice Waters. Alice has written eloquently and at length about her belief in the importance of introducing young children to the pleasures of growing and preparing fresh food. She helped establish the Edible Schoolyard in the grounds of the Martin Luther King Jr Middle School in Berkeley, California, a program that is now in its eighteenth year. Several people involved with our project have visited the Edible Schoolyard and found it inspirational.

At home and at a grassroots level, I have been influenced and inspired not only by my own food-rich childhood, but by the range of beautiful kitchen gardens I have been privileged to visit over the years, including the gardens of my friends George Biron and Prue Gill and Will Studd; the Observatory Cafe kitchen garden at Melbourne's Royal Botanic Gardens; and the kitchen gardens at Como House in South Yarra and Heide Museum of Modern Art in Bulleen. I have also been motivated by my own vegetable garden in my suburban backyard, by seeing how growing a few rows of lettuces, and some green beans, tomatoes and herbs can add so much to simple summer lunches.

Foundations

Finding the school

The first task was to investigate ways of putting my vague ideas to the test. At first I thought of linking in with an existing structure. I approached the Victorian Schools Garden Awards committee, but they did not see how my idea fitted with their more general aims of school beautification. One of the committee suggested I speak with Basil Natoli.

Basil was the Community Gardens project manager from the Office of Housing, Department of Human Services. He also worked directly with children through the Royal Children's Hospital Garden Project. As we would discover, he believes in the idea that gardens add joy and meaning to people's lives, and has demonstrated this through his work on community housing estates and elsewhere. Prior to my approach, he had already helped get some garden classes off the ground at Collingwood College, which is situated right next to a large public housing estate. I visited the estate's community gardens during its Harvest Festival, and then asked Basil: 'How do I find a school to match my vision?' Basil's answer was immediate and auspicious: 'You must meet with Frances Laurino at Collingwood College.'

Frances is Italian. Eating and sharing food with others is an important part of her culture. When I first approached her, she had been junior school principal then principal at Collingwood College for twelve years. During that time she had cause to worry about the dreadful eating habits of many of her pupils. She was

very aware of the disadvantage some of the children suffered, and was absolutely convinced that the teaching of life skills would lead to improved circumstances now and the possibility of better lives later on.

Collingwood, a couple of kilometres from the centre of Melbourne, is a suburb of mixed fortunes. Successive waves of immigrants have occupied its large public housing estates, while its tiny Victorian terraces have been the preserve of the working class for generations. In recent years the middle classes have started moving in, as has been the trend in inner-city areas around Australia, but there are still plenty of indications of disadvantage, such as youth unemployment and street crime.

Nevertheless, within the school, Frances had managed to instil a sense of pride and activity. When I visited, I was struck by a palpable sense of energy. Colourful, vigorous artwork decorated every wall. The kids were refreshingly direct, and seemed to respond well to the consistent and communicative staff. By 2001, the school had already embraced innovation in a number of areas, and actively welcomed community involvement. Frances had facilitated the setting up of a Steiner program within the school. This is a child-centred approach to learning that stresses creativity and the engagement of the whole child (intellectual, spiritual, physical, emotional). In keeping with the Steiner philosophy that a beautiful environment is central to learning, the Steiner parents

7

had torn up some asphalt to plant what would eventually become the Beautiful Garden, now an oasis of green trees and shrubs. Frances was quite relaxed at the idea of tearing up more asphalt.

In Collingwood's favour, in terms of its suitability as a site for a kitchen garden program, was that it operated both as a primary and secondary school – that is, it taught children from age five through to their final year and therefore had a home economic classroom, a standard facility for secondary schools but not primary schools. At the time that our story starts, the home economics teacher was on maternity leave, the kitchen was hardly used, the equipment was very unloved, to say the least, and the common attitude towards home economics generally was that it was a thing of the past.

Until I spied the kitchen, my notions of how the grown food would be used had been very hazy. Maybe the students would prepare a monthly lunch for the friends of the school, then perhaps a weekly lunch just for students? Or maybe they would just nibble at things in the garden.

But the existence and offer of the kitchen immediately made me see how we could create a 'seed to table' experience, a term used by Alice Waters' Edible Schoolyard in California. The idea of a continuous cycle became central to the development of the project and gave rise to what would become our mantra:

Growing Harvesting Preparing Sharing

Frances was a visionary leader, in part because she understood the importance of consensus. She discussed our fledgling idea with the staff, who gave it the thumbs-up. Later they confessed they really had no idea how it would all work and had agreed partly because they were a bit bedazzled by my public image and my interest in their school. Embarrassing to record, but nonetheless true. (Later, my 'celebrity' status would be exploited by all as a means of attracting media interest, particularly as our need for funds grew.)

We had got to the stage of finding a school, a willing principal, a supportive staff, a link to the world of community gardening (Basil), and now all we had to do was turn the idea into a reality.

Sharing the idea with staff

We formed a committee: myself; Anna Dollard; Frances and Basil; teachers Mary-Ann De Carlo and Ken Watson; and coordinator of the junior school, Kevin Conroy. The first meeting resulted in us deciding on the name – the Kitchen Garden at Collingwood College. Should the idea spread, as we hoped it would, other schools could insert their own name.

Everyone present wanted to know how the program would work. Was it to be linked to the curriculum? What classes would be involved? So we did some serious brainstorming and came up with a few initial concepts and lots of wish lists.

Anna and I were a great team. I would float a really wild idea, the central core of which Anna immediately grasped. She was able to gently point out why an idea might not work, but often countered with a really achievable compromise or added her own imaginative thoughts to the mix. We would then tease out the steps needed to take ideas from jottings on paper to reality. Anna would challenge and refine, and then she would record what was said. In this way, no detail, or conversation, or contact ever fell between the cracks. I would then be the one to present the idea to our subcommittee, or a possible funding group, or the media, or anyone who would listen.

I felt strongly that the younger the children, the more likely it was we would be able to influence their behaviour. The primary years were ideal. By a process of working out how many hours of the day the garden might be available and how many kids it could accommodate at any one time (all done long before there was even a garden plan) we hit on the idea of working with grades three, four, five and six. It was reasoned that the littlies in grades one and two would get their turn soon enough; in the meantime, they could see what the others were doing, and look forward to doing it themselves.

The program would be part of the core curriculum and each child would do gardening for one period a week, and for a

< Sunflowers grow easily and signpost the summer harvest

> Stephanie discusses plans with principal Frances Laurino and community garden advocate Basil Natoli

> The future site of the Kitchen Garden at Collingwood College

< Classroom Teacher Mary-Ann De Carlo helps make a scarecrow

maximum of four years if they were in grade three in 2001. At this early planning stage we were unsure of how much time would be needed for the cooking and eating part of the project. We envisaged the garden teacher and a classroom teacher coping with a group of twenty to twenty-four students. At Collingwood College this meant between 120 and 130 children would take part in the project every week.

Initially, the staff felt the garden and kitchen activities would need to be formally integrated into other subject areas in the curriculum, and they set about compiling an extensive list of food-related topics to explore in the classroom. After less than one year, the consensus was that with so much experiential learning taking place over so many areas (mathematics, physics, history, physical education, social sciences, art and more) there was no need for this approach, and that the Kitchen Garden should be acknowledged as a rich learning stream in its own right.

Looking back from the vantage point of four years down the track, it is amazing how accurately we pinpointed the capacity of the yet-unbuilt garden. But we were way out with our estimates of the amount of supervision needed for groups of up to twenty-four students. However, this was still all in the future.

A plan for the garden

We decided to make the construction and planting of the garden a priority for the first few months. Our wish list of equipment with which to construct the garden included:

✱ bobcat	✱ child-sized tools and
✱ post-hole digger	wheelbarrows
✱ cement and cement mixer	✱ hoses and irrigation system
✱ gravel and sand	✱ seeds and seedlings
✱ sleepers, posts and old bricks	✱ garden furniture for outdoor
✱ fencing wire and wire mesh	eating
✱ topsoil	✱ rubber boots and raincoats
✱ mulch for pathways and	✱ barbecue
working areas	✱ lots of help!

We agreed the garden should be located for maximum visual impact. We wanted passers-by to see how beautiful it was, this imagined garden, with its rows of tomato bushes, a sprawling mound of pumpkins, a strawberry patch, a bed of soft-leaved salad vegetables, rows of bush beans, fruit trees and vines climbing across fences. The fantasy included a lockable space for tools – somewhere to store our wheelbarrow at night and hang our wet coats. We needed a compost area and a place for the children to sit and eat or listen to the garden teacher, and a space for a barbecue. Once again, from the position of four years down the track, it is amazing to read this romantic, uncompromising and ambitious vision for a schoolyard, but even more amazing to record that it all happened – and more.

As well as visual impact, the siting of the garden had to take into account all the other recreational needs of the school population. The area that was of interest to us abutted the football ground. We had permission to move the goalposts a bit, but it was generally important not to eat too much into the areas the children used for physical education. This consideration pushed the site of our garden towards the school-boundary fence, which meant we would always be partially shadowed by the high-rise flats to the north. We had to accept this.

We formed a subcommittee to plan and oversee the building of the garden. Several parents came on board, most notably the wonderful Freda Thornton, an architect and landscape designer.

Freda went away to draw up plans. I had a fairly traditional idea of what a kitchen garden should look like: raised beds and geometric rows of one crop ranged alongside rows of another. So I was unprepared for – although thrilled by – Freda's hand-drawn plan, coloured in shades of apple green and gold, for what would become known as the 'first bed' – a beautiful meandering, curvy space flanked by a seating wall (a nod to Gaudi's wall in Parc Guell in Barcelona). The plan was sent to the local council, the City of Yarra, which, despite reservations about the haste of the process, approved the project.

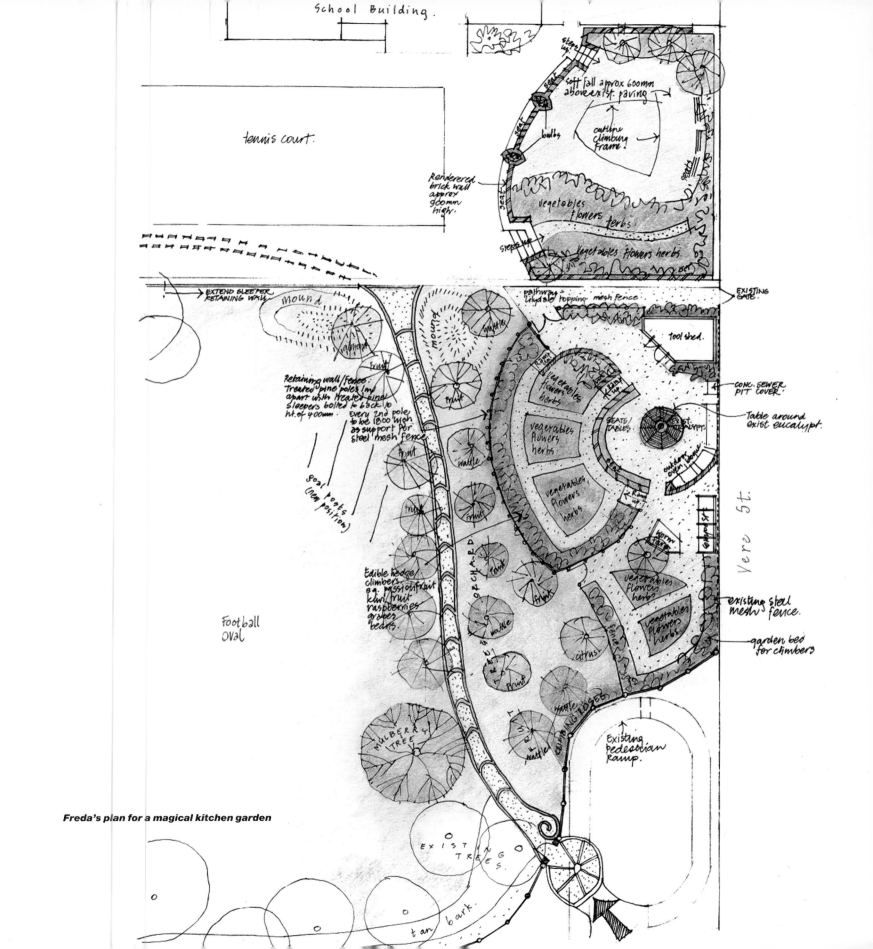

Freda's plan for a magical kitchen garden

Funding the vision

Where was the money to come from? That was the next big question for the committee, and an issue that would occupy us fairly frequently during the next few years. The school had already allocated its annual budget to existing programs – just meeting those commitments was an ongoing challenge. But we remained hopeful. I had a strong belief in the value of what we had planned, and I was convinced that money would flow from all directions as soon as the powers-that-be received our submissions. Frances felt sure that my involvement would immediately loosen purse strings, although she only confessed this later. Collectively, we spent a few moments wondering what we would do if we received money from everyone we approached! (We needn't have worried.) We drew up a list of must-haves that would need financing in the first year:

* *all items needed for the construction of the garden, as listed on page 10*
* *a garden teacher employed three days a week on contract rates*
* *a kitchen teacher employed three days a week on contract rates (as soon as the garden was established)*
* *produce for food preparation prior to harvest (and to top-up the harvest) and dry-store basics*
* *miscellaneous kitchen equipment, such as extra pots, pans and serving platters*
* *kitchen cleaning equipment*
* *office time, telephones, stationery, postage*
* *expenses for a modest public launch of the Kitchen Garden.*

We estimated a budget of $50 000 for the first year – and the date of the first working bee was already set. We thought one of our best chances in the immediate term was to try to secure donations of kitchen and garden equipment.

I wrote a submission and sent it first of all to the Premier of Victoria, an indication of how important I considered the initiative to be. State and national newspapers were regularly reporting alarming trends in the eating habits of young Australians, and we felt our proposal would be quickly taken up as a constructive way forward and an experiment worth supporting. We sent copies to various state departments and statutory bodies, several philanthropic organisations, the local council and the local Rotary club. As the weeks rolled by, we started to adjust to the reality of dealing with bureaucrats and the understanding that funding this project would require ingenuity, persistence, many hours and much energy. It was hard to avoid the conclusion that in some government departments, the process of meetings and agendas and reports seemed infinitely more important than outcomes, in contrast to our own way of going about things, best described by our catchcry: 'Just do it!'

Around this time Basil Natoli introduced us to the wonderful Peta Christensen and Cultivating Community, a not-for-profit organisation funded by the Office of Housing to support community gardens on public housing estates. Peta was passionate about involving kids in gardening and keen to undertake the role of garden teacher. Cultivating Community agreed to allocate Peta's time to the kitchen garden, and agreed to pay for one of the two days she would work there (the hoped-for third day had been sacrificed – for the moment – for budget reasons).

My own office offered to fund most of the administration costs. The City of Yarra offered free mulch. We were on our way!

The working bees

On the day before the first working bee, a big truck arrived to deliver a load of compost-rich soil, and tipped it, unceremoniously, onto the schoolyard. Like most of Melbourne, Collingwood is sited on clay, which is not at all ideal for planting. Our initial planning specified raised beds in the hope that imported soil, comprising a compost element, would be nutrient-rich and help kill off the weed base at the same time.

The delivery caused great consternation among some of the kids, who rushed to Frances' office, and, with wide eyes, informed her there had been a mistake and 'shit' had been delivered instead of soil. They could not believe this was really the stuff they were going to be spreading in the garden. (The children would eventually become big advocates of 'moo poo' and quite expert at spreading it across the garden beds.)

The day of the first working bee dawned clear, cold and dry. Everyone breathed a sigh of relief, as the prospect of shovelling mud in the rain would have tested the first show of enthusiasm. What a day of achievement. Twenty-five adults showed up and lots of kids. A few toddlers lent a hand, insisting on struggling with buckets and spades bigger than themselves. Principal Frances wielded a shovel with the best of them. The older kids started off kicking the footy and playing around the edge, but slowly gravitated towards 'the works' and were very helpful. This was to be the pattern as the project moved forward. The adults tackled the heavy-duty construction tasks, but things were planned in such a way as to ensure the students had maximum input, both physically and creatively.

The bobcats came in first and we all cheered as they began lifting the asphalt. Over the next six hours, this is what we achieved:

* We moved the goalposts, which had great symbolic significance (this was actually a very taxing job as the posts had originally been set in concrete).
* We removed the concrete slabs from a pathway, flattened the dirt underneath and laid down a layer each of gravel and sand. The kids really loved operating the heavy roller, which they could only do with two of them helping.
* We laid out the perimeter of the garden and dug a series of holes with a specially hired post-hole digger, which took two people to operate. Others then deepened the holes, digging out the loose soil with their hands.
* We set pine poles in the holes, then attached wire mesh to create a fence that could be used for growing climbing plants.

* A team of six women, armed with shovels and wheelbarrows, slowly transferred a huge pile of woodchips to the new garden bed.
* We marked out paths in the garden bed, making sure they were wide enough for wheelbarrows.

Our landscape designer, Freda Thornton, was everywhere – a Boadicea leading the charge, a true visionary. She had drawn up the plans and organised the materials, and on the day she was a powerhouse of energy as she motivated the voluntary troop. One minute she was down a hole; the next, shifting sleepers; the next, encouraging the wheelbarrow pushers and the shovellers. And always with a huge flashing smile.

A second and third working bee quickly followed. The same dedicated band built the brick wall, attaching to it used seating from other areas of the school grounds, and carted more and more compost-rich soil to build up the planting beds.

The children had created terracotta plaques depicting fruit and vegetables in their art class, and they worked with the adults embedding the plaques right along the length of the curved garden wall.

After each working bee many of us went home to soak in a hot bath. I remember feeling exhausted but marvellously stimulated, both physically and mentally, and aware of muscles that had not been used for some time.

Over time, Freda recorded her impressions of these days and what made them work. She stressed the importance of finding a dedicated core of people prepared to turn up to every working bee; people who shared a vision of a beautiful space for the children and who could remain positive despite the hard work that was involved. As it turned out, remaining positive was the easy part – everyone was always so satisfied at the end of each day, buoyed by their achievements, and, quite possibly, by the hot soup and delicious snacks that were an essential part of the experience.

We never budgeted for the input from the school groundsman, Shane Quinn, but as the project gained momentum, Shane began to play a fundamental role. He organised multiple deliveries of soil, sand and mulch, supervised the watering and dealt

< Liz Moore and Peta Christensen prepare the beds for planting

> Children dressed as carrots and corn to welcome guests to the launch

< Cultivating Community has been an important friend of the project

< Avery pushes the roller over the newly created garden path

> Hieu and Janice read up on organic gardening

with any garden damage outside kitchen garden hours. As the garden matured, his input became essential and the garden teachers came to depend on his help.

By the end of the third working bee, we had a garden with an established shape and a beautifully decorated wall, complete with seating. The next step was the official launch. With every progression and every expense, the issue of money had become more pressing. We hoped a launch would excite official interest, and thereby generate funds.

At our first launch-planning meeting, Freda created what would become known as the Beautiful Banner. The rest of us looked on in open-jawed astonishment as she took giant craft scissors and, pulling pieces of pretty cotton prints from a very large rag-bag, started cutting out half-metre tall letters without any template or guidelines or measurements. She just seemed to know how long the banner would have to be to fit all of these crazy colourful letters. When unfurled for its first public viewing on launch day, Freda's Beautiful Banner could be properly seen as the truly wondrous and extraordinary work of art that it is.

The launch of the Kitchen Garden

In the office we worked very hard at following up leads and enquiries and promises of help, and sending out information. Enquires had started trickling in as soon as news of our project made its way into the community. We thought the launch would be an opportunity to let the community know that our drawing-board idea was fast becoming a reality.

For the launch, we planned that I would stand beside the garden and give a rousing address to outline the thinking behind the project and our efforts so far; we planned tours of the garden area; we planned a barbecue lunch and a huge and wonderful salad to be mixed in a (clean) wheelbarrow. And then, on launch day, after weeks of drought, it rained. There was nothing for it but

to declare this an auspicious omen for the garden and to quickly move all the formalities to an inside location.

Despite the weather, the launch was a success. We handed out a flyer calling for volunteers and funds, as well as for donations of all sorts of necessary items – including raincoats for the children. Some of the children did the rounds dressed as vegetables. The Victorian Minister for Housing and Aged Care, Bronwyn Pike, launched the project. Other dignitaries on the day included representatives of the Department of Education and Training, who whispered excitedly there was 'a letter in the mail'. This mysterious letter took time and some prompting to eventuate, but when it did, it contained wonderful news. We had been given a one-off grant of $12 500. Together with other financial help from the Rotary Club of Collingwood, the Education Foundation, the Education Trust, the Pratt Foundation and the ANZ Felton Bequest, it was starting to look as though, despite setbacks and rejections from elsewhere, persistence was paying off and our budget, at least for the first twelve months, was secure.

Which was just as well, as our first proper garden class was scheduled for the following week. And we were about to advertise for a cook to commence work in the spring. 'Just do it!' was still pushing us forward.

ONCE UPON A TIME there was a school in a semi-industrial part of Melbourne, which was invited to take part in a bold experiment that would offer students the experiences of working in a garden and kitchen, and of coming together around a table to share food. So good would these experiences be, that the students would become seduced by the pleasures of good food, and develop an appreciation for the rituals and tastes of the table that would last a lifetime.

The experiment was the Kitchen Garden at Collingwood College and it has unfolded over weeks, months and now years; to capture the colour and vitality of this story has meant telling it as it happened. The following section unfolds in the fashion of a diary, which allows the interested reader to discover and understand the excitements, the progress and the disappointments exactly as they happened; to experience vicariously the mud, the worms and the smells – both the delicious ones emanating from the kitchen and the unusual ones from the compost heap.

This diary has drawn on a variety of resources and has been enriched by many contributing voices. Anna kept scrupulous notes, the children wrote classroom diaries and the garden and kitchen teachers recorded their own impressions and those of the children. When in full swing, the kitchen and garden classes became the source of numerous images. Soon the walls and noticeboards were thick with photos and menus, many of which now appear in the following pages.

We offer this story in the hope it convinces other schools to follow our lead. We believe in the power of pleasurable experiential education and are confident that the seeds planted – both literally and metaphorically – in the Kitchen Garden at Collingwood College will continue to bear fruit, maybe long after the students themselves have moved on from the project.

The Kitchen Garden — year by year

The first year – 2001

The first garden classes

It is August. Garden Teacher Peta Christensen supervises the first session in the garden and the kids design heart- and star-shaped garden beds, then spread the still-large supply of compost-rich soil. They rake the beds to break up any clumps of soil, in preparation for the first planting of seedlings, and they dig holes along the path to plant fruit trees to create a mini-orchard – allowing plenty of space for growth.

The first feedback is enthusiastic. Teachers report that some kids who are under-performers in other classes are shovelling and wheelbarrowing with gusto. After the first class, a few of the girls stay back during lunchtime because they enjoy the work so much. Some kids don't want to get their hands dirty. We hope this will change. Early days: we remind ourselves we must not get carried away or discouraged.

I am interviewed on the radio about the project, and I am immediately offered an eco-friendly chook house, which we're delighted to accept. The chook house is placed in the beautiful garden, and the students from the Work Education Program at the Collingwood College annexe – The Island – build an enclosure for it. Soon we have four golden bantam hens in residence. They become an instant attraction with the kids. We talk about using the eggs in the kitchen classes next term, and plan how we'll get the children to take the bantams home in the holidays.

The garden is to be 100 per cent organic. The first seedlings are from heirloom varieties. We make an early excursion to Heronswood at Dromana, home of Diggers Seeds, and come back with seeds and seedlings and a planting plan. Heritage varieties of fruit trees are grafted for planting in their prepared holes, and then inter-planted with native flowering shrubs. The natives will grow much quicker than the fruit trees, so we will be able to use them to demonstrate pruning, planting and grafting (see Orchard Planting on page 22). Peta notes that in just one month since the launch we have '. . . planted curly kale, snowpeas, broccoli, rocket, parsley, rosemary, broad beans, celery, silver beet, spinach and chives. And a bay tree.'

A New Zealand magazine photographs me planting a cumquat tree for a feature article. The media attention has been almost immediate and leads to some much-appreciated donations. Molly, a local resident, gives us a few dozen raspberry canes; olive grower Janice Hunter donates an olive tree and garlic, lettuce and potato seeds; personal friend and keen garden supporter George Biron donates a globe artichoke plant.

The children plant flowers among the fruit and vegetables. I query the existence of flowers in this kitchen garden. Peta explains the notion of companion planting: some flowers function as a natural pest control, deterring damaging pests such as the white cabbage moth and attracting useful predators to the garden beds (marigolds, for example, not only add colour to salads, but attract hoverfly, a very efficient predator of the aphid); comfrey grown underneath citrus trees can bring essential nutrients to their shallow roots; borage next to strawberries sweetens their taste. My concern was misplaced and I had learnt an important lesson.

Peta also explains that there is nothing wrong with planting flowers simply to create a beautiful space, which is what our garden soon becomes with its cosmos, sunflowers, borage, poppies, nasturtiums and pansies dotted among the green and silver leaves. In the months to come we decide we will eventually use the flowers to make posies to decorate the kitchen tables. In the meantime, the bees seem happy.

Too much water

By early September the fruit trees are in the ground. We plant the first crops with enthusiasm and high hopes and pile the compost high with green material for the first-ever batch. We then wait for the vegetables to jump out of the ground.

Within a few weeks it becomes apparent we have a problem. Nothing is growing well: our seedlings are stunted and withered; some of our precious trees have drowned in boggy soil; the artichoke plant disappears altogether; the raspberries die.

Our disappointment is huge. There are long faces and lots of head-scratching. We identify the garden's hard and compacted clay sub-structure as the problem: the tiny roots of our seedlings can't spread and the rain won't drain, which results in the boggy, soggy, sour-smelling condition of our soil. We had hoped that the rich soil that filled the raised beds would compensate, but this is clearly not the case.

We excavate parts of the garden to lay down 'aggie' pipes, which are perforated drainage pipes that remove sub-surface water. The kids love doing this – they love the digging bit, but also being part of helping solve the problem.

Soil analysis reveals serious deficiencies of some minerals, low levels of organic matter and excessive amounts of other min-erals. The challenges are coming thick and fast. There is a bright side: the children are learning about the need to feed soil and about how to be patient gardeners.

Class structure

Peta is busy working out the best way to run garden classes – how to keep twenty-four children busy for forty-five minutes at a time. Her gardening friends and volunteers from Cultivating Community come to help out regularly. This means the class can be broken up into four or five small groups. We are beginning to realise that the garden classes will be difficult if not impossible without strong volunteer support.

Before each class, Peta sources and sets up her materials (bought or scavenged!), allocates tasks for each group, allocates tasks for the volunteers, briefs the volunteers, prepares activity sheets for recording different group tasks and works achieved, and checks that the tools are in good nick.

If there are not enough volunteers on any given day, she plans activities that the kids can undertake alone: for example, seed-sorting, raking, watering, wheelbarrowing and spreading mulch or drawing.

A typical class starts with everyone gathering together for a few minutes in front of the donated whiteboard (an essential bit of garden equipment). Peta would have already set out the day's activities on the whiteboard. She explains new terms or techniques to the kids, before dividing them into small groups, allocating each group to the care of a volunteer or teacher.

Often the tasks can be completed within a single lesson; at other times, a group takes 'ownership' of the activity, and agrees to return to it the following week.

The children invent wonderful names for their groups: the 'snail trails', the 'bee stings', the 'sour cherries', the 'pea pods' and many, many more. We allocate time at the end of each class for the children to share their experiences with one another, which they do with great enthusiasm.

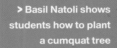
< Seedlings ready for planting on the garden wall, with the Collingwood Town Hall in the background

> Basil Natoli shows students how to plant a cumquat tree

< Flowers have an important role in the garden

< Planting an early crop

> The garden beds take shape

Building a kitchen garden

– a practical checklist for beginners

* *Involve the whole school community in the planning – students, teachers, parents.*
* *Choose the site carefully. The ideal site in Australia is north-facing, with protection from the south.*
* *Test the soil for suitability.*
* *Feed the soil and establish a compost program.*
* *Read up on permaculture (see Our Permaculture Garden on page 43)*
* *Practise crop rotation.*
* *Climbing plants save space – think passionfruit and kiwifruit and climbing beans and snowpeas.*
* *Container plantings – such as barrels, and bathtubs – are great for cumquat trees, bay trees, lemon and lime trees, and herbs and strawberries.*
* *Allow for the fully-grown size of a fruit tree when spacing trees.*
* *Provide lockable storage space near the garden.*
* *Install a rainwater tank to teach kids about sensible water usage.*
* *Provide a space for wet-weather days and shade for hot days.*
* *Plant flowers for companion planting and to adorn the kitchen tables at meal times.*
* *Have realistic expectations and keep it fun.*

Classroom Teacher Ken Watson helps out in an early garden class

Many of the children we are working with have never previously dug in soil nor delicately separated a seedling out from a clump. They are occasionally too rough with a plant or they place the plant upside down in its hole or too deeply or not deeply enough. At lunchtime, someone might kick a football onto a row of new seedlings, then the planting has to start all over again. In other words, progress is slow, but it is steady.

Orchard planting

We plant our orchard knowing that it will be some years until our first harvest. We have also had to accept that the apricots and plums will fruit over the long summer holiday period, but we console ourselves with the fact that these fast-growing trees provide wonderful shade, and that we will eventually be able to organise a summer preserving project to take care of the holiday harvest. This is our planting list.

Fruit trees

Almond
Black passionfruit
Cumquat
Emperor mandarin
Golden delicious apple
Grapefruit
Kaffir lime
Lemon
Macadamia nut
Mariposa plum
Nectarine
Newcastle early apricot
Orange tamarillo
Packham's triumph pear
Peach

Persimmon
Quince
Red fuji apple
Santa rosa plum
Sellowiana feijoa
Tilton apricot
Washington navel orange
Winter cole plum

Natives

Coastal rosemary
Hakea
Lilly pilly
Mint bush
Native trees
Wattle

Planting lists

Every garden has its own unique microclimate. Our garden does not experience much frost, which enables the most tender lettuce seedlings to grow all year round. However, we have a lot of shade throughout winter, created by the high-rise flats to the north and trees to the east and west, which means our winter crops grow a little more slowly than they otherwise might have.

The lists that follow record varieties that have been planted in the garden. Not everything was planted every season. No planting happened during the hot months of summer.

The perennials will flourish best when planted in spring, although we have planted some of these throughout the year. The winter fruits were planted as bare-rooted stock, which is a more cost effective way to purchase these plants (compared to buying them in the spring).

When reading these impressive planting lists, it should be remembered that not everything we planted flourished and many things were planted in small quantities. But the important point to make is that these bountiful food crops have all been cared for by fairly young children.

Perennials

	Spring planting		Autumn planting	Winter planting
HERBS	Bay tree	Oregano	Chives	
	Chives	Pineapple sage	Garlic chives	
	French tarragon	Rosemary	Mint	
	Garlic chives	Sage		
	Lemon balm	Thyme		
	Lemongrass	Vietnamese mint		
	Marjoram			
FRUIT	Banana	Orange	Cumquat	Almond
	Cape gooseberry	Passionfruit	Grapefruit	Apple
	Cumquat	Pepino	Lemon	Apricot
	Grapefruit	Persimmon		Blueberry
	Kaffir lime	Sellowiana feijoa		Kiwifruit
	Lemon	Strawberries		Mulberry
	Lilly pilly	Tahitian lime		Nectarine
	Macadamia nut	Tamarillo		Peach
	Mandarin			Pear
				Plum
				Quince
				Raspberry
VEGETABLES	Globe artichoke	Warrigal greens		
	Rhubarb	Watercress		
EDIBLE FLOWERS	Society garlic			

Annuals

	Spring planting	Autumn planting	All-year round
HERBS	Basil	Coriander	Parsley
	Chervil		
FRUIT	Rockmelon		
	Watermelon		
VEGETABLES	Amaranth	Beetroot	Asian greens
	Asparagus	Broad beans	– bok choi
	Beans	Broccoli	– choi sum
	Beetroot	Brussel sprouts	– gai laan
	Broccoli	Cabbage	– mizuna
	Cabbage	Carrot	– pak choi
	Carrot	Cauliflower	– tatsoi
	Cauliflower	Celery	– mustard greens
	Celeriac	Daikon	Green-manure crops
	Celery	Garlic	– broad beans
	Chilli	Kohlrabi	– fenugreek
	Corn	Leek	– lucerne
	Cucumber	Onion	– lupins
	Daikon	Peas	Radish
	Eggplant	Potato	Salad greens
	Florence fennel	Shallots	– chicory
	Jerusalem artichoke	Spinach	– endive
	Leek	Swede	– lettuce
	Parsnip	Turnip	– radicchio
	Peppers	Tuscan black kale	– rocket
	Potato	Wong bok (Chinese cabbage)	Silver beet
	Pumpkin		Spring onions
	Spinach		
	Squash		
	Tomato		
	Zucchini		
EDIBLE FLOWERS	Borage	Borage	
	Calendula	Calendula	
	Chamomile	Nasturtium	
	Marigold		
	Sunflower		

Time to start cooking

It is September. There is still plenty to do in our sprouting garden, but we need a similar level of activity in the kitchen and around the tables to complete the full circle of learning about food.

Because we have had no significant quantity of produce to pick – and therefore cook – for at least two months, we have filled in time by planning the first kitchen classes and deciding on the essential criteria for the yet-to-be-appointed kitchen teacher (see Teacher Roles on page 40).

The most important thing will be to choose an individual who is passionate about all aspects of good food and who can communicate their enthusiasm to young children.

The marvellous Peta Heine comes into our lives. Fancy having two Petas! Very quickly we come to know them as Garden Teacher Peta and Kitchen Teacher Peta. Peta Heine is a young mother who has previously operated a tourist lodge, taking responsibility for all the cooking. I am particularly impressed by the way she takes for granted that there is no special category of kids' food. We set the date for our first cooking class: Wednesday, 10 October – just two weeks away, and still a lot of work to do.

Our kitchen

In early October, Kitchen Teacher Peta and I have a two-person working bee. The kitchen has some very positive aspects: it is large and airy with central lockable cupboards for the storage of dry goods and a domestic refrigerator; it has six cooking stations, each equipped with a domestic electric stove, a single sink, benches and drawers, and overhead storage; there is a lockable office, an additional storage room for baking equipment and a laundry area with a washing machine, dryer and freezer. It's a great start but there's a lot to do.

We get to work. We empty out every drawer and every cupboard in the kitchen. We unearth an amazing collection of baking equipment: gem-scone irons, muffin pans, sponge tins, bread-loaf tins, fruit-cake tins – round and square – nut-loaf tins, rolling pins, tart tins. At some time in the past, baking must have been a major function of the kitchen.

We scrub every cupboard and wash every saucepan and measuring spoon. We count the basic equipment – wooden spoons, measuring cups, tongs, whisks, pots and pans. We create permanent homes for all measuring spoons and cups, graters, colanders, flour sifters, mixing bowls and so on. Some of the pots have definitely seen better days, so we throw them out. We also throw out bags of weevil-infested flour and rice, bottles of dried spices not opened for over a year and dried-up commercial sauces and relishes – we will be making our own!

We turn on every oven and quickly discover that some work and some do not. All are filthy. We have our heads in the ovens for quite some time. By the end of the day we have a glow of pride about our work: we now have a clean kitchen, even if the grey besser-brick walls are a bit drab, only some of the stoves work and the supply of hot water is probably inadequate.

The absence of any sort of dining equipment is a problem. We work out what we need to buy or have donated in order to set a basic table. We then add the other cooking equipment we'll need and our wish list gets quite long:

* aprons
* blenders
* bread baskets
* chargrill pans
* electric mixers
* flower vases
* food processors
* glasses
* hot-water service – bigger and better
* kitchen knives
* knives, forks, spoons
* large pots
* non-stick frying pans
* oven mitts
* pasta makers
* pepper mills
* plates
* platters
* refrigerator – extra
* rubbish and compost bins
* salad bowls
* salad spinners
* scales
* serving bowls
* tablecloths
* tea towels
* water jugs

Principal Frances promises us a technician for the ovens and some funds for basic cleaning stuff, and we find a company that will donate some glasses and crockery.

But we are still waiting for the garden to produce substantial crops. We approach Melbourne's Queen Victoria Market for assistance and they generously agree to donate weekly fruit and vegetables to the value of between $80 and $100 – with this we can push forward. Peta will set aside a budget of $1.50 per child per week for any remaining ingredients that need to be purchased.

The first-ever cooking class

Our first class is a composite of grades three, four and five. Kitchen Teacher Peta has rolled the menu into a scroll and tied it with a beautiful ribbon. She invites a student to come to the front of the class, unroll the menu and read it out loud: 'Linguine with Broad Beans, Bacon and Thyme; Wilted Silver Beet with Lemon Juice and Olive Oil; Apple Betties with Whipped Cream.' The reading is very hesitant and delivered in a tiny voice. Much prompting is needed with the words 'linguine', 'thyme' and 'wilted'.

Literacy levels at Collingwood College are an ongoing problem. Resources are stretched to the limit, and there is no doubt that some kids, especially those from non-English-speaking homes, fall through the net. So vocabulary becomes an issue within the first ten minutes of our first class. Peta writes tricky words on the blackboard and provides explanations: linguine is a thin type of pasta; wilted describes very lightly heated vegetables; the 'th' in thyme is pronounced 't' as in toffee.

I have my own vocabulary problem: despite my many years in kitchens I have never encountered an apple betty. When I first read the menu I have no idea what it is I will be helping to make. I don't want to confess my ignorance to Peta as it might look as if I lack confidence in her menu selection. Instead I consult Alan Davidson's *The Oxford Companion to Food*, which tells me the dish consists of ' . . . alternating layers of sugared and spiced fruit and buttered breadcrumbs.'

In fact, Peta's version turns out to be somewhat different, but at least I'm on the right track. Peta divides the class into four groups and each group is given a task, along with their own recipe sheets. The adults present – myself, Peta, Class Teacher Ken and Peta's mum, Barb Heine, who is roped in to help the young cooks get started – are each allocated to a group of students.

Peta has brought in her own pasta machine and I am assigned to the pasta-making and rolling group. Some children make dough for the next class, while others knead and roll the dough that Peta has made and allowed to rest before this class arrived. The kids love the pasta-making, and after a few false starts and some very ragged pieces of dough, they are rolling smooth sheets of pasta, which we then rest on semolina-scattered trays to dry until it is time to cut and cook. Every child in the group has a go at rolling and cutting. The cutting proves much more taxing: unless the pasta is carefully controlled as it comes out of the cutters, it sticks together and is hard to untangle. We end up with quite a few of these stuck-together bundles, but also with enough of the good stuff to let everyone have a taste.

Another group tackles the broad beans and silver beet, and the third and fourth groups cut the apples and toast the breadcrumbs for the dessert.

The broad beans and silver beet are, at this stage, our best crops, so they have extra significance (although the harvest will not be enough to service the five classes who will be cooking this menu during the week). The thyme is also from our own garden. The apples are from the Queen Victoria Market, as are additional broad beans. The lemons are from my own tree at home.

The group that finishes first gets to set the table. But it is immediately obvious that not one child in this group has done this before – there is no understanding of how to place the cutlery and arrange the glasses. We make a note that every group needs to have a turn at table-setting.

Table decorum is the next problem.

< A tasting of fresh broad beans dipped in extra-virgin olive oil

> Elkanah stirs and fries with confidence

> Beautiful vegetables from our garden

< Anthony concentrates on the task at hand

> Kitchen Garden Teacher Peta Heine with her mother, Barb, who came in to help out with the early classes

Good behaviour

Occasionally the kids are really challenging. All the adults involved have had to decide what is acceptable and what is not. Clearly, dangerous behaviour has to be stopped at once. The most consistent breaches of good behaviour are noise levels that prevent students listening to explanations at the start of a class and kids outright ignoring what the teachers are saying. In the kitchen, some kids are often reluctant to clean up, even though they have cooked and eaten with enthusiasm.

Early on we see how important it is that the garden and kitchen teachers develop an understanding of their roles in relation to the classroom teachers. It is the classroom teachers who lead the way in insisting on reasonable standards of attentiveness and to control disputes and outright rudeness. The specialists – the kitchen and garden teachers – are there to impart new skills and enthusiasms, and should not be diverted unduly by a few naughty children.

In the kitchen, Peta – and later teachers Karen and Desley – develop techniques to deal with unacceptable behaviour. When the preliminaries are interrupted, the teacher starts again from the beginning. The children come to realise this means less time for cooking and eating together at the table. The most devastating punishment is to tell the offending child that he or she must undertake some cleaning or tidying task instead of cooking, and to warn them that they may not be allowed to eat with the others. This is a last resort and is never invoked lightly. Peta constantly stresses her three Ts': timing, tasting, teamwork.

Many of the children develop really special relationships with the volunteers and confide their worries and their best moments to them. Some kids who are not coping very well in other areas of school excel in the kitchen.

Around the table we continually notice the weight of peer pressure. The students urge their classmates to 'Just try it!' Many of the children have seen *Jamie's School Dinners,* the marvellous television series made by British chef Jamie Oliver. Our kids express shock and superiority when discussing what the British children in the show would and would not eat: 'They wouldn't even eat roast chicken,' the kids chorus in disbelief.

I remind them that Jamie gave gold stars to the kids who tried something new, a great idea and one we think is worth copying. (Four years down the track there are very few absolute food refusers, even if there are still those children who do not like to eat most green vegetables unless they are packaged in a yummy pie or a pasta filling or a muffin, and then there is no problem at all.)

On the whole, the atmosphere in the kitchen is marvellous. It is a very happy place to be, with plenty of boisterous moments, lots of chatter and certainly lots of laughter, and many fascinating and sometimes quite bold conversations. At the time of writing, I would have eaten close to 100 meals cooked by children aged eight to twelve and, apart from the occasional slip-up with seasoning, I can honestly say I have enjoyed every one.

There are additional challenges to good behaviour in the garden. Gaining the students' attention in an outdoor environment can be difficult amid the distractions of traffic noise, other outside classes, flying and crawling insects, wet seats after rain, and hot, windy and wet weather. But again, once the children engage, these distractions seem not to matter.

Most of the children have no concept of helping themselves to a portion of food before passing the dish to someone else. If they want to fill their water glass, they lunge across the table to grab the jug. Water glasses get knocked over, water goes everywhere, and the children leap from their chairs in disgust, creating mayhem. Some children burp and make other rude noises, and there is lots of pushing and shoving and disputes about seating, and unanimous complaints about having to clear the table and tidy up the cooking areas.

It is a very lively if somewhat dismaying introduction to the cooking and eating elements of our project. It's a credit to Kitchen Teacher Peta that she does not fold up her apron and walk away from it all after day one.

But the good part is that every child positively beams as the platters of freshly made linguine come to each table, fragrant with sautéed garlic and bacon and thyme. About half the class tastes the wilted silver beet and everyone loves the apple betties.

And then the routine starts again for the next class.

Over two days, 120 children from five different classes pod and cook broad beans; sauté bacon; peel and chop garlic; chop parsley; pull thyme leaves from stalks; wash and dry silver beet; use a food processor to make simple pasta dough; roll, cut, cook and drain pasta; toss pasta with extra-virgin olive oil, bacon and herbs; peel apples; make and toast breadcrumbs; and assemble puddings. The children set tables for the first time; they wash their dishes, pots and cooking utensils; and most importantly of all, they complete all the cooking in time to sit together at the table and enjoy the fruits of their labour and feel proud.

Probably only a tiny percentage of the children have ever done any one of these tasks before. We are on the way to making changes in their lives.

> It makes my tastebuds cheer with happiness!
> Quote from Kashi

Establishing systems

By the time we get to November of the first year, Kitchen Teacher Peta and I have worked out how best to interact with one another. I want to provide as much support as possible, even from a distance. Email seems the best way and each week Peta emails me her suggested menu for feedback. Sometimes I have several comments, on other occasions I have nothing but encouragement.

Earlier, we had discussed the need to expand the children's vocabulary for describing flavour and texture. We'd agreed to ban the word 'yuck' but to encourage the kids to think of something more specific, such as 'slimy', 'bitter' or 'stringy'. We start collecting these words and writing them on the board. It soon becomes a bit of a game to see who can think of the best word to describe a dish.

Over a period, we develop the best possible format for the recipes (see the sample recipe on page 75), one that features a list of equipment, in addition to the traditional ingredients list and method. It takes us a few weeks, but eventually we convince the children that they need to set out all their equipment and ingredients before they start on the fun part of chopping and mixing.

Kitchen Teacher Peta develops her own planning systems (see Menu Planning on page 32). She takes note of what crops are ready for harvest immediately, and what will be ready for harvest in the coming week, before deciding on menus and specifying how much of each crop needs to be picked for a particular recipe. She works closely with Garden Teacher Peta. Neither teacher has much time available outside the classroom, so both are keen to use their meeting times constructively. Kitchen Teacher Peta has a weekly worksheet that she uses to plan the menus for the current week, and the following one. She keeps a record of what particular skill, technique or tip will be introduced into the coming classes, and makes notes on the cost of items purchased (adhering closely to the set budget) and any cooking preparation she has to do.

Menu planning

The principles behind the choice of each menu, like so much else in this program, have evolved over time.

It makes sense to build on what we know the children enjoy

This means that pasta, pies, pizza, muffins, breads and dips have featured regularly. Of course, our pasta is home-made and the fillings are wonderful. Our pizza dough is thin and crisp and baked on the beautiful and functional terracotta rounds made in the art department, and the toppings always include aromatic herbs and the very best extra-virgin olive oil. Our pies, tortes and tarts have thin easy-to-handle pastry and the fillings include eggs laid by our resident bantam hens, along with seasonal vegetables. We make dips with all manner of ingredients. The brilliant colour of the beetroot dip always causes comment. When we combine beetroots with chocolate chips to make muffins, the results are spectacular in terms of both look and taste.

Reinforcement of technique is very important

Although it is tempting to create an entirely new menu every week, we know if we repeat a technique for a few weeks, it is much more likely to make an impression. During the winter months we make a lot of soup. The children quickly learn that using real stock makes many soups much more delicious. They also learn to make classic puréed soups based on water, such as leek and potato soup, and come to understand how to use the food processor to achieve a smooth texture.

Basic skills and techniques are rotated from group to group so that each child does a particular dish/technique several times during the year – soup, salad dressing, salad, pasta dough, bread dough, braising, stewing, deep-frying and dessert – using a simple table to track the rotation.

Try again with dishes that seem unpopular

In the first months the salads were left largely untouched. But we persisted in offering a salad with every meal, and further down the track the children began to eat them. Some kids like them better than others, notably those with Asian or European backgrounds. We discover over time that kids like salads that contain surprises – oven-baked herb croutons, toasted nuts or seeds, or shavings of parmigiano-reggiano.

Sweet dishes are offered regularly but not every week

This is accepted without question. The children love it when we make puddings and sweet muffins and biscuits. Some are familiar with the baking process – those kids that have cooked at home, have made this type of food.

It is important to offer food that is good to eat

It is counter-productive to offer salads with tough or bitter leaves, or to allow rocket to grow to a point where it is too hot to be enjoyed. Or to include raw leaves in a salad that really need to be stir-fried to be delicious. On the other hand, we do tell students not to reject, say, a tender young cos leaf just because a snail has taken a bite first. Instead we say, wash it, dry it, dress it and enjoy it!

Ensure the recipe explanations are very clear

This is not just because of the age of the readers, but also because the various techniques and the vocabulary are often unfamiliar. Terms such as 'blanch', 'sauté', 'vinaigrette', and 'wilt' need explanation. We always discuss the spelling of words when we introduce new menus.

Identify new or unusual ingredients

Never assume that every child is familiar with all fruits and vegetables, or condiments such as fish sauce, extra-virgin olive oil, and so on.

Involve everyone

It's essential to choose dishes that involve a few different processes, rather than two quick steps and into the oven. This way everyone is kept busy, and we avoid the behaviour problems associated with idle hands.

Surprise them from time to time

Well-known children's author Mem Fox, when discussing teaching children to read, advises parents and teachers to 'enchant them'. Similarly in the kitchen we get wonderful results when we enchant or surprise the children. Their eyes open wide in disbelief when we offer blue borage flowers to eat. They are astounded at the prospect of eating battered, fried zucchini flowers and tiny sandwiches of sage leaves, pressed together with an anchovy – fiddly but well worth it. The volunteers are all pleasantly surprised at the positive reaction of the kids when we offer raw broad beans to nibble with a flake of sea salt and a dip in a shallow pool of very good olive oil. And everyone is intrigued when we propose cooking up our green tomatoes.

Stand back

The volunteers offer guidance and a helping hand and keep an eye out for safe kitchen practices – especially those involving knives, boiling water and hot stovetops – but the children do the cooking. Before launching into an instruction or a demonstration of how to use equipment, the volunteers ask the students how they might do it, instead of assuming they don't know. Overall, it is the children's work. And the results are not only delicious but look beautiful.

Sample weekly kitchen-class planning

To be harvested week beginning 6 September:	*Menu for week beginning 6 September:*
Lettuce	Three-cheese ravioli with herb butter
Rhubarb	Green salad with beetroot and croutons
Beetroots	Rhubarb custard tart
Herbs	

To be harvested in next two weeks:	*Class focus and kitchen skills for this week*
Sorrel (for soup)	Making pasta
Rocket	Salad dressings
Beans	Shallow-frying
	Oven-safety rules

Quantity of vegetables needed for each class:
Large basket of lettuce
Parsley
Thyme
Chives
2–3 beetroots
3 stalks rhubarb

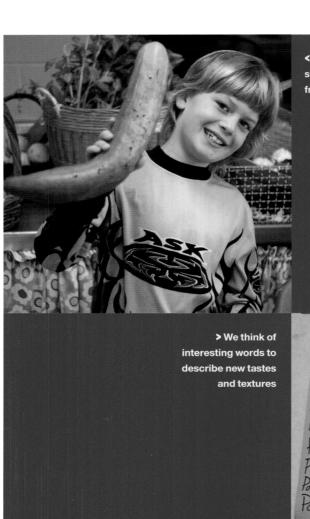

< David with an oddly shaped cucumber from the garden

> Volunteer Peter and Classroom Teacher Barbara share the meal

> We think of interesting words to describe new tastes and textures

3 March — Mary-Ann's Class

Flavour Words	Texture Words
Cucumber - 'Normal' Bland	Batter - airy
Chilli - spicy & tangy	Pasta - smooth
Pasta - yummy	Tempura - lumpy
Pasta - minty, tomato	Pasta - slippery
Pasta - tasty	
Pasta - hot (spicy) low heat	
Basil - cool	
Everything - mouthwatering	

< A basket of garden herbs

> Max brings freshly harvested basil to the kitchen

The pre-class preparation helps the day run smoothly. Peta does pre-preparation but only for the first class of the week. This includes activities such as making and proving dough for bread or making stock for soup. The first class works with the pre-prepared goods, then gets things ready for the next class. In this way, the students get an understanding of the whole process of preparing a dish from the base up.

Peta keeps her own diary. She records how dishes are received and how the class behaves, makes comments about individual kids, and makes a note of what not to do again.

Early feedback

Early November and the feedback from the classroom teachers is mostly positive. The kids say they enjoy the cooking and love the eating. In every kitchen class, they taste new food and learn new skills. But not every child tastes everything, and there is often food left uneaten at the end of a session. This is great for the kitchen and garden volunteers, who get to feast on what is left, and the kitchen quickly becomes a popular meeting-spot at recess and lunchtime – a warm and inviting place, where pretty posies of herbs and flowers decorate the tables and the wonderful smell of home cooking fills the corridors.

I am delighted to receive an email from Principal Frances, who had previously expressed doubt that the cooking part of the program needed a double period: 'I went to watch the cooking today and Peta was fabulous. I wanted to tell you that you were right – the cooking does require two periods of time!'

Being the marvellous person she is, she had agreed to try it my way initially, despite her reservations. I had made the point that in art classes it is understood it takes time to lay out materials before the painting starts and there is also cleaning up to be done at the end of each session. I saw in the art-class model a close parallel with how the kitchen classes would evolve.

After a few weeks in the kitchen, it becomes obvious we have an urgent need for volunteers (as was clear in the garden). A class with two or three adults in attendance never seems as effective as one with four or five. We work out the ideal ratio as one volunteer per group, with Peta to float and provide overall supervision. Collingwood does not have a large community of stay-at-home mothers to draw upon, and we cannot summon up an instant network of volunteers for the kitchen, as we did for the garden via Cultivating Community. We know our volunteers will need to come from the general community – people who have heard about our program and are willing to help. I write a letter and send it to various restaurants in Melbourne and this brings forth two wonderful people: Melanie Schouten and Cam Woolcock from the restaurant Pearl. Peta's mum remains one of our key volunteers, but she travels a great deal so is not always available. I go to Collingwood as often as I possibly can, but I am also the media spokesperson for the project, which is very time-consuming.

Contact with the media is proving very important: the more people that hear about what we are doing, the more support we gather. We get a lot of media coverage in just a few months: an appearance on Channel Ten's *Good Morning Australia*, radio interviews on ABC's Radio National and 774, and on the community station 3RRR; numerous articles in local, state and interstate newspapers; and profiles in almost every food magazine in Australia. In every case, the journalist on the story wants to talk to me, and I have to overcome my natural shyness to speak persuasively about this important project.

> Cooking is like magic sometimes.
> Quote from Colin

> We had lots of fun pulling up potatoes. Some of them had very crazy shapes. One even looked like a Mickey Mouse head. In cooking we made rosemary and potato pizza and frittata.
> Quote from Dominica

Kitchen and garden safety

Principal Frances has had no problem with the children handling sharp knives, electrical appliances and hot pans and oven trays, confident as she has been in our awareness of safety issues and the commonsense of the children themselves. My own message to teachers, parents, volunteers and others is this: if children are shown how to do something properly and if they are interested enough to do it carefully and attentively, then the potential for an accident is greatly reduced. In four years we have had to apply a Bandaid only about three or four times and then only for very minor nicks.

Knives

Visitors are often amazed to see our children using professional knives, which are, by definition, very sharp. The kids at Collingwood regard the knife box with a certain ambivalence. They are equally thrilled by and scared of our shiny silver, serious knives. I think they see them as slightly illicit. Many have confided that they would never be allowed to use such a thing at home. But I have always believed that one is more likely to be injured using a blunt or bendy knife than a good-quality knife.

Thanks to a donation from Mark Henry of Füritechnics, we have 25 large (East-West) and 25 small paring knives. Known as Füri knives, they are used by many chefs as well as good home cooks. Each knife is forged from a single piece of steel. Australian designed, they are well-balanced, are of appropriate but not excessive weight and are easy to sharpen.

We develop a list of rules for using knives:

* *Don't walk around with a knife in your hand.*
* *The exception to the above rule is if you have collected a knife from the box and are returning to your work station – then you walk with the knife held flat against your side.*
* *Never wave a knife in the air.*
* *Never put a knife in a sink of soapy water where it cannot be seen.*
* *When not in use, push the knife to the back of the workbench with the blade facing away from you.*
* *Learn to tuck in your fingers when slicing.*
* *Learn the proper technique for chopping.*

Other kitchen rules

* *Never run in the kitchen.*
* *Assume the handle of a pot will be hot and use a cloth.*
* *Wipe up spilled liquids immediately and thoroughly.*

Garden rules for students

* *Always carry tools facing down or in a wheelbarrow.*
* *Don't leave tools lying around; everything should be put back in its proper place once the job is finished.*
* *Don't swing tools; be aware of others when using them.*
* *Ensure tools are clean and dry before being stored.*
* *Walk and do not run in the garden.*
* *For the safety of the plants, always walk on pathways.*
* *Work well together.*
* *Sit quietly at the beginning and end of each class.*

Garden rules for garden teachers

* *Ensure the students and volunteers wear gloves at all times to avoid cuts, blisters, soil-borne diseases and the discomfort of handling prickly plants, like comfrey.*
* *Keep potting mix damp to prevent potential inhalation of Legionnaire's spores.*

> We saw Luke hold a handful of snails to feed the chooks. It looked very disgusting. We followed him to see him feed the chooks. Caitlin and me tried taking out a snail from the chook house 'cause we didn't want it to get eaten. We put it next to a puddle and it fell in. We were going to put it back in the garden but it was time to go.
> Quote from Jenni

> Today in the kitchen it was beautiful. It had other paint on the wall and the table was round, the fridge was changed and the oven too. My group made eggs with tomatoes and peppers. We all sit down in a blue chair and I ate eggs with tomatoes and peppers and it was yummy! The last food we eat was the fritters and it was FANTASTIC!
> Quote from Vy

Expansion

December is here and it is apparent that even with the best possible effort, our garden cannot supply the quantities of food we need for a full-scale kitchen program. It is necessary to expand the garden to provide more space. Our last job for the year is to build the wave bed alongside the main garden and plant it with a green-manure crop to enrich the soil. This crop will be dug in at the end of the winter in 2002, so no new vegetable planting will be possible before spring. We will continue to need help from Queen Victoria Market, which has agreed to supply us with extra produce for the first half of 2003.

We tackle some of the problems associated with running the program across two distinct areas: the garden and the kitchen. Because the specific aim of the program is to teach children about the full food cycle – as expressed by our mantra of growing, harvesting, preparing, sharing – we need to ensure the working relationships and processes run smoothly. To achieve this, the kitchen team needs to be aware of the broad learning objectives in the garden and to have realistic expectations of what can be produced. The garden team needs to be sympathetic to the aims of teaching children about new flavours and the culinary potential of crops. And the harvest must allow all students the experience of cooking with fresh food in the kitchen.

Our garden and kitchen teachers are not trained primary school teachers. There has been no thought given to specific training for this job, as nobody could really predict how it would all work. Both Petas express feelings of anxiety from time to time about whether or not they are doing their job in the right way. Both feel the strain of limited preparation time, as it becomes apparent that the success of a class depends on good planning. This project demands dedication, organisational skills and the ability to grow and be flexible. It is a very tall order, but one Peta Christensen and Peta Heine achieve with distinction.

On a very uplifting note, Principal Frances writes to me excitedly just before the start of the summer holidays:

> We have an assembly at the end of the year where we farewell each other, and the year five students give a little presentation about what they've done and what they've liked about Collingwood. It's staggering for me that every single student wrote that it was the Kitchen Garden and the cooking program – every single one! It was an overwhelming: 'This is what we like most about this school.' They were the ambassadors – they loved the gardening. They loved the cooking.

< Green zebra
heirloom tomatoes

> One of the dads helps
maintain the garden

< Volunteer Susan helps
with the barbecue

˅ We planted cosmos and
sunflowers among the vegetables

> Volunteer Jenn
Kitchen helps
out with some
of the more
difficult tasks

Teacher roles

At Collingwood College, the garden and kitchen teachers both work part-time – two days teaching and one half-day planning. Both positions report directly to the principal.

Both teachers are required to:

* liaise with one another on a weekly basis to coordinate harvesting and menu-planning activities
* liaise with one another to explore ways to integrate learning in the garden with learning in the kitchen
* facilitate classes with the aid of the classroom teacher assisting in behavioural issues
* involve classroom teachers and students in the development of the syllabus through formal and informal discussions
* be resourceful about obtaining necessary equipment: seek donations where possible; scavenge, borrow, beg and, if all else fails, make the appropriate purchases
* liaise with the wider community and nurture relationships with those donating goods to the program
* liaise with the school community regarding the development of the program and the program infrastructure
* coordinate and support volunteers, compile and update volunteer information, advertise for volunteers, respond to interest from potential volunteers
* provide encouragement, advice and inspiration to other schools by facilitating group tours and school excursions, giving presentations and responding to phone calls and emails
* attend regular meetings of the Kitchen Garden Committee to ensure round-table discussion of all aspects of the program; to plan activities and special days; and to identify and solve problems
* assist with the documentation of the project by recording comments on classes, collecting worksheets, conducting class surveys, coordinating photographic documentation and so on.

Extra duties for the garden teacher are:

* plan weekly classes, ensuring they are applicable to all participating age groups; this involves preparing up to five activities per class, creating a syllabus and preparing materials
* plan the planting of the garden and involve the students in the process
* harvest produce at the beginning of the day for the first kitchen class
* work in the garden doing general gardening tasks like weeding, pest control and completing jobs not finished by students, as well as cleaning the shed
* maintain equipment and communicate any maintenance matters to either the school groundskeeper or maintenance worker.

Extra duties for the kitchen teacher are:

* plan the weekly menu, ensuring it is suitable for all participating grades, incorporating seasonal garden produce wherever possible and reinforcing key techniques; pre-prepare elements of the menu for the first class if (absolutely) necessary
* prepare recipes in a format suitable for children to understand, and arrange photocopies for all classes
* shop for extra ingredients within budget guidelines
* maintain dry-food stores and monitor equipment needs.

Anthony and Kitchen Teacher Peta
run through the menu

The second year – 2002

Our permaculture garden

The children return from their summer holidays at the end of January raring to get back into the garden to check out what has happened over the long break.

Despite the setbacks of the year before, we have plenty of leafy salad greens to harvest and luxurious quantities of silver beet. This silver beet is our star crop, both the regular variety and the colourful rainbow chard. The herbs are growing well, too. I am envious of the health of the French tarragon, having always found it a very temperamental plant in my own garden. There are strawberries on the bushes. Few of these ever make it to the kitchen, as they are just too irresistible. We resolve to create a 'pick-me patch' in the next planting plan, featuring peas, cherry tomatoes, beans and berries.

By now every student understands that their garden is an organic garden. In addition to the 'fresh is best' philosophy we embrace in the Kitchen Garden, the garden staff from Cultivating Community are strongly committed to permaculture, a garden design system founded by Bill Mollison and David Holmgren in the 1970s. Permaculture links the concepts 'permanent', 'agriculture' and 'culture', and suggests that it is not possible for any culture to survive for long without sustainable gardening systems being followed.

One of the principles of permaculture is the planting of a diverse range of plants, many of them perennials, which can be used for more than one purpose (windbreak, pest control and food) are self-seeding and provide a strong framework to protect the more fragile annual plantings. Another is the use of raised 'no-dig' beds. These are built of thick layers of organic material, which enable plants to grow without disturbing the sub-soil and require less physical effort to create and maintain.

In our establishment year, we rushed ahead with our garden, spurred on by the catchcry 'Just do it!', and the need to plant, grow and harvest produce for our kitchen. Our main approach was simply to plant more crops and lots of them.

Looking back on the establishment period, I can see how a better understanding of philosophy and ideas would have helped us all. Slowly I have learned the significance of permaculture and more about the rationale behind practices that I had initially found a little bemusing.

In this second year, we are all getting much better at developing and communicating the philosophy of the kitchen garden as a whole. As a result, the garden is gradually becoming a place of harmony and calm, rather than one characterised by frenzied activity. The children are active learners in a very physical sense. They are encouraged to connect with the natural world in all its richness, from straightforward sensory contact with sunshine, wind and rain, to more subtle understandings of how to create healthy soil, observe nature in action, nurture plants and be involved in all aspects of growing food in a sustainable manner. Sustainability is addressed in many ways: we don't use chemical pesticides, fertilisers or other herbicides; we continually stress the importance of the compost heap and of our friends the worms; we select non-hybrid varieties of plants; we save seed from one harvest to the next.

Compost

The compost heap has become a star feature of the program. Into our three compost corrals go plants that have gone to seed or have been badly damaged by small feet or snails; vegetable and fruit scraps from the kitchen; and non-noxious weeds. Over time, these bits and pieces are transformed into a rich food for the garden beds. The compost is the heart of the garden – alive and pumping with worms and micro-organisms, which work day and night to create a rich source of fertiliser. The compost has a strong smell. Some children dislike it and complain when they feel they have had more than their fair share of composting duties. But most don't have a problem dealing with the compost once it is ready. They happily load it into the wheelbarrow, and enjoy finding the worms and other 'minibeasts' that dwell there.

We have a fast-moving compost system as well as a slow one for woody bits. Both of these compost systems act as worm farms. But in reality the whole garden is one big worm farm – the worms have colonised all the garden beds and helped enrich and aerate the soil in the process.

Compost contains a wide range of nutrients that plants need, and helps increase the water retention of soil. Elements often not found in chemical-based fertilisers, such as boron, manganese, iron, copper and zinc, are found in compost made from decomposed vegetable matter.

We use additional fertilisers to complement our compost. One is known by the children as 'moo-poo tea', a liquid fertiliser that comes courtesy of Regal, Heather and Bella, cows from the nearby Collingwood Children's Farm. Other liquid fertilisers are made from nutrient-rich plants such as comfrey and nettle.

So much happens all the time in the program that I find it hard to keep up with everything. When I discover that nettles are part of the garden fertilising system, I seize the opportunity to demonstrate how the very same nettles can be used to make a wonderful risotto or soup. This surprises Garden Teacher Peta as much as it does the students. As a child I was astonished to see my mother picking the beastly plants that stung my ankles so painfully (she wore rubber gloves) and turning them into a delicious soup. A simple example of how the expertise of each specialist can provide enlightenment for the others.

Slugs and snails

Another issue that keeps us busy in the garden is the ongoing bombardment of slugs and snails. We try everything. We fill tubs with beer. (The beer attracts the snails, which then fall in and drown.) This works well in drought conditions, but if we have a downpour the beer gets washed away and the snails use the water-filled tubs as swimming pools. The most effective system so far has been putting crushed egg shells at the base of plants, along with organically-approved Multigard pellets.

At an organic expo I hear about a snail-deterrent formula made up of one part espresso coffee diluted with ten parts water that is sprayed on the leaves. But the children's favourite method is a snail hunt, followed by a snail race, and ending with a visit to the chooks, where the snails end up as dinner.

The problem of plant protection provides ongoing opportunities for the kids to experiment with a range of solutions. For example, they discover they can stop butterflies laying their eggs on the plants by placing half an eggshell in the opened leaves of the plants, with the inside of the eggshell facing the sky. This tricks the butterfly into not landing on the plant, and it provides another example of how the use of costly chemicals can be avoided.

< Andrew and Ari getting to know the compost bays

< Volunteer Len and Oliver turning compost

> Happy gardeners Damien and Victor with Garden Teacher Liz

< Digging for potatoes

Heidi's garden themes and activities

Themes	Activities
HARVEST	Harvesting techniques and learning how to tell when plants are ready to be picked
	Touch, taste, smell
	Picking flowers for the kitchen tables
COMPOST: WORMS, MINIBEASTS, MICRO-ORGANISMS	Wanda worm show
	Making compost
	Worm olympics
	Worm song
	Making compost bins
	Collecting food scraps from the kitchen and classrooms
TOOL SAFETY, USAGE AND IDENTIFICATION	Tool relay
	Wheelbarrow licence test
	Caring for tools
	Naming tools in the garden guru quiz
	Wearing gloves
PROPAGATION, SEED DEPTH	Seed sowing through drilling seeds or broadcasting seeds
	Transplanting seedlings
	Propagating from corms, root division, runners, rhizomes and cuttings
PLANT IDENTIFICATION, BIODIVERSITY	Exploring plant stories, histories, usage and families through storytelling
	Sensory identification of plants by smell and touch as well as sight
	Seed ordering through reading catalogues
	Labelling plants
	Eye-spy or mapping activities
WATERING TECHNIQUES	Watering – when and how much
	Watering song
BUGS AND OTHER BEINGS OF THE GARDEN	Snail hunts
	Snail races
	Setting snail traps
	Pear-cherry slug investigations
	Insect identification
	Insect drawing
	Applying organic methods of pest management
	Observing the creatures

Themes	Activities
PLANT NEEDS: WATER, AIR, SOIL, NUTRIENTS, MINERALS, SUN, MOON, TLC AND SO ON	Learning about companion planting, fertilising, aerating the soil, watering and crop rotation Seed dance Watching seeds grow Plant songs and poems
SEASONS AND WEATHER	Seasonal planting Drawing a season board Rain-watchers activity: making and recording rain gauges Seasonal songs Tug-of-war at equinox Making corn dollies for autumn harvest
PLANT ANATOMY, PLANT FAMILIES	Complete/incomplete flowers: hand-pollinating pumpkins Male and female zucchini flowers Seed collecting and saving Exploring plant parts through drawing Observing/drawing similarities within plant families
SOIL STRUCTURE	Performing a soil pH test Measuring soil temperatures Soggy soil experiment: exploring clay, sand, loam and compost, drainage
GARDEN DESIGN AND BUILDING ASPECT, DRAINAGE	Designing beds Building beds Designing plantings Building pergolas
PRUNING	Pruning Making herb posies Collecting bundles of herbs for drying Making smudge sticks (dried herbs that are burned to create natural incense)
THE BIGGER PICTURE: PERMACULTURE, BIODYNAMICS, ORGANICS, ENVIRONMENTAL SUSTAINABILITY, CITIZENSHIP	Hearing stories from visitors Exploring environmental issues Creating a flow chart of the garden system World Environment Week activities
OTHER PROJECTS	Sculptures, decorations, scarecrows and so on

Our first autumn

We get a new garden teacher: Liz Moore, another Cultivating Community gardener, joins the team to work two days a week. Garden Teacher Peta is staying, but will only work one day a week. This extra day is necessary, and was always intended, but it does add a new strain to the budget. Once again, the marvellous Principal Frances agrees to 'find' the money somehow.

We draw up a planting plan at the beginning of autumn. We also intend to do one at the beginning of spring, although there are many plants that are planted throughout the year (see Planting Lists on page 24). Crop rotation is an essential aspect of successful vegetable gardening; this is how Liz explains it to her young gardeners:

If a bed has had a couple of seasons of root or heavy-fruiting crops (hungry crops), it's a good idea to give these beds a break and plant more shallow-rooted crops such as salad greens.

We pull up the spent summer crops, chop them up and add them to the compost. We prepare the ground for planting new plants for spring harvest. We have an Easter-egg hunt for potatoes, which have been planted in a separate bed so that other plants will not be damaged by enthusiastic collectors. The children collect autumn leaves from the beautiful garden and the orchard. We dampen them and keep them in a separate pile to break them down a little before they go into the compost. We give the fruit trees their first prune.

A request comes from the kitchen to plant more parsley! And to try snowpeas again – they did not grow well in the first year. As always, we need more salad leaves. The salad leaves are a big problem: the tender varieties the children like best are also a favourite with the snails. The children enjoy picking the snails from the leaves and rushing this meal to the bantam hens, but on weekends there is no one to do this and the snails have a party. In the kitchen we reassure the children that even if a leaf has a big bite taken out of it, it will still taste good.

We include potato cakes on one of our menus. They are made from mashed potato bound with an egg and some chopped parsley. We fry them in a mixture of olive oil and butter until they are golden and crisp on the outside and creamy in the middle. 'These potato cakes are much better than the ones from the fish and chip shop!' says one child.

The garden and kitchen teachers are finding it difficult to get together to discuss how best to coordinate their planning. Sometimes timetabling works against this, with classes being held at the same time in both the kitchen and garden. Lunchtimes are often the only time to get together – the teachers meet in the kitchen and talk as they lunch on delicious leftovers. Things also work well when Kitchen Teacher Peta gets to walk through the garden with garden teachers Peta and Liz; they show her what is ready for picking and what is likely to be ready in the next week or so.

As always, class planning is vital, as is making sure the children get a lot of enjoyment out of their various activities. We invent fun names for children involved in particular tasks: the 'nursery gnomes' sow, propagate and thin seedlings; the 'shifters' use wheelbarrows; the 'investigators' conduct soil or water tests, identify plants and investigate pest problems; and the 'pest busters' make traps for snails, protect plants from birds with netting and so on.

We find it necessary to give the different grades tasks suitable for the ages of the children involved. The grade-three children focus on new terms like 'harvest' and 'sow'. Their activities include composting, tool usage and safety, plant identification and basic gardening skills. They sort, save, sow and plant seeds; make compost lasagne; water the plants, and feed them with various fertilisers, including the ever-popular moo-poo tea; collect flowers for the kitchen tables; examine the garden's creatures – the worms and the many 'minibeasts'; harvest fruit; and pull out tomato vines.

The grade-four children focus on plant anatomy and plant families; the grade fives, on propagation herb identification and usage; and the grade sixes have a series of special projects, including building activities. These older children do many of

LEMON
BUTTER
"SWEET, RICH
YUMMY!"

the same activities as the younger grades, as well as tasks such as path trimming, transplanting seedlings, and building wooden bed borders. Heidi's Garden Themes and Activities chart, on page 46, shows how activities are linked to particular areas of learning, and how the kitchen and garden program gives students a broad range of experiences as well as the opportunity to acquire a range of skills, many of which are transferable to other areas of the curriculum.

The kitchen makeover

The kitchen makeover happens in the July school holidays. Channel Nine, with help from Fisher & Paykel, decide a makeover would be a wonderful addition to a story they are filming about the Kitchen Garden project for *A Current Affair*. They have already filmed the kids cooking in the old kitchen and eating at their very small, battered rectangular tables. Part of the plan is to keep me in ignorance, so that my reaction can be filmed when I discover what's been going on. This is easy to organise – I happen to be taking a family holiday while the elves are hard at it.

When I arrive for the first session of the new term, I am a bit surprised to see television cameras, but not too much so. The Kitchen Garden at Collingwood College has proved itself very appealing to the media and we have all become a bit blasé about the presence of cameras. But this is different. The lenses are right in my face as I slide open the door.

The seated children almost burst with the effort of not making a sound as they wait for my reaction. They are not disappointed – I am loudly and genuinely astonished.

We have new round tables and comfortable moulded chairs. The walls have been painted with feature panels of brilliant apple green, sunshine yellow and scarlet. We have new whiteboards,

and our new display shelving holds our collection of platters, bowls and cookery books. We have new plates and water tumblers. We have shiny new stoves, and a big new refrigerator. And, I am told, we have a completely new hot-water system.

We are thrilled. The children write thank-you letters to the sponsors concerned and tell all who will listen about the virtues of their new kitchen classroom. Kitchen Teacher Peta and I spend a brief moment wondering if we have compromised the integrity of the program by accepting so much help, but we get over it fairly quickly. Soliciting donations in kind is vital; we could never raise the sort of money we would need to re-equip the kitchen, as well as fund the program.

The round tables are an important change for us. They symbolise the coming together and sharing part of our philosophy. Round tables encourage talk and facilitate the passing of plates. As our food is always placed at the centre of the table, everyone can see and admire it equally. Yes, we could have continued to produce good food in the old kitchen, but the makeover helps reinforce the value of the program and makes the kitchen such a bright and cheerful place to be. (Because we are cooks, we sometimes wish for gas stoves instead of our electric ones, but then mentally smack the backs of our hands at such ingratitude.)

This year there are too many tomatoes!!! In the garden there are cute little rock melons with their watermelon print. Not for long they will grow Big Fat Brown and Bumpy. Pumpkins are delicious when they are in season. Pick them and put them in the pot!! In Bed One yummy strawberries live on Little hills.
From Laura's Kitchen Garden Diary

The pantry

This is a list of the commonly used dry goods in our pantry. Nearly every week we add to these basic stores as we expand our repertoire of dishes – this is just a start-up guide.

It's okay to buy some things in commercial sizes, but keep an eye on items such as flour and rice, which are prone to weevil infestation, and nuts, which turn rancid in excessive heat. Plan carefully as you approach the end of each term.

Spices must be fresh to convey full flavour. Avoid the neatly packaged supermarket jars and bottles. Buy small quantities of sealed envelopes of spices and store the packages in clean glass jars. Respect the use-by date.

Just because the consumers are children, do not compromise on quality and freshness. We are trying to engage and delight these young palates, not turn them off a dish forever because of poor-quality ingredients. We get donations of extra-virgin olive oil from Robinvale Estate, delivered in twenty-litre drums, which we decant and use for all salads and drizzling. We buy grana padano cheese, never pre-grated packages that smell like 'dirty feet', according to one child. We buy wine vinegar for dressings, not the colourless industrial vinegar widely available. When we buy ricotta for pasta fillings, we make sure it is very fresh.

Cupboard storage
Aluminium foil
Arborio rice
Baking paper
Castor sugar
Cornflour
Couscous
Cracked wheat
Cupcake cases
Currants
Granulated sugar
Haricot beans
Icing sugar
Lentils
Long-grain fragrant rice
Pappadams
Pizza flour
Plastic film
Polenta
Raisins
Self-raising flour
Sultanas
Tahini
Wholemeal flour

Spice shelf
Black peppercorns
Cinnamon sticks
Coriander seeds
Cumin seeds
Curry leaves
Fennel seeds
Ground turmeric
Paprika
Pure vanilla
Salt
Sesame seeds
Sumac

Asian shelf
Egg noodles, dried
Fish sauce
Hoi sin sauce
Mirin
Rice noodles, dried
Rice-paper wrappers
Rice vinegar
Soy sauce
Sweet chilli sauce

Freezer
Breadcrumbs
Butter
Filo pastry
Grated coconut
Nuts
Pre-rolled all-butter puff
    pastry sheets
Stock
Wonton wrappers

Refrigerator
Butter
Cheeses
Eggs
Milk
Yoghurt

First-aid and safety requirements
Aloe vera gel or
    aloe vera plant
Antiseptic cream
Bandages
Bandaids
Burn gauze dressings
Cottonwool balls
Eyewash
Fire extinguisher x 2
Safety blanket
Scissors

Laundry/cleaning
Detergent for washing-up
Dishwasher powder
Laundry powder
Liquid soap
Scourers
Wettex

A little cottage in the garden

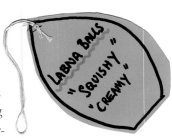

LABNA BALLS "SQUISHY" "CREAMY"

In August we get a new shed for the garden! Freda Thornton, our parent architect, hears we are trying to get hold of a cheap tin shed to lock away the garden tools, and convinces us to be more ambitious: 'If things can be beautiful, why not have a try?'

Freda designs a solid shed, but one with as much grace and style as money will allow – 'a little cottage in the garden'. It is maintenance-free, made of natural materials, and designed so it won't cast shadows on the garden beds.

We work to a budget of around $5000. Our very reliable working-bee people help with the construction, and we get some professional help from Matt, a parent and carpenter.

Our completed shed has storage space for hand tools and gumboots, a rack for hanging large tools, a rack for warm coats and sunhats, benches for potting up seedlings and plenty of parking for the wheelbarrows. There is an overhang, which will provide shelter for wet-weather classes, and the sloped roof doubles as a water-catching device.

Spring is the busiest time of the year for planting seeds and seedlings and fertilising with our own home-brewed concoctions. Pea straw is spread over the beds to act as mulch and to prepare for the summer heat. Bean pyramids are constructed to support the bean crops. The broad beans are a huge hit and look like Jack's beanstalks, reaching to a height of two metres. The corn is growing strongly, and doubles as a windbreak.

The soil analysis is very encouraging: no deficiencies. We are advised to continue with our regime of compost and liquid fertilisers. Garden Teacher Liz devises the sensory-shed activity, which proves to be a lot of fun for both the teacher and the students. Students are blindfolded and asked to guess which plants from the garden they are sniffing, touching and tasting. This sort of game is a simple evaluation tool to ascertain what the students have understood and retained.

Aspen finds an interesting way to display the harvest

In the kitchen we prepare labna balls with herbs. One of the kids, Adam, is surprised to learn that these delicious creamy balls are made from yoghurt. New Classroom Teacher Olga Jursa tells us stories about her childhood in Eastern Europe and of a happy memory of eating hot cherry-filled dumplings served with yoghurt. The children love hearing these stories of when we adults were young.

> Today at cooking we made slow-roasted tomatoes, garlic and rosemary with balsamic vinegar and olive oil served with grilled bread. It was fun until Serhat and Peter cut into a rotten tomato. It made me sick. But the part I likes was grilling the bread. So good!
> Quote from Damian

> I found a gord nearly as big as my head. I have also found that there's some sort of disease with the tomatoes. I have also found that the green house has been smashed. But on a happier note the pumpkins I planted are now massive. I also noticed the fennel is massive. At first I thought Liz had gone crazy but when I asked her she told me that she had left the fennel to go to seed on purpose so that we could get all the fennely seeds. I must say that's going to be fun. And now I enjoy gardening. It's one of my favourite sessions.
> Quote from Aspen's Kitchen Garden Diary

Equipping the garden shed

This is a list of equipment stored in our shed. We have never felt it necessary to buy (or beg) multiples of everything, as not every child does the same thing – such as digging with garden forks – at the same time. Where possible, we've purchased good-quality tools that will last for a long time. The kids struggle with bad-quality equipment and the plants suffer.

* brooms
* buckets
* forks and pitchforks
* gardening gloves
* hammers, mallets, saws, rope, wire, scissors, wire mesh for building projects
* hedge clippers
* hoes
* hoses
* measuring implements
* pots in a range of sizes
* rakes
* secateurs
* seed stamps
* small watering cans
* soap
* spray bottles
* trays
* trowels
* weed forks
* wheelbarrows

The ideal kitchen classroom

While many Australian secondary schools of a certain age will still have a home economics classroom, most primary schools will not be so lucky. Schools wanting to implement a gardening and cooking program will need to build a kitchen of some kind, possibly in an existing classroom. Ideally, this room would be located as close as possible to the garden.

In some states and in some schools there are unused or rarely-used canteen kitchens, often with adjacent space used for eating, which with a bit of creative planning could become effective kitchen classrooms.

Below is a plan by Freda Thornton that details the proposed conversion of two classrooms into a kitchen at Nunawading Primary School.

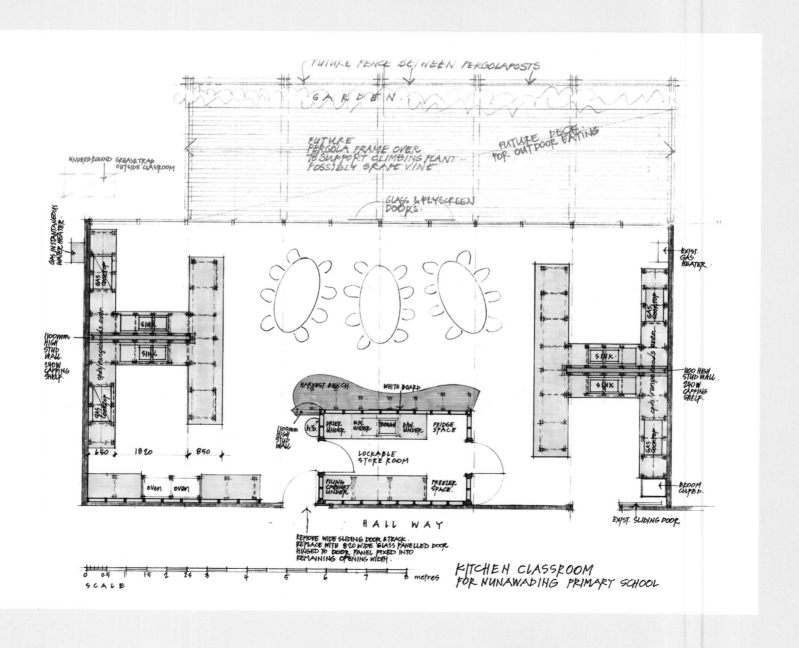

KITCHEN CLASSROOM
FOR NUNAWADING PRIMARY SCHOOL

Cooking Stations

A kitchen classroom needs four to five cooking stations (one for every four to five students) and, if space permits, a demonstration bench with its own cooktop. Each station will need a stove or a cooktop with four burners. Not every station requires an oven if cooktops have been installed. A minimum of two ovens will be needed for the class, each with an accurate thermostat and top grill. Each station needs a small double-basin sink; a generous, easily wiped workbench (with good overhang for attaching pasta machines); storage drawers; and open shelving.

Storage

A harvest table, where freshly grown produce can be displayed prominently, is essential.

A bench should be set aside for the permanent housing of a food processor, electric mixer and any other shared food appliances (make sure you have sufficient power points for all the machines to be going at any one time); underneath this bench, there should be a lockable cupboard for storing these valuable items overnight and during holidays.

We have found that centralised storage of 'like with like' is more effective than trying to create 'sets' of stuff for each station. The children quickly learn where to go for mixing bowls, baking trays, measuring spoons and cups, and graters and strainers. Conversely, we do have a set of scales at each station, and a container of wooden spoons, spatulas and tongs at the ready.

In addition, we have lockable storage for dry goods, knives and classroom notes and records.

Refrigeration

A kitchen classroom needs a large (family-sized) refrigerator (or even two refrigerators, if there is room) and a chest freezer.

Cleaning

It also needs a small area with a washing machine and a dryer – our classes at Collingwood seem to go through an amazing number of kitchen cloths, aprons and tea towels.

A luxury would be to have a dishwasher and an additional sink for scraping and rinsing plates, preferably with a closed door between this area and the classroom for noise control. Often one class is back-to-back with another class and the small amount of

time between is needed to re-set the stations, but it is often spent instead washing up the plates from the meal. The children clean up after cooking but it is best if they have plenty of time available to eat and interact in a relaxed way.

General thoughts

A whiteboard is an important piece of equipment for recording comments, and reminding students of what time the food needs to be ready for the table and so on.

Choose round tables for maximum interaction. We have found the optimum diameter for seating eight is 1500 millimetres.

Display shelves for books, platters and beautiful things help make the kitchen a pleasant place to be.

The floor should be finished with a non-slip surface, and the room should be light and well-ventilated (particularly if using gas) and protected from full sunlight.

The building should be secure at night and at other times when the school is closed.

There should be enough lockable storage space so that all equipment can be securely stored during holidays.

There should be a tap and a trough outside (or outside the garden shed) for the washing of vegetables as they are harvested.

Plan a simple barbecue area for grilling food – grilled, just-harvested sweetcorn with a little butter is so good! One barbecue should be enough, although the more the better. A barbecue area will work particularly well if it opens off the kitchen.

Multi-use potential

With sufficient storage to lock away kitchen equipment, your classroom kitchen could easily double as a delightful and spacious multi-use room for staff gatherings and school council meetings, and for other types of classes. Of course, the primary use would have to be respected. Some schools may even want to start up kitchen and gardening clubs for children who are especially keen, or, use the kitchen to prepare for special events, such as school fairs and open days. It is possible that this facility could be hired out to other community groups at weekends or during holiday periods, in the same way that many schools hire out their assembly halls.

The third year – 2003

The biggest no-dig bed ever

February and the beginning of the school year. We welcome a new grade three into the program and notice there is considerable anticipation. We subsequently find out that these children have been the custodians of a mushroom farm, donated by a visiting mushroom grower. Its original home, the garden shed, was too cold and draughty, and with lessons held on only two days of the week, the mushrooms weren't getting the care they needed. So the grade-two class took the mushroom crop into their warm classroom, where they sprayed them each day with water and referred to them as their 'little babies'. Crop after crop went into the kitchen for the cooking program, as well as into salads for the grade-two classroom.

There is much excitement as we start our enormous 'no-dig' garden, in a spot that hasn't gone well at all, due to interference from the roots of some major trees on the school's perimeter. We plan the garden so it sits a metre above the ground; a swimming-pool ladder will allow the kids easy access.

We lay down newspapers, egg cartons and recycled paper (from the school library) soaked in water to stop weeds and roots, then add a layer of pea straw and cover this with two centimetres of rich chicken manure. Next we lay twenty centimetres of loose straw, then another layer of manure and ten centimetres of compost. We water it well to settle it all down. As the matter

decomposes, the level will drop. Because of this, we will have to keep up the layering and decomposing cycle. The garden bed will be ready to plant in early winter. The children are incredulous that a garden bed can be built in this way, although it is in fact quite a standard method nowadays for building garden beds. Some schools we know have used the no-dig recipe to build beds on top of tennis courts.

The star of the summer harvest is the zucchini. The gardeners had planted the superior white zucchini, which is a delight to eat. We discover some monster zucchini that have been hiding under a leaf for a few days, and grown and grown. Such specimens are a bit tasteless but good for stuffing.

We have potatoes of every size and colour, beans, cucumbers, chillies, plenty of tomatoes, salad leaves and herbs – a marvellous time of the year. The children turn a bumper crop of superb basil into jars of pesto, and sell the surplus at the weekly school market. They also make delicious infused vinegars for their salad dressings from freshly picked herbs.

There are large quantities of weeds to be pulled out, as well as the summer annuals to be chopped and composted.

A circular table is built around a large and shady eucalypt tree in the garden so that the children can closely examine interesting or quirky plants or garden creatures.

Garden geezers

Garden Teacher Liz designed this look-and-learn activity based on the following questions:

* What do you notice has changed over the summer break? What has grown that wasn't there before? If this is your first time in the garden, just write down some of the things you notice.
* Find a smell in the garden that you like. Do you know this plant? Can you describe it in words? Can you draw it?
* Have a look at the companion-planting chart. What companion plants are growing together in the kitchen garden?
* What is your favourite plant in the garden and why?
* Do you have some ideas about what you would like to see growing in the garden this year?

He likes to cook omelettes and always goes out into our garden for herbs to add. He cooked pesto and bruschetta all by himself and served it with flair and pride. When we cook tea he often makes suggestions about interesting additions. He likes to make interesting salads . . . many thanks for a gift that will last his lifetime.

Comment from a parent survey

I love eating outside!

Quote from Elena

Lots of silver beet and broccoli

As summer gives way to late autumn there is raking and tidying and planning to be done.

At the onset of winter we pull up the spent bushes that have fed us so well during the summer and autumn terms. Routine change-of-season jobs include pruning and cutting-back deciduous vines and shrubs, and generally preparing the garden for the burst of growth in the springtime. But we still have plenty of our reliable silver beet, both the usual variety and the colourful rainbow chard, with its brilliant orange, fuchsia and golden stems and lovely crinkled leaves.

A favourite recipe using silver beet is silverbeet torte. While making it, some of the students run out of time and have to go to another class. They are quite upset, and ask if they can come back at lunchtime to eat it, which is what they do. Who would have thought that kids would rush back to eat a pie stuffed with silverbeet and a bit of cheese?

The winter harvest also yields plenty of broccoli, beetroots, Asian greens and spring onions. Some of the softer herbs die back in the cold, but the hardier ones, such as thyme, rosemary and parsley, keep growing through the winter.

On one of our winter menus we have quick-blanched broccoli, drained and drizzled with extra-virgin olive oil. 'That was scrumptious. I usually hate broccoli but that was so different,' says one of the students. There is a chorus of agreement and every little morsel is eaten. We seize the moment to talk about not overcooking green vegetables, and introduce the concept of 'texture'. We ask for some good texture words for the whiteboard. 'Crunchy', 'firm' and 'spongy' are suggested.

As the days become colder, there's less tending of the garden required, so the children make signs for the garden beds and terracotta mosaic birds for the tops of the posts supporting the passionfruit vine.

New tanks and a barbecue

Getting water to every plant continues to be a priority, as the long drought continues. By September we have had two rainwater tanks installed – thanks to a grant from City West Water secured by Garden Teacher Liz – to catch any roof run-off, but there has been no rain to fill them. The tanks have stands and sinks, rain gauges and measuring systems, which will allow for plenty of water-based activities when the rains do come.

We have a teary farewell for Kitchen Teacher Peta, who is taking maternity leave to have her second baby, but we are fortunate to find the perfect replacement in Karen Yann, who has volunteered in the program over the past year and is well-known and liked by the children.

As I am a big fan of the grill, I donate a portable barbecue to the Kitchen Garden. Karen plans a barbecue day, and in the spring sunshine we grill vegetables and tiny meatballs, then pack them into open pita bread rounds. The kids have egg-and-spoon races.

We plan a pick-me patch for the new no-dig garden. It will have lots of cherry tomatoes for summer sampling. The late-winter crops of cauliflower and cabbage are finishing.

In late November, we harvest our first raspberries and the first fruit appears on the trees. In both cases the children cannot wait: they try half-ripe raspberries, which are sour, and green fruit, which is hard and inedible. There is a meaningful moment in the kitchen as the children taste the half-ripe raspberries alongside some (purchased) perfectly ripe berries. All agree the ripe fruit tastes best. Another lesson learnt. We hope next year they will be more patient.

We have a sad incident: vandals set the pea straw alight, tear branches from a pear tree, break into the shed and steal tools, and rip entire tomato plants from the ground. The damage is so serious we have to call the police. The team's approach is to educate the students (both within and outside the program) to respect the garden, rather than put it under lock and key.

Watering cans are used to water pots and plants that are beyond the reach of the irrigation system

< Our new rainwater tank helps teach the students about water management

> Spreading tanbark over the garden paths

< Gathering summer crops

< Making ratatouille

> Seedlings receive a dose of natural liquid fertiliser

Drought and destruction

December, and the children are looking forward to a long summer holiday. There are only a few weeks of the school year left. Rosters are in place to care for the garden over the vacation. Some of the best harvests happen during holiday time and this is a bonus for those volunteers who come to check the plants, do a spot of weeding or hand-water the tubs and parts of the garden not reached by the irrigation system: they can go home with zucchini, tomatoes, beans and fresh greens.

A new problem with water threatens our summer crops. The whole country is suffering drought conditions and water use is a much-discussed topic in the garden. To make matters worse, some of our pipes burst. These are connected to our irrigation system, which is only permitted to operate during the night due to the state's water restrictions. The burst pipes lead to parched soil, which causes many salads to go to seed, resulting in much disappointment in the kitchen, and alerting the garden team to the problem. The upside of all this is that the kids have to carry water to keep the garden alive, which gives them a very good understanding of the importance of water and what happens when this flow is diminished.

We learn the following about watering our plants: always water the roots of the plant; water depending on the weather, for example the roots of a kiwi-fruit vine can be watered in the heat of the day but not the lettuce leaves; hold up the watering can or hose to create a flow like the rain; water for a good length of time to allow the water to really soak the soil – come up with a short song or count to fifteen.

Vandals strike again. Some of the girls have been very solicitous about a watermelon, which has been growing well but is not ready to pick. The girls have been careful to cover it at the end of the day with leaves and twigs. One morning they come to school to discover vandals have not only picked the prize melon, but have crudely smashed it into pieces. There are tears and anger.

The girls pick up a few of the pieces and march into various classes to display the wreckage and to vent their rage and disgust. A hard lesson, but just maybe it helps young people who tend to discard things so readily to grasp the value of something they have made or been personally responsible for. The garden team are also very sad at such wilful damage but thankful that vandalism is an occasional rather than a chronic problem. Despite the loss, we decide to leave the garden unfenced, although an external gate to the school will now be locked out of hours.

The soggy soil experiment

A fun activity, devised by Garden Teacher Liz, which dramatically demonstrates differences in soil types and how each type absorbs and drains water.

You will need:
4 transparent containers with drainage holes in the bottom (we use plastic bottles with their tops chopped off)
4 different soil types (clay, compost, sand, topsoil)
4 dishes to sit the containers in (we use baking trays)
4 bottles to be used as pourers (we use plastic bottles with a Texta mark to ensure the water amounts are equal)
measuring jug (if you don't have 4 bottles)

Instructions:
Before starting the activity, describe the different soils.
Sit the containers in the dishes or baking trays and fill each container with a different soil type. Fill the bottles up to the Texta mark with water. What do you think will happen when the water is poured into the soil containers? Will it pass through quickly, slowly or not at all? Pour a bottle of water into each container. Can you describe what happens? Which soil do you think is best for planting in and why?

The fourth and fifth years – 2004 and 2005

The seed queen

We say goodbye to Garden Teacher Liz Moore, who is travelling overseas, and welcome Heidi Sanghvi. Heidi is very interested in teaching the children about seed saving. She has the children sit around our small seed-saving table, with its odd collection of chairs. As they observe, handle, label, packet and – occasionally – eat the seeds, all sorts of wonderful conversations take place between the children and volunteers about all manner of things, from grandmothers' gardens to last night's television.

Heidi, like her predecessors, believes seed saving is a good way of ensuring the purity of plants, particularly when there are lots of different plants growing close by, as is the case in our garden. By letting plants go to seed, we can select and collect seeds from the strongest plants, and we also have a constant source of self-germinating parsley for the kitchen and handfuls of lettuce seeds to sow.

Heidi is also very committed to the growing of heritage varieties of plants, such as the purple-podded pea and Tuscan black kale. She explains that we are growing heirloom plants, some of which have been proven to produce larger yields, because these varieties have more nutritional value than hybrids. Certainly many of the heirloom tomato varieties have better flavour than the modern hybrids. We are also contributing to biodiversity at a time when, according to the FAO State of the World Report, 2000, more than 75 per cent of home-grown food varieties have been lost in the last century.

I tell the students in one of the classes about how Tuscan black kale, or 'cavolo nero', becomes a rich purple–black once cooked and that it is the traditional choice for the best minestrone. (Tuscan kale can also be slowly stewed with garlic and extra-virgin olive oil as a delicious vegetable in its own right, but each leaf must have its central stem removed as it will never soften.)

Worm olympics

You will need:
gardening gloves
seed tray full of dirt from the compost bays
small hand trowels or small garden forks for worm
    hunting in the worm farm
one worm each

What to do:
'Ready, set, go!' is the signal to drop the worms into the compost; the winner is the one that disappears first!

Afterwards:
Discuss what the worms did and why you think they did it. Discuss what you know about worms. Think of a question you have about worms. Look in the books on worms for answers to your questions. At the end of the lesson, share your thoughts with the class.

The harvest table

Another year has turned full circle. Kitchen Teacher Peta is enjoying life at home in the country, growing vegies, tending the chooks and cooking for her babies, so trained chef Desley Insall becomes our third kitchen teacher and quickly becomes known for her harvest table displays, which resemble glorious still-life paintings.

The harvest table sits just inside the door of the kitchen. A few minutes before the first class starts, the garden teacher or a student on harvesting duty brings in baskets of freshly harvested produce. It is always an exciting moment. What could be fresher than this! The harvest varies every week and depending on the season. In late summer, the table displays tomatoes, pumpkin, beans of different varieties (purple, scarlet runners, regular), red-skinned potatoes, carrots, passionfruit, eggs, herbs, green salad leaves and sorrel. Alongside is a display of different kinds of tomatoes, each labelled by variety: ponderosa, mortgage lifter, brandywine, rouge de marmande, yellow cherry, tommy toe, green zebra, roma, black krim. In class we talk about the different textures of the produce: the smoothness of tomato on one's cheek, the roughness of pumpkin skin, the dryness of harvested wheat sheaves (not from the garden).

The end of autumn is closing-down time in the garden: summer crops are pulled out and the first chill is in the air as the ground is prepared for winter brassicas and the planting for spring harvesting. Jerusalem artichokes, baby beetroots, an assortment

brown beauty beans
+ sow spring
(20 seeds)

of potatoes and the last of the green tomatoes adorn the harvest table at this time of year.

Most of the children have never seen a Jerusalem artichoke. In the early days, one child described it thus: 'Looks like ginger; tastes like dirt!' By now beetroots are very familiar, and we eat them oven-roasted and in salads and muffins. We roll thick slices of green tomato in egg and polenta and fry them like fritters – these are very popular. But nobody has heard of the movie *Fried Green Tomatoes at the Whistlestop Café* (I reflect on the fact that the children wouldn't have been born when the film was made.) One student declares, 'I'm going to get my granddad to grow green tomatoes just like these – I don't like the red ones he usually grows.' This young lady still has a bit to learn about the growing of tomatoes.

One week we have a beautiful pumpkin for the kitchen, a gift from the children at Kings Park Primary School in the Western Suburbs, which has its own lovely vegetable garden but so far no room for a kitchen. Garden Teacher Heidi worked at Kings Park before coming to us, and was replaced by another Cultivating Community member.

Kitchen Teacher Desley has enthusiastically taught the children how to make preserves of all sorts to utilise not just our own excess crops but our donations as well. We have rich tomato relish, we have green-tomato chutney and we have Moroccan-style preserved lemons. Our volunteers bring in harvests of crops we do not grow, such as medlars, crabapples and cumquats, so we then have plum jam and crabapple jelly and medlar jelly and cumquat marmalade. Our lemon supply comes from several backyard trees. My own lemon tree is very prolific. My daughter has a cumquat tree in the garden of her house that yields enough fruit for a few jars of cumquat marmalade. I spy a laden pomegranate tree in the front garden of a house I drive past frequently. I haven't asked yet, and am not sure if I should. We have a show-and-tell session in a kitchen class and display a single ripe pomegranate. The kids are fascinated; they carefully dig out the ruby kernels and scatter them over some oven-baked triangles of pita bread spread with hummas.

The corn has grown a lot since last year. The sunflowers are taller than me. The rockmelon is getting bigger. Everything is tall and bushy. Too many tomatoes. The no-dig garden is bloomed exquisitely. Darker shades of green are present.
From Jeanette's Kitchen Garden diary

< Gathering heirloom tomatoes

> Garden Teacher Heidi turning the compost

< No task is beyond even our smallest cooks

> Kitchen Teacher Desley teaches the students to preserve fruit and vegetables to sell at the school market

Compost feeds plants

EASE PUT OMPOST HERE

Volunteers in the Kitchen Garden

Some useful tips from the volunteers

✱ *RECRUIT FROM THE BROAD COMMUNITY* Try to recruit volunteers from the broader community, not just the parent body. This allows the volunteers to meet each group of students without prior knowledge of individuals and praise and encourage each student for what they do in the Kitchen Garden, regardless of what may occur elsewhere in the school.

✱ *ROLE MODELS* If possible, recruit both female and male volunteers; at Collingwood we have both, and they are important role models.

✱ *VALUE YOUR VOLUNTEERS* At Collingwood College, the volunteers have been warmly welcomed by the principal and general teaching staff, and the garden and kitchen teachers constantly check in to make sure the volunteers feel comfortable with what and how they are doing. There is always lots of praise and thanks.

Some useful tips for volunteers

✱ *CONTINUITY* It is highly desirable that as a volunteer you commit to the same class each week. It allows you to develop a relationship with the children and helps you become familiar with the environment. And it helps the teachers with their planning. Volunteers are welcome to stay for the whole day or just for one class.

✱ *PUNCTUALITY* Arrive in good time to be briefed by the kitchen or garden teacher on that day's class activities and menu.

✱ *FIRM AND KIND INSTRUCTION* Your role is one of facilitator, rather than leader. Set a good example. Everyone is there to learn and have fun. Volunteers are not expected to be the disciplinarians, so seek teacher intervention if the firm and kind approach does not seem to be working!

✱ *HANDS-OFF HELP* Encourage all the children in the group to participate and share the load. Demonstrate and supervise, but don't do all the work. Ask the children how they might do something first, then show them if necessary. Don't tell them how straightaway.

✱ *SENSORY LEARNING* Talk to the children about what they see, hear, touch, taste and smell as they go about their tasks in the kitchen and garden.

✱ *SAFETY* Practise safe bending and tool use in the garden, and care with knives and heat in the kitchen; instruct the children to do the same.

✱ *CLEANING-UP* Making a mess and getting dirty does not really matter, however, cleaning-up at the end of the class does. Often you will need to be firm with the children to ensure this is done properly.

✱ *MANY MINDS* We are all learning as we go and welcome all suggestions, ideas and feedback about how we can continue to make the Kitchen Garden a best-practice model.

✱ *HAVING FUN* The children (and staff!) eagerly anticipate the garden and kitchen sessions, and are always keen to learn more and be as hands-on as possible. Encourage a sense of enjoyment – that's what the program is about. We want every volunteer to enjoy their time in the Kitchen Garden.

What we know

By now the patterns are established. The major plantings happen at the beginning of autumn and the beginning of spring. The principles of crop rotation, companion planting, soil enrichment and water management are well understood.

The garden and kitchen are now firmly embedded in the curriculum. Every week the children have experience of both environments: forty-five minutes in the garden and ninety minutes in the kitchen.

We have visitors almost every week, as other schools and prospective sponsors and media hear about the project and arrive for a closer look. All those involved share the important task of explaining what we hope to achieve, and many of the visitors enjoy a shared lunch with the children in the kitchen. Everyone wants 'how-to' advice, but at this stage we can only show them the program in action and refer them to the school website and my own website (see page 242).

One bit of advice we do dispense very confidently is the importance of attracting volunteers from the community, something that has been critical to the success of our own program. By 2005, volunteers are collectively contributing more than 2000 hours a year of work – we can't thank them enough.

What our kids know

In one of the episodes of *Jamie's School Dinners*, Jamie asks kids to identify a leek and a stick of rhubarb. Nobody knows the answer and one child thinks the rhubarb is an onion. Our kids are scathing when they see this. They certainly know the difference between rhubarb and onion and leeks, having grown and cooked them all. They know about globe artichokes, and bulb fennel and celeriac. They know potatoes can be roundish or longish; and have skin that is red, brown, purple or yellow; and have flesh that is yellow, white, creamy or purple. And they know their salad leaves, Asian leafy vegetables and herbs and can identify many varieties of tomatoes. Now, in the kitchen at Collingwood College:

* every child can roll out pasta
* every child has mixed cakes and flat breads and kneaded bread dough
* every child has prepared salad greens and enjoyed spinning them dry in the salad spinners
* every child has combined ingredients by hand and in the food processor to make fillings, stuffings and dips
* every child has mixed salad dressings and dipping sauces and stirred herbs into yoghurt
* every child can chop and slice and whisk
* every child has tasted vegetables raw, baked, stuffed, boiled, braised and combined in curries, soups and dips
* every child can recognise a wide range of ingredients and foods never before encountered
* every child can set a table
* every child understands about presenting food on platters and sharing with others by passing food around.

And in the garden:

* every child has made compost
* every child has skills in organic gardening
* every child understands the importance of conserving water and seed saving
* every child has experimented with and understands the importance of healthy soil
* every child has been instructed in plant and animal identification, and plant anatomy and reproduction
* every child has been involved in planting, protecting seedlings, picking off predators, harvesting, and smelling and tasting
* every child knows about safe and appropriate tool use
* every child has benefited from being active for forty-five minutes in the fresh air, week after week.

Now and the future

What's happening at home?

From the beginning, we had hopes that the enjoyable hours spent in the kitchen and garden would kindle in the children a passion for good food that would extend way beyond the classroom.

With more resources we would like to do more to promote a link between the school experience and home. We imagine we could encourage students to cook a dish at home with a family member and come to school with a taste report. Or we could invite family members to a lunch or an after-school meal, from time to time, and have the children cook and wait on the tables.

But even without a formal program, there is plenty of anecdotal evidence to suggest that the children are taking home and building on their new skills and interests.

At parent and teacher nights, parents describe how their children arrive home full of news of the program, wanting to apply what they have learnt in their own kitchens and backyards. The parents comment on how meaningful the kitchen and garden activities are to the children, and seem to appreciate that through the program, the children are acquiring a full range of academic, social and practical skills. One parent says:

He has become very interested and tries to help in setting the table and preparing the ingredients when I cook. He has been helpful in washing the dishes and is proud of what he's doing.

And another:

She enjoys working in the garden and loves eating the fresh vegies in the cooking. She is more confident in the kitchen and she knows a lot more about vegetables. She likes using herbs and spices.

Izaac reports that at home he is growing chillies, basil, thyme, Vietnamese mint and tomatoes. Nick is growing thyme, chilli, broccoli and parsley in his grandfather's garden. Shaunie has planted parsley, thyme, tomatoes, rosemary and lavender. And Lucy tends tomatoes, pumpkin and lavender. In the window boxes of his flat in one of the big housing commission blocks, Victor plants herbs and spices, after attempting to grow apple and orange trees. A bold attempt indeed!

Garden Teacher Liz tells us this wonderful story:

Each group of children was allowed to decide whether they were going to take home the tomatoes they had grown or sell them at the Thursday market. There was no way the kids were going to sell the tomatoes – they wanted to take them home. They then came back the following week and told me what they'd made with them.

Classroom Teacher Ken tells us that at school camp just about all the children choose to put salad in their hamburgers, in contrast to previous years. Classroom Teacher Mary-Ann reports that a parent says her seven-year-old child 'talks on the phone to

his grandmother for ages about the program and has organised a cooking day with her.'

There are lots of stories of children trying new foods. Lucy never used to like broccoli but now enjoys it served with butter and herbs. Caitlin says she has always hated mushrooms but agrees to taste a mushroom and fennel risotto, and thinks it is wonderful. Casper has never liked brussel sprouts but learns to love them served in butter and pepper and salt.

There is one particular story that overwhelms us. The mother of a child I'll call Jenny comes to see Principal Frances to tell her of Jenny's eating problem. Jenny wants to participate in the program but is nervous she might be forced to eat. The mother is reassured that this will not happen. The child attends classes and is a great little cook – she enjoys chopping and stirring and all the other activities, but when lunch is served, she only sips water. However, in week three, Jenny takes little bites of food, and in week five, she serves herself small portions of several dishes. Her mother returns, ecstatic. She tells us the program has done more to help her child than months of therapy.

We send a simple questionnaire home to parents. When we go through the replies, we are moved and delighted to read comments such as: 'I can see what a fantastic program it is through the enjoyment my daughter shows in exploring new foods and techniques,' and 'It makes him smile and he enjoys it when other children enjoy what he makes.'

Where to now?

This part of the story finishes in 2005, but there is certainly more to come. In order to increase our capacity to raise money to expand into other schools, we set up a not-for-profit charitable organisation, the Stephanie Alexander Kitchen Garden Foundation (SAKGF). As a result, and thanks to the generous support of the Ian Potter Foundation, the Sidney Myer Foundation, the Dyson Bequest and some very generous individuals, in early 2006 we were able to part-fund two additional kitchen gardens, one in a suburban Melbourne school, the second in a regional centre. Both projects are in the first year of their exciting journey.

These are the lucky ones, but there are many others as deserving. More than fifty Victorian schools replied to our call for expressions of interest, when we had funds sufficient for just one school. Every day we hear from another school eager to start a kitchen garden, both in Victoria and in other states.

We offer the following practical advice:

* assess the degree of commitment of the principal, the school council and the classroom teachers
* accept that the bulk of the recurrent costs will be staffing
* explore whether the school is already involved in an environmental education program that has specific resources allocated (for example, water tanks, a garden of sorts) and whether this environmental education could be broadened to include edible gardening
* consider whether there is already a building on the site, ideally near the garden area, which could become a kitchen with space for the students and teachers to eat together
* develop strategies to involve the community in supporting the project; use the local newspaper, call a public meeting, ask the SAKGF to provide a speaker
* seek donations in kind from local businesses and services
* do some creative fund-raising as a school community
* become expert in applying for grants, such as Investing in Schools and Healthy School Communities Grant, to name just two of the federal grants available.

Early on, we caught the attention of philanthropist Barbara Heine. The surname is no coincidence: Barb is Kitchen Teacher Peta Heine's mother – she initially came in to help out in the kitchen. With her husband, Barb cofounded the Kids & Families Foundation (KAFF), an organisation that helps children and families at risk. Through KAFF, Barb became the Kitchen Garden's major benefactor for four years during the all-important pilot phase. Along the way, grants have been secured from the Telstra Foundation; the Strategic Partnerships Program – Department of Education and Training; the City of Yarra; and the fabulous Rotary Club of Collingwood. Not to mention the supplementary produce from the Melbourne Market Authority.

The SAKGF continues to hope that our state governments will provide some support to schools eager to take up the challenge. The Victorian government has listened to us and has been impressed enough to pledge funds for the roll-out of the program in lots more schools, although the participating schools will still be required to raise funds independently.

There is work ahead for us in developing a Kitchen Garden curriculum. In Victoria, the new guiding policy for the curriculum is the Victorian Essential Learning Standards, which stresses integrated learning; all units of work must include physical and social development, disciplinary studies and interdisciplinary studies. As a core unit of work in years three to six, a Kitchen Garden unit can offer fantastic opportunities for learning in art and design, mathematics, physics, history and cultural studies, environmental education, language, personal development and problem solving.

After reading our story we imagine that there will be enthusiastic principals and parents and school councillors who will want to 'Just do it!' We can promise them a winding and marvellous journey and we wish them all luck. The Foundation sees its ongoing role as a lobbyist, fundraiser, trainer of specialist staff, consultant, producer of creative classroom resources and an information resource that can be accessed by other schools. Our commitment to the philosophy of:

Growing Harvesting Preparing Sharing

is even stronger five years on than it was in the beginning. We have seen the results, listened to the children, been enchanted in the garden and enjoyed the lovely food. More than ever we are convinced that this is the way to introduce young children to delicious food, which just happens to be the very food they need to achieve good health.

Melissa serves the beautiful food she helped make with the produce she helped grow

OVER 100 DIFFERENT MENUS have been created for the Kitchen Garden program at Collingwood College since it began in 2001. Many dishes have been repeated due to popular demand from the children. The following thirty-two menus, arranged seasonally, have been among the most successful.

Much of the produce we use in our cooking comes from our garden. We never expected to be 100 per cent self-sufficient. This would have involved turning the entire schoolyard into a vegetable garden! So, to supplement our supplies, every week the kitchen teacher draws up a shopping list of shortfall items, in consultation with her garden colleague.

We keep the costs as low as possible. That said, we don't compromise on quality. If a recipe specifies parmesan, we buy grana padano or parmigiano-reggiano, never packets of cheese gratings. Our salads are dressed with quality vinegar and extra-virgin olive oil, thanks to the generosity of our great friends Maggie Beer, Dee Nolan and Robinvale Estate Olive Products. Mostly we avoid expensive items. For example, asparagus features only once, as we haven't yet succeeded in growing our own, and thought it too costly to buy for 120 children.

The method section of each recipe may look daunting in length, but this is because each recipe is broken into a number of detailed steps. In the classroom this allows us to keep three or four children busy at any one time. The average preparation time is usually thirty-five to forty minutes (it may be longer if you are cooking at home with fewer people). Baking time is sometimes as long as twenty-five minutes, then there is clean-up and the all-important eating time.

Many of the recipes are based on a version first published in *The Cook's Companion*, but quantities, methods and ingredients have all been substantially changed to make the recipes suitable for younger cooks.

Menus and recipes

For kids to read before they start

Almost every one of the following recipes has been cooked in a kitchen classroom by boys and girls aged eight to twelve.

In the classroom, there is always a kitchen manager, along with several volunteers to assist and answer questions. If you are cooking at home, you will need to have an adult in the kitchen with you – your mum or dad or another family member or friend, someone who is experienced with hot ovens, boiling water and sharp knives.

Once you have decided what you are going to cook, read the recipe all the way through, and talk about it with an adult: are there words or terms you don't understand, or other questions you need to ask? Think about how long things take to prepare and cook. Does anything need to be soaked, rested or cooked for a long time? If so, what can you be doing while this happens?

Before you start to cook, you should wash your hands. You will need an apron that covers your clothes really well. And you will need a dry tea towel that is used only for wiping your hands or patting dry rinsed herbs, not for cleaning up. I like to keep this tea towel tucked into the pocket of my apron or even over my shoulder.

I always have one basin of the kitchen sink half-filled with warm, soapy water so that frequently used utensils, such as boards and measuring spoons, can be given a quick swish, then dried with another tea towel and put back into use. If you only have a single sink, fill a large bowl instead and leave the sink empty for draining vegetables and the like.

The sample recipe opposite shows you exactly how most of the recipes in this book – except the basic recipes on pages 76 to 79 – are set out. Read this sample recipe thoroughly to become familiar with the various sections and stages of the process.

Always start by setting out your equipment and ingredients. (Knives must always be placed with the blade away from the front of the bench.) It's a good idea to weigh your ingredients before you begin, to make sure you have enough of everything. If you have bought an ingredient by weight, such as chicken wings, you will already have the right amount and you won't need to weigh it. But things like butter and cheese are often bought in set blocks or packets, and you will need to weigh them.

Next, follow the recipe step by step. The preparation is very important and all good cooks of whatever age follow a method.

Cleaning up is an important part of cooking and is often best done while you wait for food to cook. Rinse knives carefully and never, ever leave a knife in the bottom of a sink or basin. Clean cake tins and baking trays are best left in the turned-off but still-warm oven to make sure they are completely dry.

When it's time to eat, admire your work! Serve your tart, or curry or cake at the centre of the table so that everyone can be amazed at how delicious it smells and looks, even before they help themselves and find out how wonderful it tastes.

Decide to cook again soon . . .

Thyme-marinated fetta wrapped in vine leaves and grilled

Makes 10 pieces
Fresh from the garden garlic, bay leaves, thyme, vine leaves
In this recipe, the fetta needs time to marinate. In the classroom, we used fetta that had been marinated by the previous class, then prepared the fetta for the next class.

Equipment

scales	tray
chopping board	tongs
knives – 1 small, 1 large	kitchen paper
metric measuring spoons	kitchen scissors
large bowl	fork
plastic film	pastry brush
medium saucepan	chargrill pan
tea towel	serving plate

Ingredients

250 g fetta	3 sprigs thyme
2 cloves garlic	extra-virgin olive oil
2 bay leaves	10 fresh vine leaves
1 teaspoon black peppercorns	

BOTTOM DRAWER

Interesting terms/techniques • marinating
• cooking with a chargrill pan
Tip If you want to store this cheese, transfer it and its marinating ingredients to a large storage jar with a tight-fitting lid, and refrigerate. The marinated cheese will be good for at least 4 weeks.
Question Can you think of other foods that would work well wrapped in vine leaves?

Answer Another Greek cheese, haloumi, which contains little flecks of mint, works very well when wrapped and grilled in vine leaves. Sardines and quail are also good done this way.

What to do

✳ Using the scales, weigh the fetta. Set out the chopping board and knives. Chop the fetta into 2 cm cubes. Peel the garlic. Tear each bay leaf into 4 pieces. Place the bay leaves, peppercorns, thyme and garlic in the large bowl. Add the cubes of fetta, stir to mix, then cover with oil. Cover with plastic film and leave to marinate – 1 hour will do it, but overnight in the refrigerator is even better.

✳ Bring a saucepan of water to the boil. Spread out the dry tea towel on top of a tray alongside the saucepan. **Using tongs, dip each vine leaf into the water for 10 seconds, then lay out on the tea-towel-lined tray, rough side uppermost.**

✳ When all the leaves have been dipped and are spread out, pat them dry with kitchen paper. Snip off the stems with scissors. Using a fork, lift a piece of cheese from the bowl, allowing the excess oil to drip back into the bowl, then place the cube in the centre of a vine leaf. Fold the leaf to completely enclose the cheese, tucking in the sides of the leaf. Repeat the process until you have used all the vine leaves. Using a pastry brush, brush each little vine-leaf parcel lightly with the remaining marinade.

✳ Heat the chargrill pan on the stovetop to very hot. Place the parcels carefully on the ridges of the pan. Allow to grill for 2–3 minutes before turning with the tongs and cooking for a further 2–3 minutes. The leaves will become blackened and crisp and the cheese inside will be soft and very tasty.

✳ Place the vine-leaf parcels on the serving plate. When it comes time to eat, make sure you taste the leaves, although you may not want to eat all of them as they are a bit chewy!

Menu 7

Salade niçoise with green and yellow beans, nasturtium blossoms and bantam eggs

Thyme-marinated fetta wrapped in vine leaves and grilled

Carrot muffins with garlic butter

Master salad recipe

Serves   6 at home or 20 tastes in the classroom
Fresh from the garden   salad leaves, herbs, garlic, lemons
At Collingwood, we always serve a salad with each menu. Many of the menus that follow already include a salad, but for those that don't, use this recipe and adjust the ingredients for taste, variety and seasonal availability.

Equipment

large bowl	lemon juicer
salad spinner	tablespoon
tea towel	metric measuring cups
kitchen paper	whisk
chopping board	tongs
knives – 1 small, 1 large	salad bowl
mortar and pestle	salad servers

Ingredients

4 cups mixed salad leaves
2 cups mixed small leaves and herbs (rocket leaves [arugula], beetroot leaves, baby spinach, sorrel, mizuna, parsley)

Classic vinaigrette dressing
1 clove garlic
salt
1 lemon
⅓ cup extra-virgin olive oil
freshly ground black pepper

What to do

✴ Fill the large bowl with cold water, then tip all the leaves and herbs into the bowl to soak for a few minutes. Lift the leaves onto the draining-board of the sink and tear the stems away from the spinach leaves (or if the leaves are very small, just cut off any extra stems).

✴ Empty out the water, rinse the bowl, then add fresh water and return the leaves to the bowl. Swish the leaves again in the clean water, then lift out a small handful and place in the salad spinner. Put yellow or slimy leaves in the compost bucket, then tear any very large leaves into smaller pieces. Dry the leaves very gently in the salad spinner. Repeat this process, working in batches, until all the leaves have been dried.

✴ Lay out a dry tea towel and line it with a long piece of kitchen paper. Spread the dried leaves over the paper and roll the whole lot up like a log. Keep the rolled parcel of leaves in the refrigerator until needed. Rinse and dry the bowl well.

✴ To make the classic vinaigrette dressing, set out the chopping board and knives. Peel and chop the garlic. Place it in the mortar with a pinch of salt, then pound to a paste using the pestle. Juice the lemon and add the juice to the mortar, then stir the lot with the tablespoon and scrape it into the large bowl. Stir in the oil and add some pepper, then whisk the dressing lightly.

✴ Unwrap the parcel of salad leaves and tip them into the bowl with the dressing. Gently turn the leaves in the dressing using the tongs or your hands.

✴ Use the salad servers to transfer the salad to the salad bowl, then serve immediately.

Special touches for salads

There are so many possibilities. Have a good look in the pantry and refrigerator to see what you might be able to add to your own garden salad. Many of the extra ingredients listed here are heavier than the salad leaves, which means the extras will tend to sink to the bottom of the bowl. For that reason, it is often better to serve these kinds of salads on a wide shallow platter, then everyone can see the special touches. Always add the dressing and toss the salad well, just before serving.

Here are some ideas:

✳ Croutons (plain or garlic-rubbed, page 226)

✳ Toasted nuts (pine nuts, walnuts, almonds)

✳ Toasted seeds (pumpkin, sunflower, linseed)

✳ Shavings or crumblings of cheese (parmesan, pecorino, pressed ricotta salata, blue cheese, fetta, gruyère)

✳ Chunks of avocado

✳ Cured fish (anchovies, smoked trout)

✳ Gratings of vegetables (beetroot, carrot, radish, celeriac)

✳ Hard-boiled eggs (sliced or chopped)

✳ Bacon (cooked until crisp, and crumbled)

✳ Raw fruits (apples, pears, citrus fruits)

✳ Pickled or preserved products (preserved lemons, pickled plums or cherries)

And by season:

✳ Spring – herbs (such as flowering thyme), pine nuts, rocket leaves (arugula)

✳ Summer – tomatoes, mozzarella, basil, spinach, rocket leaves (arugula)

✳ Autumn – celeriac, gruyère, parsnip chips

✳ Winter – spinach, croutons, bacon, beetroot

Alternative dressings

While everyone has their favourite dressing, the most common formula is 1 part acid (such as lemon juice or vinegar) to 4 parts oil. (High-quality vinegars are very powerful, so you may need to use less.) Always taste the dressing and adjust the flavours as necessary.

The acid component could be: lemon juice; red- or white-wine vinegar; balsamic vinegar; verjuice; herb-infused wine vinegar. The oil component could be: 100 per cent extra-virgin olive oil; 60 per cent extra-virgin olive oil, plus 40 per cent walnut oil; 60 per cent grapeseed oil (or other neutral-flavoured oil), plus 40 per cent extra-virgin olive oil.

Additions to dressings could be: mustard; small amounts of honey or sugar; freshly chopped herbs (such as parsley, tarragon, chervil or mint); toasted spices (such as coriander seeds, cumin seeds); yoghurt. Whichever combination you choose, always season to taste with salt and freshly ground black pepper.

Four basic recipes

These are recipes for ingredients for other dishes, rather than proper dishes themselves. For example, chicken stock is not so good on its own, but is absolutely delicious when used as the base for soup or risotto. Cross-references to these recipes appear in the ingredients list of the main recipes in the following way: *1 quantity Basic Chicken Stock (page 79).*

Basic shortcrust pastry

Makes enough to line a 22 cm, 24 cm or 26 cm flan tin (with varying amounts left over)

Shortcrust pastry is used in the following recipes: Rhubarb and Scented Geranium Crumble Tart (page 102); Leek Tarts with Crumbled Fetta (page 168); Squashed Flies Slice (page 179).

Equipment   metric measuring cups, scales, sieve or sifter, food processor, chopping board, large knife, plastic film

Ingredients   ¼ cup water, 240 g plain (all-purpose) flour, salt, 180 g butter

Place the water in the freezer to get icy-cold. Weigh the flour and sift it, along with a pinch of salt, into the bowl of the food processor. Set out the chopping board and knife. Chop the butter into small pieces and add to the food processor.

Using the pulse action, briefly combine the butter and flour until the mixture looks like breadcrumbs. With the motor running, add the icy-cold water. Stop the machine as soon as the mixture forms a rough ball.

Lightly flour your workbench. Tip out the dough and knead it briefly. Divide the dough in half and flatten each piece into a disc. Wrap in plastic film and chill for 20 minutes. Use the pastry as instructed in the recipe.

Basic spicy rice filling

Makes 1½ cups

Spicy rice is used in the following recipes: Dolmades with Silver Beet (page 129); Mediterranean Vegetables Stuffed with Spicy Rice (page 143).

Equipment   kitchen paper, plate, metric measuring spoons and cups, frying pan, wooden spoon, chopping board, small and large knives, tea towel, small bowl, small saucepan with a well-fitting lid

Ingredients   ⅓ cup extra-virgin olive oil, ¼ cup pine nuts, 4 stalks dill, 6 stalks parsley, ½ onion, ½ cup long-grain rice, 1¼ cups cold water, ¼ cup currants, salt, freshly ground black pepper

Fold a piece of kitchen paper in half and rest it on the plate near the stove. Put 1 tablespoon of the oil into the frying pan and fry the pine nuts over a medium heat, stirring constantly with the wooden spoon. When the pine nuts are golden, tip them quickly onto the paper-lined plate.

Set out the chopping board and knives. Rinse the dill and parsley and dry by rolling in the tea towel. Chop the herbs finely, place in the small bowl and set aside. Peel the onion and chop finely.

Heat the remainder of the oil in the saucepan over a medium heat, and tip in the onion. Sauté, stirring with the wooden spoon, until the onion has softened.

Add the rice to the saucepan and stir for 2 minutes. Add the water, currants and pine nuts, and season with salt and pepper. Bring to the boil, stirring once or twice. Turn the heat to low, put on the lid and cook for 15 minutes.

Stir in the chopped herbs and taste the rice for salt and pepper. Allow to cool before using.

Basic chicken stock

Makes 4 litres

Chicken stock is used in the following recipes: Chicken Breasts Stir-fried with Snowpeas (page 94); Broad-bean, Leek and Fennel-top Spring Risotto (page 105); Little Cups of Sorrel Soup (page 158); Simple Hot and Sour Fish Soup with Broccoli (page 190); Minestrone with Parmesan (page 212); Jerusalem Artichoke Soup (page 227); White-bean Dip with Pita Bread (page 234).

Equipment   chopping board, small and large knives, poultry scissors, colander, stockpot or very large saucepan, peeler, kitchen string, ladle, large bowl, plastic containers for storage

Ingredients   3 chicken carcasses, 3 chicken necks, 6 chicken wings, 2 onions, 2 carrots, 1 stick celery, 1 lemon, 4 stalks parsley, 3 sprigs thyme, 1 bay leaf

Set out the chopping board, knives and scissors. Using the scissors (or knife) cut the chicken carcasses into several large pieces and place in the colander. Rinse the carcasses and drop into the stockpot. Rinse the necks and wings and drop into the stockpot.

Peel and slice the onions. Slice the carrots and celery. Add all sliced vegetables to the stockpot.

Use the small knife to slice off a piece of lemon zest. Tie a piece of kitchen string around the lemon zest, parsley stalks, thyme and bay leaf to make a little bundle, and drop into the stockpot.

Add enough water to cover the bones by about 15 cm and bring slowly to simmering point. When the stock just starts to bubble, skim off any froth from the top using the ladle. Reduce the heat so that the liquid is bubbling very gently and leave for about 3 hours.

Place the colander in a large bowl and rest the bowl in the sink. **Pour the contents of the pot into the colander.** Discard the chicken, vegetables and herbs. Any stock not used can be placed in small plastic containers and frozen.

Basic pasta dough

Makes 200 g

Pasta dough is used in the following recipes: Linguine with Broad Beans, Bacon and Thyme (page 83); Three-cheese Ravioli with Herb Butter (page 98); Fettuccine with Tomato, Sausage and Fennel Sauce (page 163); Linguine with Pesto (page 176).

Equipment   pasta machine, scales, metric measuring spoons, food processor, plastic film, large knife, pastry brush

Ingredients   200 g plain (all-purpose) flour, salt, 2 eggs

Get an adult to help you fix the pasta machine to a suitable bench. Screw the clamp very tightly.

Weigh the flour, then combine it with 1½ teaspoons of salt in the bowl of the food processor. With the motor running, add the eggs. Process for a few minutes until the dough clings together and feels quite springy.

Tip the dough onto a clean, dry workbench. Knead the dough for a few minutes, then wrap it in plastic film and let it rest for 1 hour at room temperature.

Clear a large space on the workbench alongside the pasta machine. All surfaces must be clean and dry. Press the dough into a rectangle about 8 cm wide.

Set the rollers on the pasta machine to the widest setting and pass the dough through. The dough will probably look quite ragged at this stage. Fold it in 3, turn it 90 degrees and roll it through again. Go to the next-thickest setting and pass the dough through 3–4 times.

Continue in this manner (changing the settings and passing the dough through) until the dough has passed through the second-thinnest setting. Don't use the very thinnest setting, as the dough gets too fine and is hard to manage. If the dough gets too long to handle comfortably, cut it into 2–3 pieces using the large knife, and roll each piece separately. Prepare the dough as instructed in the recipe. Clean the pasta machine by brushing it with a dry, wide pastry brush. Never wash the machine.

Spring

The first spring harvest was a celebration – the students could see that all the hard work and planning had succeeded. The dishes cooked in the kitchen made full use of our early herbs and leafy salad greens, and introduced broad beans and silver beet. By the second year, fat fennel, artichokes and sorrel were the special flavours we enjoyed in the springtime.

Master Salad with Spring Touches (page 76)

Menu 1

Linguine with broad
beans, bacon and thyme

Silverbeet and coconut
pepperpot soup

Peta's apple betties
with cream

Linguine with broad beans, bacon and thyme

Serves   4 at home or 8–10 tastes in the classroom

Fresh from the garden   broad beans, red onions, garlic, parsley, thyme

The students quickly got the hang of making homemade pasta and enjoyed using the pasta machines. To save time, we rolled and cut pasta dough that had been made by the previous class, then prepared pasta dough for the next class.

Equipment

pasta machine

2 trays

saucepans – 1 large, 1 very
   large

bowls – 6 small, 1 medium

colander

chopping board

knives – 1 small, 1 large

tea towel

medium frying pan with
   high sides

wooden spoon

grater

serving bowls – 1 small,
   1 large

Ingredients

2 quantities Basic Pasta
   Dough (page 79)

plain (all-purpose) flour for
   dusting

salt

400 g broad beans (fava
   beans) in the pod

½ red onion

3 cloves garlic

3–4 stalks parsley

8 sprigs thyme

200 g rashers (slices)
   smoked bacon

2 tablespoons extra-virgin
   olive oil

freshly ground black pepper

small wedge parmesan

BOTTOM DRAWER

Interesting terms/techniques   • making fresh pasta
• double-peeling

Questions   1 What does al dente mean?

2 Do you think double-peeling broad beans is always necessary?

Answers   1 The pasta should still taste a little firm, rather than being completely soft.   2 Double-peeling is not necessary with the very smallest, youngest broad beans or if the beans will be puréed or mashed.

What to do

✱ Make the pasta as directed on page 79. Pass the dough through the narrow cutting blades of the pasta machine to form linguine. Dust the trays with flour, lay strands of linguine in a single layer on the trays and allow to dry for 10 minutes.

✱ Bring a large saucepan of lightly salted water to the boil. Shell the broad beans (400 g will give you 1 cup shelled beans) into the medium bowl. Drop the broad beans into the boiling water and cook for 2 minutes only.

✱ Place the colander in the sink. **Tip the broad beans and boiling water into the colander and cool quickly with cold water.** Double-peel the broad beans by slipping each bean out of its tough skin and back into the bowl, using your fingers. Set aside until needed and put the tough skins into the compost bucket.

✱ As you prepare the following ingredients, place them in small bowls and set to one side. Set out the chopping board and knives. Peel and dice the onion. Peel and slice the garlic. Rinse the parsley and thyme and dry by rolling in the tea towel. Pull the parsley leaves from their stalks. Chop the parsley leaves. Pick the thyme leaves from their stalks. Cut the rind from the bacon (discard the rind). Cut the bacon into strips.

✱ Heat the oil in the frying pan over a low-to-medium heat and add the onion. Stir with the wooden spoon and allow to fry and soften. Add the bacon and garlic and stir to prevent the mixture sticking. Stir in the thyme leaves. Taste for salt and pepper and put to one side until ready to serve.

✱ Bring a very large saucepan of lightly salted water to the boil. Drop in the linguine. Cook for 4–5 minutes (taste to check if it is al dente). While the linguine is cooking, grate about 4 tablespoons of parmesan and put in the small serving bowl. Set the colander in the sink. **Tip the linguine and boiling water into the colander.**

✱ Return the linguine to the empty hot saucepan. Tip in the broad beans and shake to mix. Reheat the onion and bacon mixture briefly over a low-to-medium heat, then tip the hot sauce over the pasta.

✱ Mix well, then transfer to the large serving bowl. Scatter with parsley and offer with grated parmesan.

Silverbeet and coconut pepperpot soup

Serves   6 at home or 12 tastes in the classroom
Fresh from the garden   silver beet, onions, garlic, chillies, potatoes
This is a beautiful bright-green soup with a lovely velvety texture.

Equipment

chopping board
knives – 1 small, 1 large
salad spinner
bowls – 1 small, 2 medium
disposable gloves
peeler
small frying pan

metric measuring spoons
  and cups
mortar and pestle
medium saucepan
wooden spoon
food processor or blender

Ingredients

200 g silver beet (about
  10 leaves)
½ onion
1 clove garlic
1 small red chilli
1 medium potato
1 teaspoon cumin seeds

1 teaspoon coriander seeds
1 × 2 cm cinnamon stick
2 tablespoons vegetable oil
1 teaspoon salt
4 cups water
⅓ cup coconut milk

What to do

✱ Set out the chopping board and knives. Separate the silverbeet leaves from the stems by slicing along each side of the thick central stem. Place the stems in the compost bucket. Rinse the silverbeet leaves and spin-dry in the salad spinner. Roll the leaves into a loose bunch, then shred with the large knife. Place the shredded leaves in a medium bowl until needed.

✱ Peel and chop the onion and place in the small bowl. Peel and slice the garlic and place in the onion bowl. Slip on the disposable gloves and cut the chilli in half lengthways. Scrape the seeds into the rubbish bin. Slice the chilli finely and add to the onion bowl. Wash the board and knife and discard the gloves.

✱ Peel the potato and chop it into 1 cm cubes. Place the cubes in a medium bowl and cover with water. Place the skins in the compost bucket.

✱ Heat the small frying pan over a medium heat. Toast the cumin seeds in the dry pan until they smell fragrant. Tip the seeds into the mortar. Roast the coriander seeds in the same pan until they smell fragrant. Add these seeds to the mortar. Crumble the small piece of cinnamon stick into the mortar. Using the pestle, work the spices to a coarse powder.

✱ In the medium saucepan, heat the oil over a medium heat. Tip in the contents of the onion bowl and the contents of the mortar. Stir with the wooden spoon until the onion has softened. Drain the potato and add to the spice mixture. Stir to mix and put the lid on for 2 minutes. Add the silverbeet leaves, salt and water. Cover and simmer until the potato cubes are quite tender – check after 5 minutes.

 ✱ **Using the measuring cup, transfer a little silverbeet/potato mixture to the food processor or blender. Purée until you have a smooth, bright-green soup.** Pour the puréed soup into a medium bowl, and repeat the process with the remaining soup. This is called working in batches.

✱ Rinse out the saucepan. Return the puréed soup to the saucepan. Reheat over a low-to-medium heat to simmering point, then stir in the coconut milk. Taste for salt. Do not cover the pot at this point. Serve the soup as soon as possible to prevent the coconut milk curdling, which it may do if allowed to boil vigorously.

BOTTOM DRAWER

Interesting terms/techniques   • stemming and shredding leaves • seeding chillies • toasting spices • grinding in a mortar with a pestle • puréeing • working in batches
Safety tip   When puréeing hot soup, you need to work very carefully. The steam can force the lid to come off the blender, spraying hot soup everywhere. This will make quite a mess, but, more importantly, the hot liquid could burn you quite badly. Only blend small quantities and place a thick cloth over the blender lid to protect your hand (ask for help the first time you do it).

Peta's apple betties with cream

Makes   6 small puddings or 1 family-sized pudding
Fresh from the garden   apples
We used bought apples in this recipe. Our garden was very new and apples were still available at a reasonable cost, but really this recipe would have been better cooked in the autumn with new-season apples.

Equipment

scales
bowls – 1 small, 3 medium
peeler
chopping board
knives – 1 small, 1 large

metric measuring spoons
    and cups
6 × 150 ml pie dishes, or
    1 × 1 litre pie dish
small serving bowl

Ingredients

125 g butter
3 apples
¾ cup plain (all-purpose)
    flour
¾ cup brown sugar

1 teaspoon ground
    cinnamon
1 teaspoon ground nutmeg
¼ cup rolled oats
double cream for serving

What to do

✳ Preheat the oven to 200°C. Weigh the butter and set aside in the small bowl to allow to come to room temperature.

✳ Peel the apples. Set out the chopping board and knives. Cut the apples in half from top to bottom, then cut each in half again from top to bottom – so you have quarters.

✳ Using the small knife, cut out the core and seeds from each apple quarter and place in the compost bucket, then cut each quarter into small pieces and place in a medium bowl.

✳ Divide the following ingredients equally between the two remaining medium bowls: flour, brown sugar, cinnamon and nutmeg. Add all the rolled oats to one of the bowls.

✳ Cut the softened butter into small cubes. Use one cube to rub the inside of the dish/es. Divide the rest of the butter cubes between the two bowls. Rub the butter into the mixture, using your hands, until the mixture is crumbly.

✳ Tip half of the chopped apples into the buttered dish/es. Scatter the mixture without oats over the apples. Top with the rest of the apples. Now scatter the mixture with the oats over the apples. Bake for 35 minutes until golden brown and bubbling.

 ✳ **Remove from the oven.** Serve hot with a bowl of double cream.

BOTTOM DRAWER

Interesting techniques   • coring and seeding fruit
   • rubbing butter into mixture

Pita bread triangles

Brush rounds of pita bread with olive oil flavoured with herbs or spices. Cut the pitas into triangles with scissors or a sharp knife and spread out on oven trays. Bake at 180°C until crisp. Cool before serving.

Crudités

Make a selection of very fresh vegetables that are good to eat raw (such as snowpeas, carrots, radishes, cucumbers, zucchini [courgettes], celery and peppers). Slice the large vegetables into strips. Arrange the vegetables beautifully alongside bowls of dips or a bowl of yoghurt that has been flavoured with chopped mint.

Broad-bean dip

Makes 2 cups

Fresh from the garden   broad beans, garlic, oregano, lemons

While most students were familiar with dips, this dip and the skordalia were new experiences. The students enjoyed scooping up the dips with the vegetables.

Equipment

bowls – 1 small, 1 medium, 1 large	medium saucepan
	skewer
chopping board	colander
knives – 1 small, 1 large	dinner plate
mortar and pestle	food processor
tea towel	spatula
metric measuring spoons and cups	tasting spoon
	small serving bowl
lemon juicer	

Ingredients

1 kg broad beans (fava beans) in the pod	1 lemon
	salt
2 cloves garlic	freshly ground black pepper
salt	
2 sprigs oregano	½ cup extra-virgin olive oil
1 teaspoon ground cumin	

What to do

✱ Shell the broad beans into the medium bowl.

✱ Set out the chopping board and knives. Peel the garlic. **Place the cloves on the chopping board and flatten by thumping with the side of the large knife.** Chop the garlic roughly. Put the garlic and a teaspoon of salt into the mortar and use the pestle to work to a paste.

✱ Rinse the oregano and dry by rolling in the tea towel. Pull the oregano leaves off their stalks. Chop the oregano leaves and place in the small bowl. Add the cumin to the oregano leaves and set aside. Juice the lemon.

✱ Put the broad beans into the saucepan, along with a small pinch of salt, and just cover with cold water. Bring to the boil and cook for about 10 minutes until the beans are tender. Broad beans are cooked when a thin skewer will slip through them. Place the colander over the large bowl. **Pour the broad beans and cooking water into the colander.** Lift the colander and rest it on the plate. Save the cooking water.

✱ Put the cooked beans, oregano leaves and cumin, salt and pepper, lemon juice and ⅓ cup of the cooking water into the bowl of the food processor, along with the mashed garlic. Whiz to a smooth sauce. Stop the machine and scrape down the sides of the bowl with the spatula. Restart the machine and slowly pour the oil down the feed tube to make a mayonnaise consistency.

✱ Stop the machine and taste the sauce for salt and pepper. Spoon into the small serving bowl.

BOTTOM DRAWER

Interesting terms/techniques • flattening garlic cloves • mayonnaise consistency • grinding in a mortar with a pestle • scraping down the sides
Did you know?   1 kg of unpodded broad beans will give you about 2½ cups of podded broad beans.
Question   Why do you think the broad beans are not double-peeled in this recipe?

Answer The tough skins are chopped up finely in the food processor and the dip is good with a little bit of texture to it.

Skordalia

Makes   1 cup

Fresh from the garden   potatoes, garlic, lemons

This well-known Greek garlic-and-potato sauce is served warm
or cold. It is often enjoyed as an accompaniment to simply cooked
vegetables dressed with olive oil and lemon juice.

Equipment

medium saucepan

skewer

colander

knives – 1 small, 1 large

chopping board

mortar and pestle

metric measuring spoons
    and cups

coarse-mesh sieve or potato
    ricer or Mouli food mill

large bowl

wooden spoon

lemon juicer

small serving bowl

Ingredients

2 medium-to-large potatoes

salt

2 cloves garlic

1 lemon

½ cup extra-virgin olive oil

¼ cup milk

freshly ground black pepper

What to do

✱ Put the potatoes into the medium saucepan, add a pinch of salt
and cover with cold water. Bring to the boil and cook until potatoes
are tender (15–20 minutes) – potatoes are cooked when a thin
skewer will slip through them.

✱ Place the colander in the sink. **Tip the potatoes and cooking
water into the colander and leave to cool.** When cool enough to
handle, peel the skins off the potatoes using your fingers or a small
knife. Place the skins in the compost bucket.

✱ Peel the garlic. **Place the cloves on the chopping board and
flatten by thumping with the side of the large knife.** Chop the
garlic roughly. Put the garlic and a teaspoon of salt in the mortar
and use the pestle to work to a paste.

✱ Press the peeled potatoes through the coarse sieve (or potato ricer
or food mill) into the large bowl. Scrape the garlic paste into the
potatoes and mix well with the wooden spoon.

✱ Juice the lemon. Add the oil and lemon juice to the potato mixture
a little at a time, mixing very well after each addition. The sauce
should be thick, with a mayonnaise consistency. If it is too thick,
add a little milk. Taste for salt and pepper. Spoon into the serving
bowl.

BOTTOM DRAWER

Interesting terms/techniques   • flattening garlic cloves
• grinding in a mortar with a pestle   • mashing with a potato
ricer or Mouli food mill   • mayonnaise consistency

Menu 3

Grilled asparagus with extra-virgin olive oil

Warm beetroot and dill salad

Cauliflower with cheese sauce and crusty topping

Grilled asparagus with extra-virgin olive oil

Snap off the woody ends of a bunch of asparagus spears. Brush the spears with olive oil and grill in a chargrill pan on the stovetop or under a preheated grill. The asparagus will develop black grill marks and look a bit blistered. Drizzle with a few drops of really good olive oil and add a little sprinkle of salt. Serve with a few lemon wedges.

Warm beetroot and dill salad

Serves   6 at home or 12 tastes in the classroom
Fresh from the garden   beetroots, dill

Beetroot was a star crop, and we had to think of many different ways to use it. We wore disposable gloves when peeling the beetroots to stop our hands being stained purple with beetroot juice.

Equipment

chopping board
knives – 1 small, 1 large
mixing bowls – 1 small,
   1 large
kitchen paper
peeler
baking dish

metric measuring spoons
aluminium foil
2 tea towels
skewer
disposable gloves
serving plate

Ingredients

4 medium-to-large beetroots, or 18 small beetroots
   (golf-ball sized)
3 tablespoons extra-virgin olive oil
2 teaspoons balsamic vinegar
1 teaspoon brown sugar
8 stalks dill

What to do

✳ Preheat the oven to 200°C. Wash the beetroots very well – make sure all the sand and grit is removed. Set out the chopping board and knives. Cut off the beetroots' leafy tops. Soak the leafy tops in a large bowl of cold water. Dry the beetroot with kitchen paper.

✳ If you are using large beetroots, peel them using the peeler, then cut into wedges with the large knife. Place the wedges in the baking dish. If you are using small beetroots, trim the root ends with the small knife and place the beetroots whole and unpeeled in the baking dish.

✳ To make the sauce/dressing, mix the oil, balsamic vinegar and brown sugar in the small bowl. Drizzle this mixture over the beetroots and shake so that each beetroot or piece is coated. Cover the baking dish with aluminium foil or a lid and bake for 20–45 minutes until tender.

✳ While the beetroots are baking, inspect the leaves. Place any that are ragged or yellow in the compost bucket. Dry the good leaves by rolling in a tea towel, then chop roughly with the large knife. **Open the oven 10 minutes before the beetroots are cooked and remove the baking dish. Add the leaves to the beetroots, stir or shake to mix, then return the dish to the oven for 10 minutes.**

✳ While waiting, rinse the dill and dry by rolling in a tea towel. Chop the dill leaves and fine stems roughly.

✳ Check the beetroots – they are cooked when a thin skewer will slip through them. **Remove from the oven.** If baking small beetroots, wait until they cool, then pick up each beetroot and slip off its skin (use disposable gloves to stop the juice staining your skin). Return the beetroots to the baking dish and place the discarded skins in the compost bucket.

✳ Scatter the chopped dill over the cooked beetroots and beetroot leaves and spoon onto the serving plate, making sure the juices are drizzled over the top.

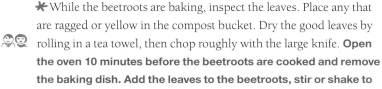

BOTTOM DRAWER

Interesting technique   •   testing with a skewer
Question   Why would you peel big beetroots before cooking and little beetroots after cooking?

Answer   Small beetroots can be very fiddly to peel before cooking (if you feel like a challenge, you can try), but once the beetroots are cooked, their skins just slip off.

Cauliflower with cheese sauce and crusty topping

Serves 6 at home or 12 tastes in the classroom
Fresh from the garden cauliflower
This simple dish is a great favourite, and the smell
of baking cheese is irresistible.

Equipment

chopping board	scales
knives – 1 small, 1 large	kitchen paper
metric measuring spoons and cups	large or small ovenproof pie dish/es
saucepans – 1 small, 1 large	jug (to hold 1 litre)
food processor	bowls – 3 small, 1 large
skewer	grater
colander	wooden spoon
dinner plate	heatproof board or mat

Ingredients

½ cauliflower	1½ cups milk
2 litres water	2 tablespoons plain (all-purpose) flour
1 teaspoon salt	150 g gruyère
2–3 slices day-old bread	freshly ground black pepper
40 g butter, plus a little extra for the crust	½ fresh nutmeg

What to do

✱ Preheat the oven to 180°C. Set out the chopping board and knives. Cut the cauliflower into 'florets'. Bring the water and 1 teaspoon of salt to the boil in the large saucepan. Drop in the cauliflower and cook, uncovered, for about 10 minutes.

✱ Meanwhile, remove the crusts from the bread (place crusts in the compost bucket). Put the bread in the bowl of the food processor, then run the motor to make breadcrumbs.

✱ Test the cauliflower. You can tell it is cooked when a thin skewer will slip through it quite easily. Place the colander in the sink.

Pour the cauliflower and cooking water into the colander. Stand the colander on a plate and leave to drain.

✱ Using the scales, weigh out 40 g of butter. Use some kitchen paper and a small slice of the butter to grease the ovenproof dishes.

✱ **Place the milk in the small saucepan and heat to scalding point.** Tip the hot milk into the jug. (Milk can also be heated in a non-metal jug in the microwave for 1 minute.) Rinse the saucepan and dry it.

✱ Put the flour in a small bowl near the hot milk. Grate the cheese. Set aside 1½ tablespoons of the grated cheese in a small bowl to use later as a topping. Put the rest of the cheese in another bowl near the milk and flour. Put the butter in the saucepan and melt over a medium heat. When the butter starts to froth, add all the flour. Stir well with the wooden spoon for a minute. This is called making a roux.

✱ Gradually add the hot milk, stirring all the time to prevent lumps. Continue stirring until the sauce comes to the boil. Tip in the grated cheese and stir until the cheese has melted. Remove from the stove and add salt and pepper to taste. Grate in the fresh nutmeg.

✱ Tip the drained cauliflower into the large bowl. Add the cheese sauce and gently mix to coat each piece of cauliflower. Pour the cauliflower into the buttered ovenproof dish/es. Scatter with the fresh breadcrumbs, then the reserved cheese. Dot with extra butter. Bake for about 20 minutes until golden brown and bubbling.

✱ **Remove from the oven.** Place the board or mat on the table and serve the cauliflower in the ovenproof dish/es at the table.

BOTTOM DRAWER

Interesting terms/techniques • making fresh breadcrumbs
• testing with a skewer • making a roux • grating fresh nutmeg
Tip Cheese sauce is very useful and can be used in other ways. You can use it with other vegetables, such as fennel or silverbeet stems (cooked in the same way as the cauliflower). Or you can mix it with cooked pasta (choose a chunky pasta such as macaroni or penne) and cook it in the oven. To make a thicker sauce, add more flour; to make a richer sauce, add a dollop of cream.

Lemon delicious pudding

Serves   8 at home or 16 tastes in the classroom
Fresh from the garden   lemons, eggs
This pudding is truly delicious. In my house it's a family favourite.

Equipment

scales
kitchen paper
ovenproof pudding mould
   (2½-cup capacity)
bowls – 2 small, 2 large
lemon juicer
grater
metric measuring spoons
   and cups

electric mixer
spatula
electric hand beater
large metal spoon
ladle
baking dish with high sides
electric jug
heatproof board or mat
small serving bowl

Ingredients

60 g butter
2 lemons
3 eggs
1½ cups castor (superfine)
   sugar

3 tablespoons self-raising
   (self-rising) flour
1½ cups milk
cream for serving
icing (confectioners')
   sugar for dusting

What to do

✴ Preheat the oven to 200°C. Use the scales to weigh the butter. Use some kitchen paper and a small slice of the butter to grease the pudding mould. Set the rest of the butter aside in a small bowl to come to room temperature. Juice the lemons. Grate the zest from each lemon.

✴ Set out a large bowl and a small bowl. To separate the eggs, crack them, one at a time, and tip each egg into your cupped hand held over the large clean bowl. Slightly open your fingers and let the white slip into the bowl, then place the yolk in the small bowl.

✴ Cream the butter and sugar in the electric mixer until the mixture turns pale. Beat the egg yolks into the butter and sugar one at a time. Using a spatula, scrape down the sides of the mixing bowl to ensure the whole lot is properly mixed.

✴ Add the flour and milk alternately, a little at a time, to the butter, sugar and egg mixture, mixing lightly after each addition until just combined. (Too much mixing will certainly curdle the mixture at this point, which doesn't seem to matter but it can look alarming.) Scrape down the sides of the bowl again.

✴ If you have an electric hand beater, use it to whisk the eggwhites until they form soft peaks. If not, transfer the pudding mixture from the electric mixer bowl into another large bowl. Wash and dry the electric mixer bowl and the beaters. Place the eggwhites into the mixer bowl and beat until soft peaks form.

✴ Mix the lemon juice and zest into the pudding batter. Using the large metal spoon, fold in the eggwhites as delicately as possible. Using the ladle, transfer the mixture to the buttered pudding mould. Carefully place the pudding mould into the baking dish.

✴ Have the electric jug full of boiling water. Transfer the baking dish to the oven and settle it on the rack. **Pour enough boiling water into the baking dish to come halfway up the pudding mould.** This is called cooking au bain-marie. Gently close the oven door and bake for 35–40 minutes until the pudding top is golden and feels springy in the centre when touched.

✴ **Remove from the oven.** Allow to cool a little. Place the board or mat on the table and serve the pudding in its cooking dish with a bowl of cream alongside. Sprinkle the top of the pudding with a little icing sugar.

> **BOTTOM DRAWER**
>
> **Interesting terms/techniques**   • separating eggs   • creaming butter and sugar   • whisking eggwhites to form soft peaks   • cooking au bain-marie   • feeling a surface to see if it's springy
> **Tip**   You can make individual puddings with this recipe. The mixture here would be enough for 8 × 150 ml pudding pots; puddings this size would take 25–30 minutes to cook.

Chicken breasts stir-fried with snowpeas

Serves   4 at home or 8 tastes in the classroom
Fresh from the garden   snowpeas, garlic, spring onions, chillies

Stir-frying is a very fast way of cooking. Because of this, everything must be prepared and placed nearby before you start to cook.

Equipment

metric measuring spoons
   and cups
bowls – 3 small,
   2 medium
fork
chopping board

knives – 1 small, 1 large
disposable gloves
wok with lid
wok sang or
   large slotted spoon
serving plate

Ingredients

2 skinless chicken breasts
250 g snowpeas
4 flat mushrooms or
   8 button mushrooms
2 cloves garlic
1 × 2 cm piece fresh ginger
2 spring onions (scallions)
1 red chilli
2 teaspoons oyster sauce
½ cup Basic Chicken Stock (page 79)
2 tablespoons vegetable oil

Marinade

2 tablespoons light soy sauce
2 tablespoons mirin
2 tablespoons vegetable oil
2 teaspoons cornflour (cornstarch)

What to do

✶ Place all the ingredients listed under *Marinade* in one of the medium bowls and mix with the fork.

✶ Set out the chopping board and knives. Slice the chicken breasts into thin slices, diagonally across the breast, and drop the slices into the marinade. Mix lightly with the fork and set aside.

✶ Wipe down the chopping board and knives. Remove the string from each snowpea and place the snowpeas in a small bowl. Finely slice the mushrooms and place in a second small bowl. Peel and chop the garlic and place in a third small bowl. Peel and chop the ginger and add to the garlic bowl. Trim the outside layer from the spring onions and cut off the tops and ends, then slice the spring onions and add to the garlic bowl. Slip on the disposable gloves and cut the chilli in half lengthways. Scrape the seeds into the rubbish bin, slice finely, and add to the garlic. Discard the gloves. Wash the board and knives very well.

✶ Place the oyster sauce in the second medium bowl with the chicken stock. Mix with the fork and set aside.

✶ **Heat the wok over a high heat to very hot. Tip in the oil and straightaway add the garlic, ginger, spring onion and chilli.** Toss quickly with the wok sang for 30 seconds. Tip in the snowpeas and toss until they are bright-green and shiny. Add the mushroom slices and the chicken in its marinade and toss to keep everything moving. Tip in the chicken stock and oyster sauce mixture, then cover the wok with the lid.

✶ Lower the heat and cook for 3 minutes. Lift the lid and stir. Transfer to the serving plate and serve hot.

BOTTOM DRAWER

Interesting terms/techniques
• marinating • seeding chillies
Something to think about   Have you heard of a wok sang before? Do you think it makes stir-frying easier?

Caesar salad

Serves   6 at home or 12 tastes in the classroom
Fresh from the garden   cos lettuce, eggs, parsley, garlic, lemons
This salad featuring cos lettuce, anchovies and eggs is one of the best-known salads in Australia (and other places) and is on the menu of almost every cafe.

Equipment

salad spinner	grater
2 tea towels	metric measuring spoons
kitchen paper	and cups
medium saucepan	bowls – 2 small
teaspoon	jug for dressing
food processor	dinner plate or tray
chopping board	non-stick frying pan
knives – 1 small, 1 large	egg lifter
lemon juicer	large serving plate

Ingredients

2 cos lettuces, or 32 loose	*Dressing*
cos leaves	2 eggs
3 eggs	1 clove garlic
6 stalks parsley	2 anchovy fillets
small wedge parmesan	1 lemon
3 thick slices bread	small wedge parmesan
¼ cup extra-virgin olive oil	1 tablespoon Dijon-style
1 clove garlic, unpeeled	mustard
3 rashers (slices)	½ cup extra-virgin olive oil
streaky bacon	salt
6 anchovy fillets	freshly ground black pepper

BOTTOM DRAWER

Interesting terms/techniques   • storing salad leaves in a parcel   • flattening garlic cloves   • mayonnaise consistency   • making croutons   • cooking in batches
Something to think about   Why do you think this is such a popular salad? What are the tastes that people like in this salad?

What to do

✱ Rinse the cos leaves and dry very gently in the salad spinner. Lay out a dry tea towel and line it with a long piece of kitchen paper. Spread the dried leaves over the paper and roll the whole lot up like a log. Keep refrigerated until needed.

✱ Fill the saucepan with water and bring to the boil. **Add all 5 eggs and boil for 4 minutes. Remove from heat.** Run under cold water.

✱ To make the dressing crack 2 of the eggs and scoop the insides into the food processor, then process until smooth.

✱ Set out the chopping board and knives. Peel the garlic. **Place the garlic on the board and flatten by thumping with the side of the large knife.** Chop the 2 anchovies. Juice the lemon. Grate the parmesan – you'll need 2 tablespoons. Place the garlic, anchovies, lemon juice, parmesan and mustard in the bowl of the food processor with the eggs.

✱ Process the ingredients until smooth. With the motor running, slowly dribble in the ½ cup of oil until the dressing is like mayonnaise consistency. Stop the machine. Taste for salt and pepper. Pour the dressing into the small jug and set aside.

✱ Rinse the parsley, dry by rolling in a tea towel, chop, then place in a small bowl. Shave off pieces of parmesan using either the grater or a normal potato peeler then place in a small bowl.

✱ Make the croutons. Cut the crusts from the bread. Cut the bread into 1 cm cubes. Line the dinner plate or tray with a double piece of kitchen paper. Heat ½ the oil in the frying pan over a medium heat. Add the unpeeled clove of garlic and half the bread. Use the egg lifter to turn the bread so it crisps and browns on all sides. Transfer to the paper-covered plate. Use the remaining oil to fry the second batch of bread.

✱ Cut the rind from the bacon. Add the bacon to the pan and cook until crisp. Break the bacon into smaller pieces, then add to the croutons. Peel the 3 reserved eggs and cut each egg into quarters.

✱ Arrange the salad leaves on the serving plate, with the croutons, bacon pieces and quartered eggs. Drizzle on the dressing. Finish with chopped parsley, the 6 anchovies and the shaved parmesan.

Baked potatoes with grilled cheese and spring onion

Makes   1 potato per person, ½ potato per person for tastes in the classroom

Fresh from the garden   potatoes, spring onions

Because the potatoes in this recipe take 1 hour to cook, and another ½ hour or so to cool, we had the children at Collingwood prepare the potatoes for the class ahead. If you are cooking at home, you might like to get to work on one of the other recipes while the potatoes are cooking, or you could bake the potatoes the day before and keep them covered in the refrigerator.

Equipment

small brush or scourer   metric measuring spoons
skewer   teaspoon
baking tray   small bowl
chopping board   fork
large knife   tablespoon
grater   heatproof board or mat

Ingredients

1 medium-to-large potato per person
1 spring onion (scallion) per potato
1 small piece cheddar-style cheese
   (allow 1 tablespoon grated per half potato)
1 tablespoon butter per potato, plus extra for topping
salt
freshly ground black pepper

What to do

✳ Preheat the oven to 200°C. If the potatoes are unwashed, rinse well in cold water (you may have to scrub them with a small brush or scourer). Prick each potato a few times with a fine skewer. Place the potatoes on the baking tray and bake for 1 hour (set timer).

 Remove potatoes from the oven. Allow to cool.

✳ Set out the chopping board and knife. Finely chop the spring onion, including most of its green top. Grate the cheese.

 ✳ Take a cold cooked potato and cut it in half lengthways. **Carefully scoop out the centre using the teaspoon.** Put the scooped potato into the small bowl.

✳ Crush the scooped potato with a fork and work in the butter, spring onion and half of the cheese. Taste and add salt and pepper if needed. Carefully spoon the filling back into the potato skins and return them to the baking tray. Scatter the last of the cheese over the top, then add a thin slice of butter to each. Bake for 15 minutes until golden and bubbling.

 ✳ **Remove from the oven.** Serve immediately on the heatproof board or mat. Remember, the skins are the best part!

BOTTOM DRAWER

Interesting technique   •   testing with a skewer
Something to think about   Did you like the crunchy potato skins?

Beetroot and chocolate muffins

Makes 12
Fresh from the garden   beetroots, eggs
The children loved this combination of flavours.

Equipment

scales
small saucepan
pastry brush
1 × 12-hole muffin tin
peeler
grater
food processor

bowls – 2 medium, 1 large
metric measuring spoons
   and cups
sieve or sifter
whisk
spoons
wire rack

Ingredients

80 g butter
1 large beetroot (over 250 g)
175 g plain (all-purpose)
   flour
1 teaspoon baking powder
2 tablespoons cocoa
1 large egg, or 2 bantam
   eggs

¼ cup milk
¼ cup vegetable oil
¼ cup castor (superfine)
   sugar
½ cup well-packed
   brown sugar
100 g dark chocolate
   (enough for 12 squares)

What to do

✱ Preheat the oven to 180°C. Use the scales to weigh the butter, then set it aside to come to room temperature. Melt 1 tablespoon of the butter in the small saucepan, then use the pastry brush to grease the holes of the muffin tin.

✱ Peel and grate the beetroot. (Your food processor may have a grating attachment, which will make this task much easier.) You will need 250 g of peeled and grated beetroot (use the scales).

✱ Sift the flour, baking powder and cocoa into a medium bowl, then sift again (this is called double-sifting) into a second bowl. Set the sifted ingredients aside. Rinse and dry the now empty bowl, and use it to lightly whisk together the egg/s and milk.

✱ In the clean bowl of the food processor combine the softened butter, oil and 2 kinds of sugar, and process until creamy. Gradually add the egg and milk mixture. Transfer the batter to the large mixing bowl.

✱ Fold the sifted dry ingredients into the wet ingredients, then stir in the grated beetroot. Spoon the mixture into the greased muffin tin. Break the chocolate into 12 squares and poke a square of chocolate into the top of each muffin.

✱ Bake for 20–25 minutes until the muffins are well-risen and feel springy. **Remove from the oven.** Allow to cool in the tin for a few minutes, before turning out onto the wire rack.

Three-cheese ravioli with herb butter

Makes   60 filled ravioli to serve 6 at home
or 20 tastes in the classroom
Fresh from the garden   parsley, oregano, chives,
sorrel, eggs

Everyone loves filled pasta, especially when it is made
with tender hand-rolled pasta and is freshly cooked.
In the classroom, it disappeared very fast. Once the
technique was learnt, we made this dish over and
over again, sometimes changing the filling. Because
pasta dough needs to rest for 1 hour after it has been
made, we used dough that had been made by an earlier
class, then made more dough so that the next class
could begin rolling and filling straightaway.

Equipment

chopping board	tall jug
knives – 1 small, 1 large	(if using piping bag)
tea towel	kitchen paper
bowls – 1 small,	wide ovenproof dish
2 medium	2 large trays
scales	very large saucepan
grater	pastry brush
metric measuring spoons	teaspoon
wooden spoon	slotted spoon
teaspoon, or piping bag	frying pan
with plain nozzle	heatproof board or mat

Ingredients

semolina flour for dusting
salt
1 quantity Basic Pasta Dough (page 79)

Herb butter
20 stalks parsley
4 sprigs oregano
15 chives
25 sorrel leaves (enough
    for 1 cup chopped)
150 g butter

Filling
250 g parmesan
500 g ricotta
200 g blue cheese
2 eggs
salt
freshly ground
    black pepper
½ fresh nutmeg

What to do

✱ To begin the herb butter, set out the chopping board
and large knife. Rinse the parsley, oregano and chives
and dry by rolling in the tea towel. Chop the herbs,
then place in one of the medium bowls.

✱ Fold each sorrel leaf along the stem line, with the
rough side uppermost, then pull the stem up and along
the leaf (a bit like pulling up a zip). The stem end and
the central stem will come away leaving you with two
pieces of leaf. Put the stems in the compost bucket.

✱ Rinse the sorrel leaves and dry by rolling in the tea
towel. Roll the leaves into a loose bunch, then shred
using the large knife. Add the sorrel to the bowl with
the other herbs and toss lightly to combine.

✱ Now make the pasta filling. Using the scales,
weigh the parmesan, ricotta and blue cheese. Grate
the parmesan into the second medium bowl. Crumble
the ricotta and the blue cheese into the same bowl. ❯❯

✱ To separate the eggs, set out a small bowl. Crack each egg, one at a time, tipping it into your cupped hand held over the small bowl. Slightly open your fingers and let the white slip into this bowl, then place the yolk with the cheese mixture. Set the whites aside for later.

✱ Add salt and pepper to the cheese mixture, then grate in the fresh nutmeg. Add 3 tablespoons of the chopped herbs and mix all ingredients together using the wooden spoon. If you have a piping bag, place it in a tall jug for support, then spoon in the cheese filling.

✱ Using the scales, weigh 150 g of butter. Use 1 tablespoon of the butter and a bit of kitchen paper to grease the ovenproof dish. Heat the oven to 120°C and place the dish in the oven to keep warm. Scatter the 2 trays with semolina flour.

✱ Fill the saucepan with water, add 1½ teaspoons of salt and bring to the boil.

✱ Cut the pasta sheets in half lengthways (you should have strips that are about 7–8 cm wide). Brush the strips lightly with the reserved eggwhite (you probably won't need all the eggwhite).

 If using a piping bag, pipe small mounds of the filling at regular intervals along one side of each strip of pasta dough. If using a spoon, place teaspoonfuls of the filling in exactly the same way as described above. Fold the pasta strip to enclose the filling. Press firmly between the mounds of filling to get rid of trapped air. Using a small knife, cut between each filled shape to separate the ravioli.

 ✱ Place the completed shapes on the semolina-dusted trays and continue until all are made. **Drop a batch of the filled pasta shapes into the boiling water (not too many at once) and cook for 6 minutes. Lift the ravioli from the water with the slotted spoon and allow to drain for a moment.** Slip the cooked shapes into the buttered ovenproof dish, then return the dish to the oven. Continue with the next batch until all the filled shapes have been cooked.

✱ Melt the remaining butter in the frying pan. When the butter is bubbling, toss in the remaining herbs. Stir to mix evenly.

✱ **Remove the ovenproof dish from the oven.** Pour the herb butter over the cooked pasta in the dish and shake to mix evenly. Place the heatproof board or mat on the table and serve the pasta in its ovenproof dish.

BOTTOM DRAWER

Interesting terms/techniques   • making fresh pasta
• stemming and shredding leaves   • separating eggs
• grating fresh nutmeg   • using a piping bag
• cooking in batches
Something to think about   Sorrel and spinach look a bit similar and can be prepared in the same way. Do they taste similar?
Variation   Substitute 1 cup of chopped young borage leaves for some of the cheese in this recipe.
Question   What is semolina flour made from?

Answer   The large, hard part of the wheat grain.

Waldorf salad with variations

Serves 6 at home or 16 tastes in the classroom
Fresh from the garden celery, radishes, apples
This salad is not seen much these days and might be thought of as old-fashioned, yet the combination of flavours is delicious.

Equipment

tea towel	frying pan
chopping board	wooden spoon
knives – 1 small, 1 large	serving bowl
large bowl	
metric measuring spoons and cups	

Ingredients

4 sticks celery	½ cup walnut halves
5 radishes	¼ cup sour cream
3 oranges	salt
2 eating apples	freshly ground black pepper
1 tablespoon extra-virgin olive oil	

What to do

✷ Rinse the celery sticks and radishes and pat dry with the tea towel. Set out the chopping board and knives. **Using a small or large knife – whichever feels comfortable – carve the skin from each orange. Holding an orange in one hand, over the large bowl to catch the juice, slip the knife down one side of a single segment and then down the other side of the segment, cutting the flesh away from the membrane.** Drop the segment into the bowl. Repeat, until all the segments are in the bowl, then work on the other oranges in the same way. As you go, squeeze the orange 'skeletons' (what is left in your hand after all the segments have been removed) so that the juice falls over the orange segments.

✷ Using the large knife, halve the apples from top to bottom. Halve the apple pieces again. Using the small knife, remove the cores and seeds from the apple quarters and place the cores and seeds in the compost bucket. Chop the quarters into small pieces and add to the bowl with the oranges.

✷ Slice the celery sticks crossways into 5 mm slices and add to the fruit. Slice the radishes thinly and add to the bowl.

✷ Place the frying pan over a medium heat. Add the oil and walnuts and stir with the wooden spoon until the walnuts are lightly toasted. Remove from the heat and set aside until needed

✷ Add the sour cream to the salad ingredients and stir to mix. Taste for salt and pepper, add the toasted walnuts, then transfer the salad to the serving bowl.

BOTTOM DRAWER

Interesting terms/techniques • segmenting oranges • orange skeletons • coring and seeding fruit • toasting nuts

Rhubarb and scented geranium crumble tart

Serves   6–8 at home or 16 tastes in the classroom
Fresh from the garden   rhubarb, rose-scented
geranium leaves, eggs
The combination of rhubarb and rose-scented leaves is lovely.
Because the pastry in this recipe needs to be refrigerated for 1 hour,
we used pastry that had been prepared by the previous class,
then prepared the pastry for the next class.

Equipment

rolling pin
22 cm flan tin
knives – 1 small, 1 large
aluminium foil
pastry weights (or generous
    handfuls dried chick
    peas)
chopping board
bowls – 2 medium

wooden spoon
food processor
scales
metric measuring spoons
tea towel
spoons – 3 large
serving plate or board
small serving jug

Ingredients

1 quantity Basic Shortcrust
    Pastry (page 78)
plain (all-purpose) flour for
    dusting
cream for serving

Almond cream
60 g butter
60 g castor (superfine) sugar
1 egg
60 g ground almonds

Rhubarb filling
10 stalks rhubarb
2 tablespoons brown sugar
3 rose-scented geranium
    leaves from the garden

Crumble topping
100 g plain (all-purpose)
    flour
50 g brown sugar
1 teaspoon baking powder
1 teaspoon ground
    cinnamon
60 g butter

What to do

✴ Make the pastry as instructed on page 78 and refrigerate for 1 hour.

✴ Preheat the oven to 200°C. Take the pastry out of the refrigerator
and dust a clean work surface with flour. Roll the pastry to fit the
flan tin, dusting with flour as needed. Line the tin with the pastry,
trimming the edges with the small knife. Cover with aluminium
foil. Place pastry weights (or dried chick peas) on the foil and bake
blind – which means bake without a filling – for 20 minutes.

✴ Meanwhile, use the chopping board and large knife to slice the
rhubarb into very thin slices. Place the rhubarb in the medium bowl,
along with the brown sugar, and mix with the wooden spoon.

 ✴ **Remove the cooked tart 'shell' from the oven.** Don't turn off
the oven. Allow the tart to cool for a few minutes, then remove the
foil and pastry weights.

✴ Make the almond cream. Weigh the butter and sugar, place in the
bowl of the food processor and cream together. Drop in the egg and
mix, then add the ground almonds and mix.

✴ Make the crumble topping by mixing the flour, sugar, baking
powder and cinnamon in the second medium bowl. Rub in the
butter using your hands, but very roughly so that the crumble
is quite lumpy.

✴ Rinse the scented geranium leaves and dry by rolling in the tea
towel. Use the chopping board and large knife to chop the leaves
very finely, then add the leaves to the rhubarb.

✴ Using the large spoons, cover the pastry case with all the almond
cream, then cover the almond cream with the rhubarb, then cover
the rhubarb with the crumble mixture.

 ✴ Bake for 20–30 minutes until golden brown. **Remove the
tart from the oven.** Allow it to settle for a few minutes, before
transferring to the serving plate or board.

✴ Serve warm with a small jug of cream alongside.

BOTTOM DRAWER

Interesting terms/techniques • pastry weights • baking
blind • creaming butter and sugar • cooking with flowers

Menu 6

Broad-bean, leek and
fennel-top spring risotto

Spinach and
beetroot-leaf salad with
avocado and a lemon
and garlic dressing

Lemon crêpes

Broad-bean, leek and fennel-top spring risotto

Serves 4 at home or 10 tastes in the classroom
Fresh from the garden broad beans, onions, parsley, fennel, leeks
The students became really skilled at making risotto and some have made it at home for their families. It is a great way of using small quantities of home-grown vegetables and herbs.

Equipment

medium saucepan	knives – 1 small, 1 large
bowls – 3 small, 2 medium, 1 large	tea towel
	salad spinner
colander	½ cup ladle
grater	scales
metric measuring spoons and cups	frying pan with 5 cm sides
	wooden spoon
chopping board	

Ingredients

salt	1 large leek, or 2 small leeks
500 g broad beans (fava beans) in the pod	4 cups Basic Chicken Stock (page 79)
small wedge parmesan	80 g butter
1 small onion	1 cup arborio rice
10 stalks parsley	freshly ground black pepper
handful fennel tops	

What to do

✳ Fill the saucepan with water, add a pinch of salt and bring to the boil. Shell the broad beans into a medium bowl. Place the colander in the sink. Drop the beans into boiling water for 30 seconds. **Tip the broad beans and water into the colander and cool quickly with cold water.**

✳ Double-peel the broad beans by slipping each bean out of its tough skin into a medium bowl, using your fingers. Place the tough skins in the compost bucket.

✳ Grate the parmesan into a small bowl – you'll need about 3 tablespoons. Set aside. Set out the chopping board and knives. Peel and finely chop the onion and place in a small bowl. Rinse the parsley and fennel tops and dry by rolling in the tea towel. Chop both the parsley and the fennel tops and place in a small bowl for later.

✳ Cut the leek into fine rings and soak in a large bowl of cold water, swishing the rings with your fingers to release any dirt or sand. Lift the washed leek rings into the salad spinner and give them a quick spin. Empty the bowl of water and give it a rinse, then place the leeks in the bowl and set aside for later.

✳ Rinse the saucepan used to boil the beans. Pour in the stock and heat over a medium heat. Turn the heat to low and leave the stock, with the ladle in it.

✳ Using the scales, weigh the butter, then divide it into 2 equal pieces. Heat 1 piece in the frying pan over medium heat and tip in the onion and leek. Stir with the wooden spoon until vegetables are well-softened. Tip in the rice and stir to ensure that every grain is well coated with buttery juice. **Add a ladleful of hot stock, stirring all the time. The rice will absorb the hot stock and start to swell. Continue to add a ladleful of stock as the last one disappears, stirring all the time.** Use all but a couple of ladlefuls of stock (you'll use this later).

✳ After 15 minutes, taste the rice. It should be just a little bit nutty in the centre of each grain. Add the broad beans and the last 1–2 ladlefuls of stock, stirring. Taste for salt and pepper.

✳ After an extra 5 minutes, stir in the second piece of butter and the fennel tops, herbs and parmesan, and give the risotto a final stir. Cover the pan for 3–4 minutes before serving.

Spinach and beetroot-leaf salad with avocado and a lemon and garlic dressing

Serves 4 at home or 8–10 tastes in the classroom

Fresh from the garden spinach, beetroot leaves, garlic, lemons

When you buy beetroot from the shops, the leaves are often very large, yellowing and in poor condition. Such leaves are only good for the compost bucket. This recipe is for the delicate inner leaves or for the tops of home-grown beetroot. Even if only a few of the beetroot leaves are useable, they will be delicious with the spinach, and you could even toss in other salad greens, such as rocket or mizuna. If you do buy beetroot by the bunch (rather than getting it out of the garden) you can use the actual beetroot in other recipes, such as Warm Beetroot and Dill Salad (page 89) and Beetroot and Chocolate Muffins (page 97).

Equipment

knives – 1 small, 1 large
chopping board
bowls – 2 large
salad spinner
tea towel
kitchen paper

lemon juicer
mortar and pestle
whisk
tongs
serving bowl or plate

Ingredients

2 or 3 good handfuls (about 200 g) spinach leaves
1 good handful (about 100 g) small beetroot leaves
1 clove garlic
1 lemon
salt
¼ cup extra-virgin olive oil
freshly ground black pepper
1 avocado

What to do

✱ Stem the spinach by tearing the leaves from the stems. (If the leaves are very small, just trim away the extra stem using the small knife.) Set out 2 large bowls of cold water. Place the beetroot leaves in one bowl and the spinach leaves in the second bowl, and allow to soak for a few minutes.

✱ Lift the beetroot leaves and the spinach leaves from the water, one by one, and place in the salad spinner, putting any leaves that are yellow or slimy in the compost bucket and tearing the larger leaves into smaller pieces. Spin very gently.

✱ Lay out a dry tea towel and line it with a long piece of kitchen paper. Spread the spinach and beetroot leaves over the paper and roll the whole lot up like a log. Keep the rolled parcel of leaves in the refrigerator until needed. Tip the water out of the bowls and dry well.

✱ Set out the chopping board and knives. Peel and chop the garlic. Juice the lemon. Put the garlic cloves and a pinch of salt in the mortar and use the pestle to work to a paste. Add the lemon juice, stir and scrape the mixture into one of the large bowls. Whisk in the oil and add some pepper. This is the dressing for the salad.

✱ Peel the avocado and cut into slices or chunks, then drop the chunks into the dressing. Unwrap the parcel of greens and place them in the bowl with the dressing. Turn the leaves very gently using tongs, then lift onto a flat plate or a shallow bowl to serve.

BOTTOM DRAWER

Interesting terms/techniques • stemming leaves • storing salad leaves in a parcel • grinding in a mortar with a pestle

Lemon crêpes

Makes   10 crêpes

Fresh from the garden   eggs, lemons

Pancakes seem to be everyone's favourite treat and they are so simple to make. With this recipe you need to allow 2 hours for the batter to rest in the refrigerator. At Collingwood, we used batter prepared by the previous class, then prepared ahead for the next class.

Equipment

shallow ovenproof dish	fork
scales	jug
non-stick 18 cm frying pan	kitchen paper
sieve or sifter	small ladle
bowls – 1 medium, 1 large	egg lifter
metric measuring cups	baking tray
whisk	lemon juicer

Ingredients

30 g butter	1½ cups milk, plus ½ cup
150 g plain (all-purpose)	extra
flour	2 lemons
pinch of salt	½ cup castor (superfine)
2 eggs	sugar

What to do

✳ Preheat the oven to 120°C and put the ovenproof dish in the oven to keep warm. Weigh the butter and melt in the frying pan over a medium heat, then allow to cool.

✳ Sift the flour and salt into the large bowl and make a well in the centre. Break the eggs into the medium bowl, add the milk and whisk together lightly. Add the cooled, melted butter to the milk and eggs.

✳ Tip the egg/butter mixture into the well in the flour and gradually fork in the flour. Using the whisk, mix until smooth. Pour into the jug and refrigerate for 2 hours before cooking. The consistency of the rested batter should be like cream. If the batter is too thick, add a little of the extra milk.

✳ To cook the crêpes, put a dab of butter on a piece of kitchen paper and grease the base of the frying pan. Heat the pan over a high heat.

✳ Spoon one ladleful of batter into the pan and immediately lift and tilt the pan so the batter flows evenly all over the base of the pan. Place the pan flat on the stove again, reduce the heat to moderate and leave for 1 minute. Shake the pan to ensure the pancake is not sticking and, using the egg lifter, flip the pancake over. After less than a minute on this side, slide the pancake onto the waiting baking tray.

✳ Continue until you have used all the batter. Try to make your pancakes as thin as possible. You may need to re-butter the base of the frying pan after every 2 or 3 pancakes.

✳ When all the pancakes are cooked, juice the lemons. Take one pancake at a time, drizzle it with lemon juice, sprinkle it with sugar and roll it up tightly like a sausage. Place the rolled pancakes in a stack in the ovenproof dish in the oven until you are ready to serve.

BOTTOM DRAWER

Interesting terms/techniques • making a well in dry ingredients • cooking in batches
Something to think about   Why do you think we roll the pancakes up before we eat them?

Menu 7

Salade niçoise with
green and yellow beans,
nasturtium blossoms
and bantam eggs

Thyme-marinated fetta
wrapped in vine leaves
and grilled

Carrot muffins with
garlic butter

Salade niçoise with green and yellow beans, nasturtium blossoms and bantam eggs

Serves   4 at home or 10 tastes in the classroom
Fresh from the garden   salad leaves, potatoes, green and yellow beans, eggs, nasturtium blossoms

This is a classic combination of ingredients and a perfect use for our small bantam eggs. On another occasion, you could try this recipe with pan-fried quail eggs, which are really tiny. To be truly delicious the salad should be gently mixed while the potatoes and beans are both still warm.

Equipment

large bowl	colander
salad spinner	whisk
tea towel	chopping board
kitchen paper	knives – 1 small, 1 large
large saucepan	serving plate or bowl
metric measuring spoons	salad servers
skewer	

Ingredients

2 cups well-packed salad leaves (about 6 handfuls)
4 medium potatoes, or 8 small kipfler potatoes
salt
1 tablespoon red-wine vinegar
⅓ cup extra-virgin olive oil
freshly ground black pepper
4 tomatoes (hydroponic at this time of year)
2 × 200 g cans tuna packed in olive oil
250 g assorted beans
½ cup black olives
4 bantam eggs (or other eggs)
4 nasturtium blossoms

What to do

✱ Fill the large bowl with cold water and soak the salad leaves for a couple of minutes. Remove any yellow or slimy leaves and place in the compost bucket. Place the good leaves in the salad spinner and spin gently. Lay out a dry tea towel and line it with a long piece of kitchen paper. Spread the dried leaves over the paper and roll the whole lot up like a log. Keep the rolled parcel of leaves in the refrigerator until needed.

✱ Wash the potatoes, but do not peel them. Place the potatoes in the saucepan and cover with cold water. Add a teaspoon of salt, bring to the boil and boil for 15–20 minutes. Potatoes are cooked when a thin skewer will slip through them. Place the colander in the sink. **Tip the potatoes and boiling water into the colander and leave to cool a little.**

✱ Dry the bowl used to soak the salad leaves and put the wine vinegar and oil into it. Mix with the whisk. Season with salt and pepper.

✱ Set out the chopping board and knives. Use the small knife or your fingers to peel the cooked potatoes and place the skins in the compost bucket. Cut the potatoes into bite-sized chunks and drop into the dressing. Cut the tomatoes into chunks and add to the dressing. Open the cans of tuna, drain the excess oil from the can and tip the tuna chunks in with the dressing.

✱ Rinse the saucepan used to cook the potatoes, then fill it with plenty of water. Add a teaspoon of salt and bring to the boil. Meanwhile, top and tail the beans, and string if necessary. If the beans are very large, cut into smaller pieces. Drop the beans into the rapidly boiling water and leave uncovered on full heat for about 8 minutes – they should be tender and not crunchy. Place the colander in the sink. **Tip the boiling water and the beans into the colander.**

✱ Do not soak the beans in cold water (see Bottom Drawer, next page). While they are still warm, drop them into the large bowl with all the other salad ingredients. Add the olives to the bowl (I always leave the stones in, but you can stone them if you prefer). ➤➤

✹ Fill the saucepan with water again and bring to the boil. **Place the eggs in the boiling water. Boil for exactly 4 minutes, then remove from heat.** Run under cold water to cool. Tap the shells against the side of the sink to allow a bit of air to enter the eggs. This will make them easier to peel neatly. Peel the eggs and cut into quarters. Set aside until needed.

✹ Remove the salad leaves from the refrigerator and arrange on the serving plate. Gently mix all the ingredients in the bowl, using the salad servers, and taste for salt and pepper. Arrange the dressed ingredients on top of the salad leaves. Place the egg quarters around the salad and decorate with nasturtium flowers and a few of the smaller nasturtium leaves.

BOTTOM DRAWER

Interesting techniques • storing salad leaves in a parcel • cooking with flowers

Question 1 Why do we cook beans in so much water?

2 Why are the beans not put in cold water?

Answers 1 The chlorophyll (this is what makes beans green) reacts with the acids in the cooking water and turns the beans grey–green. If you use lots of water, the acids are diluted and by leaving the lid off, the acids can disperse. 2 If you put beans briefly into cold water or iced water they will remain brilliantly green but I believe they lose their 'bean' flavour and taste more like cold water than water than beans.

Thyme-marinated fetta wrapped in vine leaves and grilled

Makes   10 pieces

Fresh from the garden   garlic, bay leaves, thyme, vine leaves

In this recipe, the fetta needs time to marinate. In the classroom, we used fetta that had been marinated by the previous class, then prepared the fetta for the next class.

Equipment

scales	tray
chopping board	tongs
knives – 1 small, 1 large	kitchen paper
metric measuring spoons	kitchen scissors
large bowl	fork
plastic film	pastry brush
medium saucepan	chargrill pan
tea towel	serving plate

Ingredients

250 g fetta	3 sprigs thyme
2 cloves garlic	extra-virgin olive oil
2 bay leaves	10 fresh vine leaves
1 teaspoon black	
peppercorns	

BOTTOM DRAWER

Interesting terms/techniques   • marinating
• cooking with a chargrill pan

Tip   If you want to store this cheese, transfer it and its marinating ingredients to a large storage jar with a tight-fitting lid, and refrigerate. The marinated cheese will be good for at least 4 weeks.

Question   Can you think of other foods that would work well wrapped in vine leaves?

Answer   Another Greek cheese, haloumi, which contains little flecks of mint, works very well when wrapped and grilled in vine leaves. Sardines and quail are also good done this way.

What to do

✳ Using the scales, weigh the fetta. Set out the chopping board and knives. Chop the fetta into 2 cm cubes. Peel the garlic. Tear each bay leaf into 4 pieces. Place the bay leaves, peppercorns, thyme and garlic in the large bowl. Add the cubes of fetta, stir to mix, then cover with oil. Cover with plastic film and leave to marinate – 1 hour will do it, but overnight in the refrigerator is even better.

✳ Bring a saucepan of water to the boil. Spread out the dry tea towel on top of a tray alongside the saucepan. **Using tongs, dip each vine leaf into the water for 10 seconds, then lay out on the tea-towel-lined tray, rough side uppermost.**

✳ When all the leaves have been dipped and are spread out, pat them dry with kitchen paper. Snip off the stems with scissors. Using a fork, lift a piece of cheese from the bowl, allowing the excess oil to drip back into the bowl, then place the cube in the centre of a vine leaf. Fold the leaf to completely enclose the cheese, tucking in the sides of the leaf. Repeat the process until you have used all the vine leaves. Using a pastry brush, brush each little vine-leaf parcel lightly with the remaining marinade.

✳ Heat the chargrill pan on the stovetop to very hot. Place the parcels carefully on the ridges of the pan. Allow to grill for 2–3 minutes before turning with the tongs and cooking for a further 2–3 minutes. The leaves will become blackened and crisp and the cheese inside will be soft and very tasty.

✳ Place the vine-leaf parcels on the serving plate. When it comes time to eat, make sure you taste the leaves, although you may not want to eat all of them as they are a bit chewy!

Carrot muffins with garlic butter

Makes 12

Fresh from the garden   carrots, parsley, eggs, garlic

When baking muffins (or cupcakes) I often put a paper cupcake case inside each hole in a standard muffin tin. Even if the mixture is rather runny it will bake without sticking to the tin, and by setting the paper cases inside the holes, the muffins or cupcakes will keep their shape, rather than collapsing with the weight of the mixture. But I have given instructions for both in case you have no paper cupcake cases.

Equipment

metric measuring spoons and cups	tea towel
small saucepan	scales
pastry brush	bowls – 1 small, 2 medium
12 cupcake cases (if using)	whisk
1 × 12-hole muffin tin	tablespoon
grater	fork
chopping board	baking paper
knives – 1 small, 1 large	wire rack

Ingredients

1 tablespoon butter

1 medium carrot

15 stalks parsley

60 g cheddar or gruyère

220 g self-raising (self-rising) flour

1 egg

¾ cup buttermilk

½ cup vegetable oil

Garlic butter

2 cloves garlic

salt

125 g butter

What to do

✳ Preheat the oven to 180°C. If you are using cupcake cases, drop one into each of the holes in the muffin tin. Otherwise, melt the 1 tablespoon of butter in the small saucepan, then use the pastry brush to grease the holes of the muffin tin.

✳ Set out the grater, chopping board and knives. Peel and grate the carrot – you'll need about ½ a cup. Rinse the parsley, dry by rolling in the tea towel, then chop. Using the scales, weigh the cheese, then grate it. Mix the grated cheese, parsley and flour in a medium bowl, then add the carrot.

✳ In the second medium bowl, whisk the egg, buttermilk and oil. Make a well in the dry ingredients and tip in the liquid mixture. Mix lightly, then spoon the batter into the cupcake cases or the holes of the greased muffin tin, filling them two-thirds full. Bake the muffins for 20–25 minutes until browned on top.

✳ While the muffins are cooking, make the garlic butter. Peel the garlic. **Place the cloves on the chopping board and flatten by thumping with the side of the large knife.** Sprinkle the garlic with salt, then chop finely. Place the butter in the small bowl and soften with the fork. Work in the garlic and mash until smooth. **Spoon the garlic butter onto a piece of baking paper and roll up tightly like a small sausage, twisting the ends.** Place the roll in the refrigerator (or freezer) to firm up so it can be sliced.

✳ **Remove the muffins from the oven.** Allow them to sit for a minute in the tin, before turning out onto the wire rack to cool. Take the garlic butter roll out of the refrigerator and slice finely. When the muffins are nearly cold, split them in half or make a slit in the top of each muffin and insert a slice of garlic butter.

BOTTOM DRAWER

Interesting terms/techniques   • making a well in dry ingredients
• flattening garlic cloves   • making a roll of butter or dough
Question   What is buttermilk?

Answer   Once upon a time buttermilk was the liquid that resulted after one churned cream to make butter. Nowadays it is made by adding a culture to skimmed milk, which ferments the milk a little, giving it a slightly sour flavour.

Baked eggs with tomato, herbs and spinach

Serves 4 at home or 8 tastes in the classroom
Fresh from the garden parsley, onions, garlic, spring onions, spinach, eggs, mint
We used my homemade tomato relish for this recipe, and presented the baked eggs on the beautiful wooden boards made by the woodwork class.

Equipment

non-stick frying pan
metric measuring spoons
wooden spoon
mortar and pestle
chopping board
knives – 1 small, 1 large
tea towel

bowls – 4 small
salad spinner
dishes – 4 small
aluminium foil
heatproof board or mat
large serving spoon

Ingredients

1 teaspoon coriander
  seeds
1 teaspoon cumin seeds
10 stalks parsley
1 small onion
1 clove garlic
2 spring onions
  (scallions)
1 handful spinach leaves
1 tablespoon extra-virgin
  olive oil

1 × 500 g jar tomato
  relish, or 1 × 400 g
  can chopped tomatoes
1 teaspoon paprika
8 small pita bread
  rounds
4 eggs
6 mint leaves
freshly ground black
  pepper

What to do

✳ Preheat the oven to 150°C. Place the frying pan over a medium heat. Tip in the coriander seeds and stir with the wooden spoon until they start to smell fragrant. Tip the seeds into the mortar. Add the cumin seeds to the same pan and stir until they smell fragrant. Tip the seeds into the mortar. Using the pestle, grind the toasted seeds to a coarse powder and set aside until later.

✳ Set out the chopping board and knives. Rinse the parsley, dry by rolling in the tea towel, chop, then place in a small bowl. Peel and dice the onion. Peel the garlic and chop finely. Trim the outside layer from the spring onions and cut off the tops, then slice the spring onions finely. Place the onion, garlic and spring onion in a small bowl.

✳ Rinse the spinach leaves and dry in the salad spinner. Roll the leaves into a loose bunch, then shred using the large knife.

✳ Heat the oil in the frying pan over a medium heat. Add the onion, garlic and spring onion and stir with the wooden spoon until the onions are well softened. Open the relish or canned tomatoes and tip the contents into the pan. Add the paprika and cook until the tomato is bubbling and starting to thicken. Drop the shredded spinach leaves into the pan and stir.

✳ Place the pita bread rounds on the oven rack to warm through. This should take 5–8 minutes.

 ✳ Break an egg carefully into a small dish. **Make a hole in the tomato sauce and slide the egg into the hole. Repeat with the remaining eggs.** Cover the pan with a sheet of foil and cook for 3 minutes.

✳ Uncover the pan and scatter with the chopped parsley and torn mint leaves. Grind over some black pepper. Place the board or mat on the table. **Take the pan from the stove and place on the table.** Using the large serving spoon, serve onto plates. Use the warmed pita bread for scooping up the sauce.

BOTTOM DRAWER

Interesting techniques • toasting spices
• grinding in a mortar with a pestle
• shredding leaves

Orange, fennel, spinach and black olive salad

Serves 6 at home or 12 tastes in the classroom
Fresh from the garden oranges, spinach, fennel, orange flowers
This is such a pretty salad. On another occasion, you could add some small salad leaves, in addition to the spinach, to increase the quantity. The orange-flower water adds an exotic Middle Eastern flavour to the salad. You can add a couple of orange flowers as decoration, if you know someone with a tree that has plenty of flowers.

Equipment

chopping board	vegetable-slicing gadget
knives – 1 small, 1 large	(such as a mandoline)
bowls – 2 large	metric measuring spoons
salad spinner	and cups
tea towel	tongs
kitchen paper	serving bowl

Ingredients

3 oranges	½ teaspoon orange-flower
4 handfuls spinach leaves	water (optional)
1 small bulb fennel	salt
½ cup black olives	freshly ground black pepper
¼ cup extra-virgin olive oil	orange flowers (if available)
2 teaspoons red-wine vinegar	

What to do

✱ Set out the chopping board and knives. **Using a small or large knife – whichever feels comfortable – carve the skin from each orange. Holding an orange in one hand, over a large bowl to catch the juice, slip the knife down one side of a single segment and then down the other side of the segment, cutting the flesh away from the membrane.** Drop the segment into the bowl. Repeat, until all the segments are in the bowl, then work on the other oranges in the same way. As you go, squeeze the orange 'skeletons' (what is left in your hand after all the segments have been removed) so that the juice falls over the orange segments.

✱ Fill the second large bowl with cold water and soak the spinach leaves. Remove any slimy leaves and place in the compost bucket. Place the good leaves in the salad spinner and spin gently. Lay out a dry tea towel and line it with a long piece of kitchen paper. Spread the dried leaves over the paper and roll the whole lot up like a log. Keep the rolled parcel of leaves in the refrigerator until needed.

✱ Take the fennel and remove any outside leaves that are brown or cracked, and place in the compost bucket. Cut the fennel bulb in half from top to bottom. Slice the fennel as thinly as possible using either a knife or a vegetable slicer, such as a mandoline. **If using a vegetable slicer, you will definitely need a grown-up around, as these can be dangerous.** Tip the sliced fennel into the bowl with the oranges and orange juice.

✱ Place an olive on the chopping board and press down on it with the flat side of the large knife. The olive will squash and the stone can be easily removed. Do this with all the olives and then add to the bowl with the oranges and fennel.

✱ Tip the dried spinach leaves into the bowl, drizzle over the oil, vinegar and orange-flower water (if using) and mix gently with the tongs. Taste for salt and pepper. Transfer to the salad bowl, garnish with orange flowers (if available) and serve.

> **BOTTOM DRAWER**
>
> **Interesting terms/techniques** • segmenting oranges
> • orange skeletons • storing salad leaves in a parcel
> • squashing olives to remove the stone • using a vegetable-slicing gadget (mandoline) • cooking with flowers
> **Did you know?** Orange-flower water is a specialist product made from bitter Seville oranges. It is used to flavour syrups for pastries and puddings, as well as sprinkled in salads. Availability varies, but most good delis and specialist food stores sell it, as well as some supermarkets.

Hummus with paprika oil

Makes 3 cups

Fresh from the garden parsley, garlic, lemons

This recipe convinced the students that homemade dips, using freshly picked herbs, taste better than store-bought dips. Chick peas must be soaked overnight, then cooked for 1 hour, so the students prepared ahead for following classes.

Equipment

colander	tea towel
large saucepan	chopping board
bowls – 1 small, 1 large	knives – 1 small, 1 large
metric measuring spoons and cups	lemon juicer
	food processor
frying pan	teaspoon
wooden spoon	spatula
mortar and pestle	shallow plate for serving

Ingredients

150 g chick peas, soaked overnight in water	4 parsley leaves
	2 cloves garlic
1 teaspoon paprika	2 lemons
1 tablespoon extra-virgin olive oil	⅔ cup tahini paste
	salt
1 teaspoon cumin seeds	freshly ground black pepper

What to do

✳ Drain the soaking chick peas in the colander and rinse with cold water. Tip chick peas into the large saucepan and cover with water. Bring to the boil and simmer for 1 hour, or until cooked. Chick peas are cooked when they are soft. Place the colander in the large bowl.

👧👦 **Tip the chick peas and boiling water into the colander.**
Save ½ a cup of the cooking water.

✳ Mix the paprika and oil in the small bowl and set aside. Heat the cumin seeds in the frying-pan over medium heat, stirring with the wooden spoon until they smell fragrant. Tip the seeds into the mortar and use the pestle to grind to a powder.

✳ Wash the parsley leaves and pat dry with the tea towel. Set out the chopping board and knives. Peel and chop the garlic. Juice the lemons.

✳ Place the chick peas, lemon juice, cumin and garlic in the food processor, along with half of the reserved cooking water, and process to a smooth cream. Spoon in the tahini and blend again. Add more cooking water if the mixture is too thick. Taste for salt and pepper.

✳ Use the spatula to scoop the paste onto the shallow plate. Mark a channel all around the paste with the teaspoon, then drizzle the paprika oil into this channel. Decorate the plate with the parsley leaves.

BOTTOM DRAWER

Interesting techniques • toasting spices
• grinding in a mortar with a pestle
Questions 1 Why do you soak chick peas overnight before using? 2 What is tahini made from?

Answers 1 Soaking softens the tough outer skin, which means the chick peas will cook faster. 2 Sesame seeds.

Summer

We discovered that the summer dishes often work best when grilled. The zucchini proved astonishingly prolific and the children found it hard to believe that a vegetable could grow so fast. Sweetcorn waved in the breeze and we enjoyed many different salads. The art department made terracotta stones, and we used them for baking pizza.

Bruschetta with Tomato and Roasted Red Pepper (page 137)

Chicken marinated in yoghurt, paprika and lemon juice

Makes   6 skewers

Fresh from the garden   mint, lemons, salad leaves
This is a simplified version of an Indian marinade.
The yoghurt forms a lovely crust and is said to
tenderise tough meats (not a problem in Australia
with our very tender poultry).

Equipment

6 bamboo skewers
2 bowls – 1 medium,
   1 large
aluminium foil
chopping board
large knife
tea towel

lemon juicer
metric measuring spoons
   and cups
large gratin dish
large spoon
serving plate

Ingredients

15 mint leaves
½ lemon
¾ cup plain yoghurt
1 teaspoon paprika, plus extra to garnish
1 tablespoon extra-virgin olive oil
500 g skinless chicken thighs or breasts
salt
freshly ground black pepper
salad leaves to garnish

What to do

✳ Soak the skewers in cold water in the large bowl.
Heat the grill to maximum and line the grill tray with
aluminium foil to catch drips.

✳ Set out the chopping board and knife. Rinse the
mint leaves, dry by rolling in the tea towel, then chop.
Juice the lemon. Place the mint, lemon juice, yoghurt,
paprika, oil and salt and pepper in the medium bowl
and mix well.

✳ Cut the chicken into 3 cm cubes. Lift the skewers
from the water and pat dry on the previously used tea
towel. Thread the chicken pieces onto the skewers.
Place each skewer into the large gratin dish as you
complete it. Spoon the yoghurt marinade evenly over
the skewers. The chicken can be grilled at once or
you can leave it in the marinade for an hour.

✳ Lift the skewers onto the grill tray – do not move
them around. **Grill until the chicken looks golden
brown – a couple of minutes – then turn the skewers
to grill the other side.**

✳ When cooked, arrange the skewers on the serving
plate and decorate with a sprinkle of paprika and a few
salad leaves.

BOTTOM DRAWER

Interesting term   •   marinating
Question   Why do we soak bamboo skewers
in cold water?

Answer   So the skewers don't burn as they cook.

Zucchini slice

Makes   16 squares
Fresh from the garden   zucchini, onions, eggs, tomatoes
This slice is very popular with all ages. The recipe came to me from an Italian woman who grew her own zucchini and tomatoes and was always inventing interesting things to do with her bountiful crop.

Equipment

metric measuring cups	bowls – 1 medium, 1 large
pastry brush	scales
baking dish	chopping board
baking paper	knives – 1 small, 1 large,
pencil	1 serrated
scissors	whisk
grater	wooden spoon
2 tea towels	

Ingredients

½ cup olive oil	150 g self-raising
500 g zucchini (courgettes)	(self-rising) flour
150 g parmesan	3 eggs
1 onion	salt
150 g streaky bacon	freshly ground black pepper
	2 large tomatoes

What to do

✱ Preheat the oven to 180°C. Measure out the oil, then use a little to lightly brush the base and sides of the baking dish. Place the dish on a sheet of baking paper and trace the outline with a pencil. Cut out the shape and place the paper in the dish.

✱ Grate the zucchini using the largest hole of the grater. Tip the gratings into a clean tea towel and twist over the sink to remove the excess moisture. Tip the zucchini into the large bowl. Weigh the cheese, grate it, then tip into the large bowl. Set out the chopping board and knives. Peel and chop the onion as finely as you can and

chop the bacon into tiny pieces, then add both to the zucchini bowl. Finally, add the flour.

✱ In the medium bowl, lightly whisk the eggs, then add to the ingredients in the large bowl. Mix well and season with salt and pepper.

✱ Spoon the mixture into the prepared baking dish and smooth the top. Using the serrated knife, cut the tomatoes into thick slices and lay the slices on top of the mixture. Drizzle the remaining oil over the top. Bake for about 25–30 minutes until firm.

 ✱ **Remove from the oven.** Allow the slice to cool a little before cutting into squares or fingers.

BOTTOM DRAWER

Interesting terms/techniques • squeezing liquid from an ingredient using a cloth • cutting tomatoes with a serrated knife

Ricotta pancakes with sugared strawberries

Makes   10 pancakes

Fresh from the garden   strawberries, eggs

Thick, fluffy pancakes like these ones are often served with maple syrup or honey, and are quite different from crêpes.

Equipment

baking tray

chopping board

small knife

bowls – 1 small, 2 medium,
    1 large

metric measuring spoons
    and cups

scales

sieve or sifter

small saucepan

whisk

wooden spoon

pastry brush

non-stick frying pan

small ladle

egg lifter

serving plate

Ingredients

30 strawberries

¼ cup castor (superfine)
    sugar

300 g self-raising (self-
    rising) flour

salt

60 g butter

1¼ cups milk

2 eggs

150 g ricotta

cream to serve

What to do

✳ Preheat the oven to 120°C and place the baking tray in the oven to keep warm. Set out the chopping board and knife. Hull the strawberries and slice each one into 2 or 3 pieces. Place in one of the medium bowls and add 2 tablespoons of the castor sugar.

✳ Weigh the flour, then sift it, along with the remaining 1 tablespoon of sugar and a pinch of salt, into the large bowl.

✳ Melt the butter in the saucepan over a medium heat. Pour half into the small bowl and set aside. Pour the other half into the second medium bowl. Add the milk and eggs and whisk together.

✳ Make a well in the flour and pour in the egg and milk mixture. Using the wooden spoon, mix until you have a smooth batter. Crumble the ricotta into the batter in small lumps.

✳ Use the pastry brush to brush the base of the non-stick frying pan with some of the melted butter, and place the pan over a medium heat. Drop a ladleful (or a couple of spoonfuls) of batter into the pan, allowing room for the pancake to spread a bit. Cook for 2–3 minutes until bubbles form on the uncooked side. Flip the pancake using the egg lifter, and cook for a further minute on the second side.

✳ **When the pancake is done, slip it onto the warm tray in the oven.** Before you cook another pancake, brush the pan with a little more melted butter. Continue until you have used all the batter. Arrange the pancakes on the serving plate, then top each one with a quantity of sliced strawberries and a dollop of cream.

BOTTOM DRAWER

Interesting techniques   • hulling strawberries

• making a well in dry ingredients

Question   What does ricotta mean?

Answer   Ricotta means re-cooked. This refers to the fact that ricotta is made by reheating the whey that remains after the curds have been lifted out to be pressed for cheese.

Polenta and rosemary bread with fresh sweetcorn

Makes   16 small slices

From the garden   sweetcorn, rosemary, eggs

This bread makes a great snack and is good fresh from the oven or toasted. It can also be baked in a shallow tin, such as a Swiss-roll tin, so that the squares are thinner, and then topped with a slice of tomato or a roasted and peeled pepper. The baking time for a thinner slice will be shortened by about 10 minutes.

Equipment

metric measuring spoons and cups	scales
bowls – 2 small, 1 medium, 1 large	grater
	chopping board
pastry brush	knives – 1 small, 1 large
1 × 20 cm square baking dish	fork
	whisk
baking paper	wooden spoon
pencil	skewer
scissors	wire rack

Ingredients

1 tablespoon extra-virgin olive oil

60 g parmesan

¼ cup cream

2 cobs sweetcorn

2 cups coarse polenta (cornmeal)

2 teaspoons salt

1 teaspoon bicarbonate of soda (baking soda)

6 × 3 cm stalks rosemary

2 cups buttermilk

2 eggs

What to do

✳ Preheat the oven to 220°C. Measure the oil into a small bowl, then use the pastry brush to lightly grease the base and sides of the baking dish. Place the dish on a sheet of baking paper and trace the outline with a pencil. Lift off the tin and cut out the shape, then place the paper in the dish.

✳ Weigh the cheese, then grate it. Combine the cheese with the cream in a small bowl.

✳ Set out the chopping board and knives. Stand the cobs on the board and, using the fork, rake the kernels to split the skins. **Cut the kernels from the cob.** Put the polenta, salt and bicarbonate of soda into the large bowl and mix well. Add the corn kernels to this mixture.

✳ Strip the needles of rosemary from the stalks and chop finely. Put the rosemary, buttermilk and eggs into the medium bowl and whisk well. Make a well in the polenta and tip in the buttermilk/egg mixture. Use the wooden spoon to mix well to form a batter.

✳ Tip or spoon the batter into the prepared dish. Spread the cheese/cream mixture over the batter.

✳ Bake for 30 minutes. Test by inserting a skewer – the polenta bread is cooked if the skewer comes out dry and clean.

✳ **Remove the polenta bread from the oven.** Allow to cool in the dish for at least 10 minutes, then turn out onto the wire rack. Cut the polenta bread into slices and serve as is, or toasted with butter.

BOTTOM DRAWER

Interesting terms/techniques   • stripping rosemary needles from the stalk   • cutting corn kernels from a cob   • making a well in dry ingredients   • testing with a skewer

Safety tip   Cutting kernels from a corn cob can be difficult because the kernels are slippery.

Grilled quail marinated in lemon juice, olive oil and herbs

Serves   6 at home or 12 tastes in the classroom
Fresh from the garden   parsley, oregano, garlic, lemons
The quails caused much excitement in the class, as some of the
students thought they were frogs! But once marinated and grilled,
the students loved them. Quail tastes very similar to chicken.

Equipment

aluminium foil	metric measuring cups
tea towel	kitchen paper
chopping board	poultry scissors/shears
knives – 1 small, 1 large	tongs
large bowl	serving plate
lemon juicer	

Ingredients

15 stalks parsley
8 sprigs oregano
1 clove garlic
2 lemons
¼ cup extra-virgin olive oil
salt
freshly ground black pepper
6 quails

What to do

✱ Heat the grill to maximum and line the grill tray with
aluminium foil to catch drips.

✱ Rinse the parsley and oregano and dry by rolling in the tea towel.
Set out the chopping board and knives. Chop the herbs and place in
the large bowl. Peel the garlic, slice and add to the bowl. Juice 1 lemon,
then add the juice to the bowl. Add the oil then complete the
marinade by adding salt and pepper.

✱ Set out the quail and pat dry all over with kitchen paper. **Cut each
bird in half using scissors, being very careful not to damage the
breasts.** Put the quail halves in the bowl and swish to coat well with
the marinade. Leave for 15 minutes.

✱ Pull out the grill tray from the oven. Using the tongs, arrange
the quail pieces on the tray.

✱ Return the tray to the oven, lower the heat to medium and grill
for 10 minutes until the quail pieces look golden brown and are
bubbling. Turn the quail and grill the other side for 5 minutes.
Test with a skewer – the quail is cooked when a skewer will slip
easily through the thigh and the juices that emerge are clear.

✱ Meanwhile, cut the second lemon into wedges. Pile the quail
pieces onto the serving plate and add a few lemon wedges.
You could also line the plate first with large lettuce leaves.

> **BOTTOM DRAWER**
>
> **Interesting terms/techniques**   • marinating
> • using poultry scissors/shears   • testing with a skewer
> **Did you know?**   Quails are found in the wild in Europe,
> Asia and Africa. They are small and plump, and are known as
> ground-dwellers, preferring to run rather than fly. In Australia,
> they are bred on special poultry farms.

Dolmades with silver beet

Makes   16 rolls

Fresh from the garden   lemons, silver beet

Dolmades are traditionally made using fresh vine leaves. If you have fresh vine leaves, follow the instructions for preparing them in Thyme-marinated Fetta Wrapped in Vine Leaves (page 113). We had such a lot of silverbeet leaves that the recipe below was a very successful variation.

Equipment

large saucepan	6 tea towels
lemon juicer	teaspoon
metric measuring cups	frying pan with 5 cm sides
bowls – 1 small, 1 medium,	aluminium foil
1 large	plate to fit inside frying pan
chopping board	simmer mat
small knife	serving plate
tongs	

Ingredients

1 lemon
1 cup tomato juice
16 medium-to-large silverbeet leaves
1½ cups Basic Spicy Rice Filling (page 78)

BOTTOM DRAWER

Interesting terms/techniques   • blanching   • refreshing

Question   1 Why did the recipe suggest putting a ball of aluminium foil into the frying pan?   2 Why would you use a simmer mat ?

Answers   1 So the dolmades don't move around as they cook.   2 So the rolls don't get burnt as they cook, as there is not very much liquid in the pan.

What to do

✳ Fill the saucepan with water and bring to the boil. Juice the lemon and mix it with the tomato juice in the small bowl.

✳ Fill the large bowl with cold water. Set out the chopping board and knife. Separate the silverbeet leaves from the stems by slicing along each side of the thick central stem. Place the stems in the compost bucket.

✳ **Using the tongs, plunge 3 or 4 leaves into the boiling water for just a few seconds, then drop them into the cold water.**

✳ Lift the leaves from the cold water immediately and lay on a dry tea towel. Cover with another dry tea towel. Continue with this process of blanching and refreshing until all the leaves are done.

✳ Put the spicy rice filling into the medium bowl. Lay a dry leaf on the chopping board and place 2 teaspoons of rice filling on the leaf, about 4 cm in from the lengthways edge. **Roll sideways over the filling, tucking in the sides of the leaf, and continue to roll firmly to the end of the leaf.** Continue until all leaves are filled and rolled.

✳ Tuck the rolls tightly together in the frying pan. If there is still space in the pan, fill the gap with a crumpled ball of aluminium foil.

✳ Pour the tomato/lemon liquid over the rolls, then settle a plate on top of the rolls to stop them floating. Place the frying pan on a simmer mat on the stovetop and cook over a medium heat for about 15 minutes.

✳ When done, allow the rolls to cool a little before lifting out and arranging on the serving plate.

Peach cakes with cinnamon sugar

Makes 10 muffin-sized cakes

Fresh from the garden eggs, yellow peaches

The peach trees in the garden were still very small but peaches are the very essence of summer so we wanted to use them. Other stone fruits, such as plums or apricots, could be used instead.

Equipment

scales	bowls – 1 small, 1 medium,
small saucepan	1 large
pastry brush	whisk
1 × 12-hole muffin tin, or	chopping board
oval-holed friand tin	large knife
sieve or sifter	wooden spoon
metric measuring spoons	tablespoon
and cups	wire rack

Ingredients

140 g butter

150 g plain (all-purpose) flour

1 teaspoon baking powder

3 teaspoons ground cinnamon

3 eggs

½ cup castor (superfine) sugar,
   plus extra 2 tablespoons for topping

3 ripe yellow peaches

What to do

✱ Preheat the oven to 200°C. Use the scales to weigh the butter, then melt it in the small saucepan over a medium heat. Using the pastry brush, grease 10 holes of the muffin tin (or friand tin) with the melted butter (the mixture will probably only make 10 cakes). Put the remaining butter to one side.

✱ Sift the flour, along with the baking powder and half the cinnamon, into the large bowl.

✱ Put the eggs and the ½ cup of sugar into the medium bowl and whisk well. Add the rest of the melted butter to the egg mixture and stir. Make a well in the dry ingredients, pour in the egg/butter mixture and stir to combine.

✱ Set out the chopping board and knife. Chop 2 of the peaches and add to the large bowl. Using the wooden spoon, mix everything together well.

✱ Using the tablespoon, divide the mixture equally between the greased holes of the muffin or friand tin, filling each one only three-quarters full.

✱ Slice the third peach into 10 slices (1 slice per cake), then press a peach slice into the top of each cake.

✱ Bake for 20 minutes or until the cakes are golden and feel firm to the touch.

 ✱ **Remove the cakes from the oven.** Allow them to cool for a few minutes in the tin, before turning out onto the wire rack.

✱ Combine the extra castor sugar and remaining cinnamon in the small bowl and sprinkle a little over each cake.

BOTTOM DRAWER

Interesting terms/techniques • making a well in dry ingredients • testing a cake by feeling its surface

Did you know? A friand tin makes oval or rectangular cakes. Friands are a specialised French cake made with ground almonds.

Menu 11

Chargrilled Middle
Eastern lamb burgers
with pita breads

Roasted sweet potato
and pumpkin
with peanuts

Tabbouleh

Fresh cantaloupe
wedges with mint and
lemon juice

**Fresh cantaloupe
wedges with mint
and lemon juice**

Halve a cantaloupe and
scoop out and discard the
seeds. Cut into neat wedges
and arrange on a plate.
Squeeze over lemon juice
and add freshly picked mint
leaves. You can serve the
wedges peeled or unpeeled.

Chargrilled Middle Eastern lamb burgers with pita breads

Makes   10 small burgers

Fresh from the garden   onions, lemons, parsley, thyme

So that all the students could enjoy these delicious hamburgers, we went to Melbourne's Middle Eastern shopping strip in Sydney Road, Coburg, and purchased our lamb from a specialist Halal butcher. Halal describes meat from animals that have been slaughtered in the ritual way according to Islamic law.

Equipment

2 baking trays	knives – 1 small, 1 large
frying pan	grater
metric measuring spoons and cups	lemon juicer
	tea towel
wooden spoon	tongs
mortar and pestle	fork
kitchen paper	chargrill pan
large bowl	pastry brush
chopping board	

Ingredients

2 teaspoons coriander seeds	500 g minced (ground) lamb
2 teaspoons cumin seeds	2 teaspoons salt
½ onion	freshly ground black pepper
1 lemon	¼ cup extra-virgin olive oil
15 stalks parsley	10 small pita pocket breads
10 sprigs thyme	½ cup yoghurt

What to do

✳ Preheat the oven to 150°C and put one of the baking trays in the oven to keep warm.

✳ Heat the frying pan over a medium heat. Tip in the coriander seeds and stir with the wooden spoon until they start to smell fragrant. Tip the seeds into the mortar. Toast the cumin seeds in the same pan until they, too, smell fragrant. Add these seeds to the mortar and wipe out the frying pan with a piece of kitchen paper.

✳ Using the pestle, grind the toasted seeds to a coarse powder. Tip the powder into the large bowl. Set out the chopping board and knives. Peel and chop the onion finely (or grate it) and tip into the bowl. Juice the lemon and grate the zest, adding both to the bowl.

✳ Rinse the parsley and thyme, dry by rolling in the tea towel, then chop. Add the herbs to the bowl. Now add the lamb and salt, along with a good grind of black pepper. Make sure your hands are very clean, then use your hands to mix everything together very well.

✳ Heat the frying pan over a medium heat and add a tiny dash of the oil. Take a walnut-sized piece of the mixture and fry it in the frying pan for a couple of minutes. Using the tongs, lift this sample out of the frying pan. Allow to cool a little, then taste it to decide if the mixture needs more salt or pepper.

✳ Form the mixture into 10 equal balls. Flatten each ball a bit with the back of a fork and place on the cold baking tray. Using the pastry brush, brush the lamb burgers with oil. Heat the chargrill pan over a medium-to-high heat. **Place the burgers carefully on the hot grill – do not try to move them once they have been placed. Turn after 8–10 minutes and cook the other side for about 5 minutes.** As the burgers are cooked, transfer them to the baking tray that has been in the oven.

✳ While the burgers are grilling, brush the pita pocket breads with oil, then place on the oven rack to warm through. This should take 5–8 minutes. Serve the burgers and warm breads at the table, where your guests should open the pocket breads, spoon in some Tabbouleh (page 135) and then top with the lamb burger and a dollop of yoghurt.

BOTTOM DRAWER

Interesting terms/techniques   •   toasting spices
•   grinding in a mortar with a pestle   •   cooking with a chargrill pan

Roasted sweet potato and pumpkin with peanuts

Serves   6 at home or 12 tastes in the classroom

Fresh from the garden   sweet potatoes, pumpkin, garlic, rosemary

It is very important to make sure that no one in your class or your family is allergic to peanuts before choosing to make this dish. The dish could also be made by substituting sunflower seeds or pumpkin-seed kernels for the peanuts.

Equipment

baking dish	metric measuring spoons
chopping board	large spoon
knives – 1 small, 1 large	skewer
peeler	serving plate
bowls – 1 small, 1 large	

Ingredients

500 g sweet potato
500 g pumpkin
6 cloves garlic
3 × 3 cm stalks rosemary
2 tablespoons extra-virgin olive oil
½ teaspoon salt
freshly ground black pepper

Dressing

¼ cup unroasted peanuts,
    or sunflower seeds or pumpkin-seed kernels
1 clove garlic
2 × 3 cm stalks rosemary
1 teaspoon balsamic vinegar
2 tablespoons extra-virgin olive oil
salt
freshly ground black pepper

What to do

✳ Preheat the oven to 220°C. Tip the peanuts (or seeds) for the dressing into the baking dish and roast until they turn a deep golden colour (about 10 minutes). **Remove the peanuts from the oven.** Transfer to the small bowl and leave to cool.

✳ Set out the chopping board, knives and peeler. Peel the sweet potato and cut into 1 cm slices, then put the slices into the large bowl. Peel the pumpkin and cut into 1 cm thick pieces, then put the pieces into the same bowl. Put the scraps into the compost bucket.

✳ **Place the garlic cloves, unpeeled, on the chopping board and flatten with the side of the large knife.** Add the crushed unpeeled garlic to the bowl. Drop in the rosemary stalks. Drizzle the vegetables with the oil, then season with salt and pepper. Mix together with the large spoon.

✳ Tip everything into the baking dish used to roast the peanuts, making sure the vegetables are spread out in a single layer. Bake for 20 minutes. **Lift the baking dish out of the oven and carefully turn the pieces over.** Return the baking dish to the oven for an extra 20 minutes or until the vegetables are soft (you can use a skewer to test).

✳ While the vegetables are baking, make the dressing using the ingredients listed under *Dressing*. Chop the previously roasted peanuts coarsely and return to the small bowl. Peel and finely chop the garlic and add to the bowl. Strip the rosemary needles from their stalks, chop the needles finely and add to the bowl. Mix in the vinegar and oil. Stir together and season with salt and pepper.

✳ **When the vegetables are ready, remove the baking dish from the oven.** Arrange the vegetables on the serving plate and spoon over the peanut dressing.

BOTTOM DRAWER

Interesting terms/techniques   • roasting nuts
• flattening garlic cloves   • testing with a skewer
Did you know?   Sweet potato is native to Central America but is now eaten around the world.

Tabbouleh

Serves 6 at home or 12 tastes in the classroom

Fresh from the garden tomatoes, cucumbers, spring onions, garlic, parsley, mint, lemons

Tabbouleh needs plenty of parsley. When ready to serve, the mixture should look brightly coloured with the red of the tomatoes and the green of the herbs. Use it to fill pita pocket breads and then add some Falafel (page 236), Chargrilled Middle Eastern Lamb Burgers (page 133) or Labna Balls (page 156).

Equipment

metric measuring spoons and cups	chopping board
bowls – 1 small, 1 medium	knives – 1 large, 1 serrated
tablespoon	peeler
large strainer	lemon juicer
2 tea towels	serving bowl

Ingredients

½ cup cracked wheat	15 mint leaves
3 tomatoes	1 lemon
1 long cucumber (green ridge or telegraph variety)	2 tablespoons extra-virgin olive oil
2 spring onions (scallions)	salt
1 clove garlic	freshly ground black pepper
10 stalks parsley	

What to do

✱ Place the cracked wheat in the medium bowl and cover with cold water. Soak for 10 minutes, then tip into the strainer. Press out as much liquid as possible with the back of the tablespoon.

✱ Tip the cracked wheat into one of the tea towels (choose one that's thick) and roll it like a sausage. **Two people are now needed to each hold one end of the tea-towel sausage, and to twist in opposite directions to squeeze even more liquid from the grains.** Rinse and dry the bowl used to soak the cracked wheat, then unwrap the 'sausage' and carefully shake the cracked wheat into the bowl.

✱ Set out the chopping board and knives. As you chop the following ingredients, place them in the bowl with the cracked wheat. Cut the tomatoes into small dice using the serrated knife. Peel and dice the cucumber. Trim the outside layer from the spring onions, cut off their tops and ends, then finely slice the rest. Peel and finely chop the garlic.

✱ Rinse the parsley and mint and dry by rolling in the second tea towel. Chop the herbs and add to the other ingredients. Juice the lemon. In the small bowl, mix the oil and lemon juice to make a dressing, then add to the medium bowl. Mix everything together and taste for salt and pepper. Spread the parsley evenly throughout. Transfer the tabbouleh to the serving bowl and serve.

BOTTOM DRAWER

Interesting technique
• squeezing liquid from an ingredient using a cloth

Questions 1 What are the names of the different types of cucumber? 2 Which cucumber has the largest seeds?

Answer 1 Apple, telegraph, Lebanese, regular and green ridge. 2 Apple.

Raw broad beans with sea salt and extra-virgin olive oil

Pick young broad beans, shell them, then carefully tear open the outer skin and pop out the brilliantly green inner bean. These double-peeled broad beans are delicious dipped into a saucer of very fruity extra-virgin olive oil and then topped with a single flake of sea salt.

Zucchini agrodolce

Serves   6 at home or 12 tastes in the classroom
Fresh from the garden   basil, zucchini, onions, garlic, celery

This way of serving vegetables in a sweet-and-sour sauce comes from Sicily, in the south of Italy. Small onions are often treated in the same way. The dish can be enjoyed on its own, as here, or served alongside grilled fish.

Equipment

metric measuring spoons	tea towel
non-stick frying pan	tongs
slotted spoon or egg lifter	dinner plate
kitchen paper	wooden spoon
chopping board	aluminium foil
knives – 1 small, 1 large	serving plate
7 small bowls or plates	

Ingredients

½ cup extra-virgin olive oil	6 large green olives
2 tablespoons pine nuts	1 tablespoon tomato paste
3–4 basil leaves	2 tablespoons sultanas
6 small zucchini (courgettes)	¼ cup sugar
1 onion	¼ cup red-wine vinegar
2 cloves garlic	salt
2 anchovy fillets	freshly ground black pepper
2 sticks celery	

BOTTOM DRAWER

Interesting terms/techniques
• toasting nuts   • stoning olives
Question   What does agrodolce mean?

Answer   Bittersweet.

What to do

✱ Put 1 tablespoon of the oil into the frying pan, and toast the pine nuts over a medium heat. When golden, scoop out with the slotted spoon and drain on kitchen paper. Set aside.

✱ Set out the chopping board and knives. Halve the zucchini lengthways. As you prepare the following ingredients, place them in small bowls/plates and set to one side. Rinse the basil leaves, dry by rolling in the tea towel, then tear into pieces. Peel the onion, halve it from top to bottom, turn the cut side down and cut into fine half circles. Peel and chop the garlic. Chop the anchovy fillets. Chop the celery into 5 mm (very fine) slices. **Place an olive on the chopping board and press down on it with the flat side of the large knife – this makes it easier to remove the stone.** Do this with all the olives. Chop the stoned olives into several pieces.

✱ Heat half the remaining oil in the frying pan over a medium heat. Fry the zucchini, cut side down, for about 5 minutes – the cut side should be a rich brown colour. Using tongs, turn the zucchini and fry for 2 minutes on the other side. Remove the zucchini to the dinner plate.

✱ Add the onion and garlic to the pan and fry, stirring with the wooden spoon, until soft – add a few more drops of oil during cooking, if necessary. Add the tomato paste, celery and sultanas and cook gently for 5 minutes. Add the anchovies and olives and stir to mix well. Return the zucchini to the pan, cut side up.

✱ Increase the heat. Scatter in the sugar, followed by the vinegar, and shake the pan to mix. Reduce the heat to medium. Cover with aluminium foil and cook for a further 5 minutes. Uncover and taste for salt and pepper. Spoon onto the serving dish and scatter with the toasted pine nuts and torn basil leaves.

Bruschetta with tomato and roasted red pepper

Serves   6 (1 piece of bread each)
Fresh from the garden   red peppers, tomatoes, basil, garlic
This Italian snack tastes wonderful when the tomatoes are ripe, the bread is chewy and crusty, and the olive oil is full-flavoured.

Equipment

aluminium foil	pastry brush
chopping board	tongs
knives – 1 large, 1 serrated	plastic or brown paper bag
metric measuring spoons and cups	tea towel
	chargrill pan
bowls – 2 small, 1 medium	serving plate

Ingredients

1 red pepper	salt
½ cup extra-virgin olive oil	freshly ground black pepper
3 tomatoes	1 clove garlic
10 basil leaves	sourdough loaf

What to do

✳ Heat the grill to maximum and line the grill tray with aluminium foil. Set out the chopping board and knives. Slice off the top of the pepper, then halve the pepper lengthways. Cut each piece in half again – you should now have 4 pieces – and scrape all the seeds into the compost bucket or grill the pepper whole. Place the oil in one of the small bowls, and brush the shiny side of the pepper with oil.

✳ Arrange the pepper on the grill tray and grill until it has lots of black blisters. **Using the tongs, remove the blackened pieces (or the whole pepper) and place immediately in the plastic bag or brown paper bag. Close the bag and allow the pepper to cool completely.**

✳ Using the serrated knife, cut the tomatoes into 1 cm dice and put into the medium bowl. Rinse the basil leaves, dry by rolling in the tea towel, then tear into small pieces and add to the bowl.

Add 1 teaspoon of salt and some black pepper to the bowl, then pour in half the remaining oil and mix very well. Set aside.

✳ Transfer a piece of cooled, blackened pepper from the bag to the chopping board. Peel away the skin and place it in the compost bucket. Place the peeled pepper in the second small bowl. Cut the whole pepper or each of the 4 pieces into 1 cm dice and add to the bowl with the tomatoes. Mix well. Peel the garlic clove, cut it down the middle and set aside.

✳ Cut 6 slices of bread, about 1 cm thick. Heat the chargrill pan over a medium heat. Brush the slices of bread with the remaining oil and grill on both sides, using the tongs to turn. The bread will probably develop lovely stripes from the ridges of the chargrill pan.

✳ Remove the grilled bread from the pan and rub each slice lightly with the cut garlic. Cut each slice of bread in half, spoon a generous amount of tomato/basil/pepper mixture onto the bread, then arrange on the serving plate.

BOTTOM DRAWER

Interesting terms/techniques
- roasting and peeling peppers
- cooking with a chargrill pan
- cutting tomatoes with a serrated knife

Zoi's chocolate cupcakes

Makes   12

Fresh from the garden   eggs

Zoi is a very talented pastry chef who worked with me for some time. Her cakes are always very tempting. This recipe will make 12 cupcakes, but there may be a small amount of mixture left over.

Equipment

metric measuring spoons and cups	bowls – 2 medium, 1 large
saucepans – 1 small, 1 medium	chopping board
	large knife
pastry brush	mixing spoon
1 × 12-hole muffin tin	plastic container
12 cupcake cases (optional)	teaspoon
scales	whisk
sieve or sifter	wire rack

Ingredients

80 g butter, plus 1 tablespoon extra	1 cup castor (superfine) sugar
200 g plain (all-purpose) flour	⅓ cup vegetable oil
	80 g cocoa
¼ teaspoon salt	¾ cup water
¾ teaspoon bicarbonate of soda (baking soda)	2 eggs
	¾ cup buttermilk
	¾ cup cream

What to do

✱ Preheat the oven to 180°C. Melt the 1 tablespoon of butter in the small saucepan, then use the pastry brush to grease the holes of the muffin tin. If you prefer, you can line the muffin tin with cupcake cases instead of greasing it.

✱ Use the scales to weigh the flour, then sift it, along with the salt and bicarbonate of soda, into the large bowl. Stir in the castor sugar.

✱ Set out the chopping board and knife. Chop the butter into small pieces. Select a medium-sized bowl that will sit comfortably on top of a similarly sized saucepan. Half fill the saucepan with water and bring to a simmer over a medium heat. Place the butter, oil, cocoa and water in the bowl, then set the bowl over the simmering water. This is called cooking au bain-marie. The water should not touch the bottom of the bowl.

✱ **Once the butter has completely melted, remove the bowl from the water.** Stir the mixture gently until completely smooth.

✱ Set out the plastic container. Separate 1 egg by cracking it, then tipping it into your cupped hand, which should be held over the plastic container. Slightly open your fingers and let the white slip into the container. Place the yolk in the bowl with the cocoa/butter mixture, along with the second unseparated egg, and lightly whisk. (You can freeze the unused eggwhite. Remember to cover and label the container.)

✱ Make a well in the dry ingredients and tip the cocoa/butter mixture into the well. Stir or whisk to thoroughly combine. Stir in the buttermilk.

✱ Spoon the mixture into the prepared muffin tin, filling each hole three-quarters full. Bake for 12–15 minutes until the cakes are well-risen and feel springy. Meanwhile, place the cream in a medium bowl and whip with the whisk.

✱ **Remove the cakes from the oven.** Allow to cool completely in the tin, before turning out onto the wire rack.

✱ Slice off the top of each cupcake and place a generous teaspoonful of whipped cream on the cut surface, before replacing the top, so that it looks like a little hat on top of the cake.

BOTTOM DRAWER

Interesting terms/techniques   • cooking au bain-marie
• separating eggs   • making a well in dry ingredients
• testing a cake by feeling its surface

Potato and rosemary pizza with rocket leaves

Summer salad

To make a great summer
salad, follow the instructions
in the Master Salad Recipe
(page 76). You can then use
a variety of fresh summer
ingredients, such as tomato
and basil, as well as discs
of bocconcini, with your
choice of dressing
(pictured on page 142).

Serves   6 at home or 12 tastes in the classroom

Fresh from the garden   rocket, rosemary, potatoes

At Collingwood College, the students made and fired
large flat terracotta platters about 32 cm in diameter,
in their pottery class. These platters were placed in
the oven and the pizzas were shaped on squares of
lightweight three-ply wood so that they could be easily
shaken onto the very hot platters. In professional pizza
stores, these wooden squares have a long handle for
pushing the pizza deep into a large oven and are
known as 'peels'. Simple pizza trays are much easier
but the base will never be as crisp. Pizza dough has
to rest or 'prove' for a total of around an hour and a
half. At Collingwood, each class prepared the dough
ahead for the next class.

Equipment

metric measuring spoons
and cups
bowls – 1 small, 2 large
fork
scales
electric mixer with a
dough hook
pastry brush
2 tea towels
salad spinner
kitchen paper
pizza stone, or 1 × 28 cm
pizza tray

chopping board
grater
peeler
vegetable-slicing gadget
(such as a mandoline)
pizza peel or baking tray
(if using pizza stone)
wide egg lifter
large board for serving
pizza
large knife

Ingredients

Pizza dough

½ cup lukewarm water
2 teaspoons instant
dry yeast
½ teaspoon sugar
2 teaspoons extra-virgin
olive oil, plus extra
for greasing
200 g plain (all-purpose)
flour, plus extra
for flouring
½ teaspoon salt
1 tablespoon semolina
flour (if using
pizza stone)

Topping

2 handfuls rocket
(arugula) leaves
50 g parmesan
4 × 3 cm stalks rosemary
2 medium-to-large
potatoes
¼ cup extra-virgin
olive oil
1 teaspoon salt
freshly ground
black pepper

What to do

✱ First of all make the dough. Place the water, yeast
and sugar in the small bowl, mix with the fork and
leave for 5–10 minutes until the mixture looks frothy.
Add the 2 teaspoons of oil to the yeast mixture,
and mix well.

✱ Using the scales, weigh the flour, then place it,
along with the salt, in the bowl of the electric mixer.
Add the yeast mixture and beat for at least 8 minutes
until the dough looks smooth. Brush the inside of a
large bowl with a little of the extra olive oil, and turn
the dough into the oiled bowl. Cover with a clean,
dry tea towel and put in a draught-free place until
the dough has doubled in size. This process, which
is called 'proving', will take at least 1 hour. ▸▸

using the vegetable-slicing gadget. Tip the sliced potatoes into a large bowl and drizzle with most of the oil. Add the rosemary and salt and pepper, then mix together so that all the slices are lightly oiled.

✱ Scatter some flour on the workbench and roll the dough to form a thin disc about 26 cm in diameter. If you are using a preheated pizza stone, you will first have to assemble the pizza on a light piece of wood – a peel (see introduction) – or an upside-down baking tray (you don't want any edges that could prevent the prepared dough slipping easily onto the preheated stone). Flour the tray first. If you are using a pizza tray, you can assemble the pizza directly onto the tray (again, flour the tray first).

✱ Place the rolled-out pizza dough onto either the floured pizza tray or wooden peel (or upside-down baking tray). Arrange slices of potato on the pizza, overlapping as you go, then sprinkle most of the parmesan over the potato, keeping some aside.

✱ If you are using a pizza tray, drizzle the pizza with the last of the oil, then place the pizza in the oven. **If you are using a pizza stone, pull out the rack with the very hot pizza stone. Scatter the pizza stone with semolina, then firmly shake and slide the pizza from the wooden peel or baking tray onto the stone, and drizzle with the last of the oil.** Bake the pizza for 15 minutes or until the edges are very crusty and the cheese is bubbling.

✱ **If you are using a pizza tray, you may want to slip the pizza off the tray onto the rack for the last few minutes, so that you get a really crusty base. Whether you are using a stone or a tray, once the pizza is done, transfer it to the board using the wide egg lifter.**

✱ Cut the pizza into 8–12 pieces. Serve topped with a handful of the washed rocket leaves and remaining parmesan.

✱ Tip the risen dough onto the workbench and knead briefly, then shape into a round ball, return to the bowl, cover with the tea towel, and leave, this time for at least 20 minutes.

✱ While this is happening, rinse the rocket leaves and dry them very gently in the salad spinner. Lay out a dry tea towel and line it with a long piece of kitchen paper. Spread the dried leaves over the paper and roll the whole lot up like a log. Keep the rolled parcel of leaves in the refrigerator until needed.

✱ Preheat the oven to maximum. If using a pizza stone, place it on a rack in the oven to get very hot.

✱ Meanwhile, prepare the topping. Set out the chopping board. Shave off pieces of parmesan using either a grater (if it has a wide slicing option) or a normal potato peeler. Strip the rosemary needles from the stalks. Peel the potatoes. **Slice the potatoes very thinly**

BOTTOM DRAWER

Interesting terms/techniques • proving dough • storing salad leaves in a parcel • using pizza stones and pizza peels
Question Why are we using pizza stones?

Answer Pizza stones absorb and retain heat, so the crust gets an instant 'lift' as it hits the hot stone and starts to cook and blister immediately. Also, because the stone is quite porous, it absorbs excess moisture from the pizza dough, which makes the crust very crispy.

Mediterranean vegetables stuffed with spicy rice

Serves   6 at home or 12 tastes in the classroom
Fresh from the garden   onions, zucchini, tomatoes, parsley
Because the spicy rice takes a little while to prepare, each class at
Collingwood College prepared the rice ahead for the next class.
Finished spicy rice can be packed into plastic takeaway containers
and frozen for another day. Remember to label and date the
container.

Equipment

large saucepan
chopping board
knives – 1 small, 1 large
slotted spoon or egg lifter
2 tea towels
bowls – 2 small, 1 large
teaspoon (with sharp edges)

wooden spoon
metric measuring cups
pastry brush
ovenproof dish
food processor
aluminium foil
heatproof board or mat

Ingredients

salt
6 medium onions
3 medium zucchini
   (courgettes)
6 roma tomatoes

1 quantity Basic Spicy Rice
   Filling (page 78)
15 stalks parsley
½ cup extra-virgin olive oil
3 slices sourdough bread

What to do

✱ Preheat the oven to 200°C. Fill the saucepan with water,
add a pinch of salt and bring to the boil.

✱ Set out the chopping board and knives. Halve the unpeeled onions
crossways and drop into the boiling water for 10 minutes. **Lift out
with the slotted spoon.** Drain the onions, cut side down, on a tea
towel.

✱ Turn the onions right side up and extract the centre of each onion,
leaving a 'wall' of 2–3 rings. Strip away and discard the skin and put
the onion centres into a small bowl. **Carefully cut the zucchini in
half lengthways.** Using a teaspoon, scoop out the seeds and some
of the flesh, so that each zucchini half resembles a dugout canoe,
and place the scooped-out bits in the onion bowl. Halve the roma
tomatoes lengthways and scoop the seeds and flesh into the onion
and zucchini bowl using the teaspoon.

✱ Place the spicy rice filling in the large bowl. Chop the tomato flesh,
zucchini flesh and onion centres together and use the wooden spoon
to stir the chopped vegetables into the spicy rice filling. Rinse the
parsley and dry by rolling in a tea towel. Chop the parsley, place in
a small bowl and set aside until needed.

✱ Measure out the olive oil. Use the pastry brush to grease the
inside of the ovenproof dish. Brush the skin of the zucchini and
tomatoes and the outside surface of the onions with oil, then place
the vegetable halves in the ovenproof dish. Fill the halves with the
rice mixture, mounding the tops a little.

✱ Remove the crusts from the bread, place in the bowl of the food
processor, then run the motor to make breadcrumbs. Place the crusts
in the compost bucket.

✱ Add the breadcrumbs to the parsley, mix well, then scatter the
mixture over the vegetables. Drizzle with the remainder of the oil.
Cover loosely with aluminium foil and bake for 15 minutes. **Remove
the foil, then bake for a further 15 minutes. When done, remove
the dish from the oven.** Place the board or mat on the table and
serve the vegetables in their ovenproof dish.

Wilted cucumber and borage flower salad

Serves   4 at home or 8 tastes in the classroom

Fresh from the garden   cucumbers, borage flowers, parsley, chives

The students were very intrigued by the idea of eating flowers. Borage self-seeds so we always had a scattering of these lovely blue star-shaped flowers. Some people have suggested that if you close your eyes and eat the blue part of the flower, it tastes similar to oysters. What do you think?

Equipment

chopping board
peeler
vegetable-slicing gadget
    (such as a mandoline)
bowls – 2 small, 1 large
metric measuring spoons
    and cups

colander
dinner plate
2 tea towels
large knife
serving bowl or plate

Ingredients

1 cucumber
2 teaspoons salt
10 borage flowers
10 stalks parsley
10 chives
½ cup yoghurt
freshly ground black pepper

What to do

 ✳ Set out the chopping board. Peel the cucumber. **Slice the cucumber very thinly using the vegetable-slicing gadget.**

✳ Put the sliced cucumber into the large bowl, along with the salt, and mix well. Transfer the salted cucumber to the colander and stand the colander on the plate to catch the drips. Leave for at least 20 minutes.

✳ Carefully detach the blue flowering part of the borage from the rest of the stem. Set aside the flowers in a small bowl and place the stems in the compost bucket.

✳ Rinse the parsley and chives and dry by rolling in a tea towel. Chop the parsley and chives and set aside in a small bowl.

✳ Place the colander in the sink and rinse the cucumber well under cold water, moving the slices around to ensure all the salt is washed away. Give the colander a good shake, then tip the cucumber slices onto a tea towel and pat dry.

✳ Rinse out the large bowl used to hold the cucumber and dry it well. Return the cucumber to the bowl. Stir in the yoghurt and three-quarters of the parsley and chives. Taste for salt (although it probably won't need any) and pepper.

✳ Tip the salad into the serving bowl and garnish with the remaining parsley and chives and the borage flowers, which are completely edible.

Menu 14

Golden bantam tea eggs

Thai cucumber,
coriander and
peanut salad

Cold white-cooked
Chinese chicken breast

Green beans with
fermented black beans

Summer fruit salad

Summer fruit salad

Hull some strawberries
(this means remove their
green topknots) and slice
them in half. Use a melon
baller to make small balls
of watermelon. Peel some
peaches by scoring the
skin with a knife and then
dropping the fruit into
boiling water for a minute
(get an adult to help). Lift
away the skin and slice the
peach. Put the strawberries,
watermelon and peach slices,
along with 2 or 3 spoonfuls
of sugar, into a shallow bowl.
Stir to mix, cover with plastic
film and refrigerate for half
an hour before serving.
During this time, the sugar
and fruit juice will blend
to a delicious syrup.

Golden bantam tea eggs

Makes   8 eggs

Fresh from the garden   eggs

This recipe can be made with eggs of any size. I used quail eggs on one occasion. The ingredients tend to stain an aluminium saucepan, so choose a stainless-steel or enamelled saucepan. Several of these ingredients are best found in an Asian grocery store.

Equipment

saucepans – 1 small, 1
   medium (not aluminium)
colander
large bowl
tablespoon or teaspoon
peeler

chopping board
large knife
metric measuring spoons
serving plate
small bowl for
   dipping sauce

Ingredients

8 eggs (bantam if possible)
1 orange, or 1 piece dried
   mandarin peel
¼ cup black tea leaves
2 sticks cassia bark
2 whole star anise
½ teaspoon salt
¼ cup dark soy sauce

Dipping sauce
1 × 4 cm piece fresh ginger
2 tablespoons sugar
2 tablespoons red
   rice vinegar
2 tablespoons light
   soy sauce

What to do

✱ Place the eggs in the medium saucepan, cover with water and bring to the boil. Reduce the heat and simmer for 8 minutes.

Drain the eggs in the colander. Fill the large bowl with cold water and place the eggs in the bowl to cool down.

✱ Drain the eggs again and tap each egg with the back of a tablespoon or teaspoon, until the shell is covered with small cracks. If using an orange, remove a strip of orange peel from the orange with the vegetable peeler.

✱ Return the eggs to the saucepan and cover with fresh water. Add the orange peel, tea leaves, cassia bark, star anise, salt and dark soy sauce. Simmer the eggs for at least 30 minutes – and up to 1 hour. **Remove from the heat.** Allow the eggs to cool down in the cooking liquid.

✱ While the eggs are cooling, make the dipping sauce. Set out the chopping board and knife. Peel the ginger, then chop finely – you'll need 2 tablespoons. In the small saucepan, stir the sugar and rice vinegar over a medium heat until the sugar has dissolved. Stir in the ginger and light soy sauce and pour into the dipping-sauce bowl.

✱ Peel the eggs carefully to reveal the beautiful patterns and arrange on the serving plate with the dipping sauce alongside.

BOTTOM DRAWER

Did you know?   Pieces of fresh mandarin peel can be strung like a necklace and hung up to dry in places where there is good airflow. The peel may take more than a week to be really dry and can then be stored in a screw-top jar.

Thai cucumber, coriander and peanut salad

Serves   4 at home or 10 tastes in the classroom
Fresh from the garden   cucumbers, limes, chillies, shallots, coriander, Vietnamese mint

This is another recipe where getting the balance between salty, spicy, sweet and sour is very important. Also important is making sure that no one you are cooking for has a peanut allergy. If they do, leave out the peanuts.

Equipment

chopping board	disposable gloves
peeler	scales
knives – 1 small, 1 large	non-stick 20 cm frying pan
teaspoon	small strainer
bowls – 2 small, 1 large	plate
small saucepan	kitchen paper
metric measuring spoons	tea towel
wooden spoon	kitchen scissors
lemon juicer	flat serving plate

Ingredients

2 cucumbers	¼ cup vegetable oil
2 teaspoons brown sugar, or palm sugar	2 shallots
1 tablespoon rice-wine vinegar	1 handful coriander (cilantro) leaves
½ lime	5 Vietnamese mint leaves
1 red chilli	1 unsprayed dark-red rose
50 g peanuts (optional)	1 tablespoon fish sauce

What to do

✳ Set out the chopping board, peeler and knives. Peel the cucumbers and halve lengthways. Using the teaspoon, scrape out most of the seeds from the centre of the cucumber and place in the compost bucket. Dice the cucumber and put into the large bowl.

✳ In the small saucepan, stir the sugar and vinegar over a medium heat until the sugar has dissolved, then pour over the cucumber.

✳ Juice the lime and pour the juice over the cucumber. Slip on the disposable gloves and cut the chilli in half lengthways. Scrape the seeds into the rubbish bin. Slice the chilli finely, then add to the cucumber bowl. Discard the gloves. Wash the chopping board and knife and dry well.

✳ Use the scales to weigh the peanuts, then sauté in 1 tablespoon of the oil in the frying pan over a medium heat. When the peanuts smell 'toasted', tip into the bowl with the cucumber.

✳ Peel the shallots and slice finely. Heat the rest of the oil in the frying pan over a medium heat and fry the shallots, stirring, until they are an even golden brown. **Tip the oil and shallots into the small strainer held over a small bowl (do this over the sink).** Tip the small amount of discarded oil into the sink and rinse it down with hot water. Line the plate with kitchen paper and place the shallots on the paper – this will allow them to crisp up.

✳ Rinse the coriander and mint, dry by rolling in the tea towel, chop roughly and place in a small bowl. Snip off the white part of each rose petal with scissors and discard it. Tear each petal into 3 pieces. Mix the rose petals with the herbs, reserving 2 or 3 petals for garnish. Add the fish sauce to the cucumber and mix well. Stir the herbs and rose petals into the cucumber. Taste for seasoning. You may like to adjust the taste with extra fish sauce, sugar or lime juice.

✳ Arrange the salad on the flat serving plate. Sprinkle with the fried shallots and the reserved rose petals.

BOTTOM DRAWER

Interesting terms/techniques   • scooping out vegetable seeds • seeding chillies   • toasting nuts   • cooking with edible flowers
Did you know?   Fish sauce has been used in this recipe instead of salt. Palm sugar is obtained by boiling the sap of various palm trees, and is usually sold as small solid discs, which are caramel-coloured or much darker. These discs can be grated or chopped.

Cold white-cooked Chinese chicken breast

Serves   4 at home or 12 tastes in the classroom

Fresh from the garden   spring onions

When buying your chicken, remember to ask for chicken breast fillets, otherwise you may get the whole breast, which contains 2 fillets. This recipe also works very well for whole chickens. As with chicken breasts, simmer the whole chicken for 10 minutes, but leave it in its covered saucepan for 45 minutes (rather than 15 minutes), before chilling in cold water for 1 hour.

Equipment

chopping board

peeler

large knife

large saucepan with tight-
    fitting lid

ladle for skimming stock

large bowl

egg lifter

plate

Ingredients

1 × 6 cm piece fresh ginger

2 spring onions (scallions)

4 chicken breast fillets, skin on, preferably free-range

2 trays ice cubes

What to do

✱ Set out the chopping board, peeler and knife. Peel and slice the ginger. Trim the outside layer from the spring onions and cut off the tops and ends, then cut the spring onions into 6 cm pieces. Place the scraps in the compost bucket.

✱ Fill the saucepan with water, add the ginger and spring onions and bring to the boil. **Plunge in the chicken breasts and wait for the liquid to return to boiling point. Use the ladle to skim off any froth that rises to the surface.** Reduce the heat to a simmer and put the lid on tightly.

✱ Cook for 10 minutes. **Remove the tightly closed saucepan from the heat.** Do not lift the lid. Set the timer for 15 minutes. Tip the ice cubes into the large bowl and half fill the bowl with very cold water. **When the 15 minutes is up, remove the lid from the saucepan and, using the egg lifter, lift the chicken breasts out of the pot, then plunge into the iced water.** Set the timer again for 15 minutes.

✱ When the 15 minutes is up, lift the chicken from the ice-cold water and place on the plate. Put the plate in the refrigerator. When ready to serve, place the chicken breasts on the chopping board and cut into very thin slices.

✱ Serve with a dipping sauce (see Golden Bantam Tea Eggs on page 147 or Thai Cucumber, Coriander and Peanut Salad on page 148).

BOTTOM DRAWER

Tip   This is a fantastic way to cook chicken. Try the poached chicken in sandwiches or in a salad, or a slice or two makes a good after-school snack.

Question   Why do we plunge the chicken into icy water?

Answer   Chilling the chicken quickly like this solidifies the layer of juices under the skin, which makes the chicken moist and very tasty.

Green beans with fermented black beans

Serves   6 at home or 12 tastes in the classroom
Fresh from the garden   green beans, chillies, garlic
Fermented black beans have a pungent, salty flavour, and are used in many Asian dishes. They can be bought in jars or vacuum packs at Asian grocery stores.

Equipment

chopping board
knives – 1 small, 1 large
disposable gloves
bowls – 2 small, 1 medium
metric measuring spoons
  and cups

fork
non-stick frying pan
  with lid (or use any
  lid that fits)
wooden spoon
serving bowl

Ingredients

350 g green beans
1 red chilli
2 teaspoons sugar
2 cloves garlic
2 teaspoons fermented black beans
2 tablespoons vegetable oil
½ cup water

What to do

✶ Set out the chopping board and knives. Top and tail the green beans, then cut the beans on the diagonal into 4 cm pieces. Place the scraps in the compost bucket.

✶ Slip on the disposable gloves and cut the chilli in half lengthways. Scrape the seeds into the rubbish bin. Slice the chilli finely, then place it in a small bowl, along with the sugar. Discard the gloves.

✶ Rinse the board and knives thoroughly and dry well. Peel and chop the garlic and put into the second small bowl, along with the fermented black beans. Mash the black beans and garlic with the back of the fork.

✶ Heat the oil in the frying pan and sauté the garlic and black bean mixture over a high heat for 30 seconds, stirring with the wooden spoon.

✶ Add the green beans and stir to coat with the black bean mixture. Stir in the chilli and sugar mixture and, after 1 minute, add the water. Cover the frying pan, reduce the heat and cook for 4 minutes.

 ✶ **Remove the pan from the heat.** Allow to cool for a few minutes, then transfer the bean mixture to the small bowl to serve.

> **BOTTOM DRAWER**
>
> **Interesting technique**   • seeding chillies
> **Did you know?**   Here is another recipe where an ingredient – in this case fermented black beans – has been used instead of salt.

Menu 15

Thai-style fish cakes
with sweet chilli sauce

Antonio's stuffed peppers
with eggplant

Greek salad

Chilled lychees

Chilled lychees

Lychees are so beautiful in
their red coats that it is best
to leave them for the diner
to peel. They are most
refreshing when they have
been chilled for half an
hour before serving.

Thai-style fish cakes with sweet chilli sauce

Makes   12 walnut-sized cakes
Fresh from the garden   limes, lemongrass, coriander, Vietnamese mint, red onions, garlic, kaffir lime leaves, chillies
The balance between salty, spicy, sweet and sour is considered very important in Thai cooking. To check you have the right balance here, roll and fry one small ball and taste it, then adjust the mixture.

Equipment

chopping board
knives – 1 small, 1 large
tweezers (or fish-bone pliers)
bowls – 1 small, 1 large
lemon juicer
metric measuring spoons
   and cups
tea towel
peeler
disposable gloves
large spoon

food processor
tray
dinner plate
kitchen paper
non-stick frying pan
fine sieve
spatula suitable for
   non-stick frying pan
serving plate
small bowl for dipping
   sauce

Ingredients

350 g white fish fillets
1 lime
2 teaspoons fish sauce
1 teaspoon brown sugar or
   palm sugar
1 × 4 cm piece lemongrass
1 large bunch coriander
   (cilantro), with roots
15 Vietnamese mint leaves

¼ red onion
1 × 3 cm piece fresh ginger
6 cloves garlic
2 kaffir lime leaves
2 red chillies
½ cup vegetable oil
2 tablespoons cornflour
   (cornstarch)
sweet chilli sauce for serving

What to do

 ✳ Set out the chopping board and knives. **Skin the fish by placing the fillets skin-side down on the board. Hold the left tip of the skin very firmly in your left hand and wriggle and slide the large knife between the skin and the flesh from left to right. If there are still**

pin bones in the fillets, remove these using tweezers that have been sterilised in boiling water. Cut the fish into 2 cm cubes and place in the large bowl.

✳ Juice the lime and add half to the bowl. Add the fish sauce and sugar to the bowl. Remove and discard the tough outer layers of the lemongrass, chop finely and put into the bowl. Rinse the coriander and mint and dry by rolling in the tea towel. Set aside some coriander leaves in the small bowl as a final garnish. Chop the remainder of the coriander and the mint, then add to the large bowl.

 ✳ Peel the red onion, ginger and garlic, then chop all three and add to the bowl with the fish. **Fold the kaffir lime leaves in half and cut away the central rib.** (This is quite tricky to do, so ask for help.) Slice the leaves finely and add to the bowl.

✳ Slip on the disposable gloves and cut the chillies in half lengthways. Scrape the seeds into the rubbish bin. Slice the chilli finely, then add to the bowl. Do not remove the gloves. Using a large spoon, mix everything together very well, then transfer to the food processor.

✳ Process the mixture using the pulse action, so that the ingredients are mixed in short bursts – you do not want a totally smooth paste. Using your hands, form the mixture into small balls, the size of golf balls. Put the balls on the tray and refrigerate for 10 minutes. Discard the gloves and wash the chopping board and knives well.

✳ Line the plate with kitchen paper. Heat about half the oil in the frying pan. Sift the cornflour over the balls and place as many balls in the frying pan as will fit. Cook over a medium heat for 4 minutes. Use the spatula to turn the balls and cook on the other side for 3–4 minutes, then lift with the spatula onto the paper-lined plate.

✳ Continue cooking in batches until all the balls are cooked. Place on the serving plate and decorate with the coriander leaves. Fill the dipping-sauce bowl with sweet chilli sauce and place alongside the fish cakes.

BOTTOM DRAWER

Interesting terms/techniques   •   skinning fish
• removing pin bones   •   seeding chillies   •   working in batches

Antonio's stuffed peppers with eggplant

Serves   6 at home or 12 tastes in the classroom

Fresh from the garden   peppers, eggplants, garlic, tomatoes, parsley

You may have seen Antonio Carluccio on the television. Antonio's grandmother prepared this dish for him when he was a young boy and he has remembered it ever since. It is absolutely delicious.

Equipment

chopping board

knives – 1 small, 1 large,
   1 serrated

tablespoon

metric measuring spoons
   and cups

pastry brush

baking dish

bowls – 2 small, 2 medium

tea towel

food processor

non-stick frying pan

wooden spoon

Ingredients

3 large yellow, orange or red
   peppers (or 1 of each)

½ cup extra-virgin olive oil

1 medium eggplant
   (aubergine) (about 350 g)

2 cloves garlic

3 tomatoes

3 anchovy fillets

1 tablespoon small capers

6 black kalamata olives

10 stalks parsley

3 slices sourdough bread

salt

freshly ground black pepper

What to do

✳ Preheat the oven to 200°C. Set out the chopping board and knives. Halve the peppers lengthways, so that each resembles a boat. Scoop out the seeds using the tablespoon, being careful to leave the stalks intact so that the peppers keep their lovely shape.

✳ Measure out the oil, then use the pastry brush to brush the inside and outside of the peppers with a little oil. Put the remaining oil aside for later. Place the peppers in the baking dish and bake for 20 minutes.

✳ Now make the stuffing. Cut the eggplant into 5 mm slices, then cut each slice into 5 mm cubes. Place in one of the medium bowls.

✳ Chop the garlic finely and place in one of the small bowls. Using the serrated knife, cut the tomatoes into 5 mm slices, then cut each slice into 5 mm cubes. Place in the second medium bowl. Chop the anchovies finely and add to the tomato bowl, along with the capers. **Press the flat side of the large knife onto each olive to squash it – the pip can now be removed easily.** Slice each olive into 2 or 3 pieces and add to the tomato bowl. Rinse the parsley, dry by rolling in the tea towel, then chop and add to the tomato bowl.

✳ Remove the crusts from the bread. Put the bread in the bowl of the food processor, then run the motor to make coarse breadcrumbs. Tip the breadcrumbs into the second small bowl and place the crusts in the compost bucket.

✳ Heat half the remaining oil in the frying pan and fry the eggplant until it is golden and soft. (Dribble in a bit more oil during cooking if the pan looks dry.) When the eggplant is soft and golden in colour, add the garlic. Stir with the wooden spoon to combine.

✳ Remove the frying pan from the heat and stir in the contents of the tomato bowl. Tip all the ingredients back into the tomato bowl and taste for salt and pepper. Stir in the breadcrumbs.

✳ **Take the peppers out of the oven.** Spoon the tomato and eggplant stuffing into the peppers and sprinkle with the rest of the oil (watch your fingers – the peppers will be hot). Bake for 25 minutes until the stuffing looks a bit crisp. **Remove from the oven.** Serve each person half a stuffed pepper as part of a meal.

Greek salad

Serves 6 at home or 12 tastes in the classroom

Fresh from the garden cucumbers, tomatoes, spring onions, green peppers

Ingredients vary a little depending on availability, but a Greek salad should always be a celebration of ripe tomatoes and, as such, will always be colourful. Mostly it is topped with fetta, as here.

Equipment

chopping board	metric measuring spoons
knives – 1 small, 1 large	fork
peeler	wooden spoon
teaspoon	scales
bowls – 1 small, 1 large	

Ingredients

1 cucumber	2 teaspoons red-wine
6 tomatoes	vinegar
2 spring onions (scallions)	salt
or 1 small red onion	freshly ground black pepper
1 green pepper	60 g fetta
12 kalamata olives	
2 tablespoons extra-virgin	
olive oil	

What to do

✳ Set out the chopping board, knives and peeler. Peel the cucumber and halve lengthways. Using the teaspoon, scoop out most of the seeds from the centre of the cucumber. Cut the cucumber into 2 cm dice and transfer to the large bowl.

✳ Cut the tomatoes into chunks or wedges and add to the bowl. If using spring onions, trim the outside layer and cut off the tops and ends, then cut the spring onions into 1 cm pieces. If using red onion, halve and peel, then place the flat side down on the board and cut crossways as finely as you can. Add the onion to the cucumber bowl. Cut the green pepper into 1 cm dice and add to the bowl. Place all the scraps in the compost bucket.

✳ **Press the flat side of the large knife onto each olive to squash it – the pip can now be removed easily.** Add the olives to the salad.

✳ In the small bowl, combine the oil and vinegar to make the dressing. Whisk lightly with a fork, then pour over the salad and mix all the ingredients very well with the spoon. Taste for salt and pepper (remember the cheese is quite salty). Weigh the fetta, crumble it over the salad, then serve.

BOTTOM DRAWER

Interesting terms/techniques   • scooping out vegetable seeds
• stoning olives

Did you know?   Most cheeses have salt added to them. Some cheeses are also stored in brine, such as fetta, which makes them even saltier.

Cheese and herb calzone

Labna balls

Line a strainer resting over a large bowl with a very large sheet of damp, wrung-out muslin or a damp, wrung-out clean tea towel. Tip a quantity of yoghurt into the cloth. Gather the cloth and tie it at the top. Transfer the yoghurt, strainer and bowl to the refrigerator and leave for at least 24 hours or even 2 days. Discard the liquid (the whey) in the bowl, and tip the firm yoghurt mixture into a bowl. Season with a little salt and your choice of garlic and herbs. Roll into small balls and finish with a grind of pepper. These little balls are lovely served with roasted or barbecued vegetables.

Makes   8 pieces

Fresh from the garden   basil, thyme, parsley, oregano, rocket, garlic

Calzone is an envelope of dough stuffed with tasty fillings. Here we use the same pizza dough recipe as described in Potato and Rosemary Pizza (page 140). Read both recipes all the way through before starting.

Equipment

2 pizza stones (or trays)

2 pizza peels (if using
  pizza stones)

salad spinner

bowls – 1 small,
  1 medium

chopping board

large knife

scales

grater

fork

wooden spoon

rolling pin

metric measuring cups

pastry brush

heatproof board or mat

Ingredients

1 quantity pizza dough,
  see Potato and
  Rosemary Pizza
  (page 140)

10 basil leaves

3 sprigs thyme

10 stalks parsley

3 sprigs oregano

1 handful rocket
  (arugula) leaves

100 g ricotta

100 g blue cheese

100 g cheddar

50 g parmesan

1 clove garlic

salt

plain (all-purpose) flour
  for rolling

½ cup extra-virgin
  olive oil

freshly ground
  black pepper

BOTTOM DRAWER

Interesting technique
- working with pizza stones and peels

What to do

✱ Make the pizza dough as described on pages 140–42, including setting the dough aside twice to prove. Preheat the oven to 220°C. If using pizza stones, place them on a rack in the oven to get very hot.

✱ Rinse the basil, thyme, parsley, oregano and rocket leaves, and dry in the salad spinner. Place any damaged or slimy leaves in the compost bucket. Pick out the rocket and set leaves aside until later.

✱ Set out the chopping board and knife. Roughly chop the herbs and place in the medium bowl. Weigh out the cheeses and crumble the ricotta and blue cheese into the bowl. Grate the cheddar and parmesan and add to the bowl. Peel and chop the garlic. Place in the small bowl, along with a pinch of salt, and work to a paste using the fork. Add to the other ingredients and mix everything together with the wooden spoon.

✱ Flour the workbench. Halve the pizza dough and roll out each half to form a 26 cm circle. Flour the pizza peels or baking trays and transfer the rolled-out dough to them. Measure out the oil, then brush both circles of dough with oil. Spread the cheese mixture evenly over the two circles of dough. Grind a little black pepper over the cheeses. Fold each circle of dough in half to enclose its filling. Press the edges of the dough together to seal very well. Pierce a few holes in the top with the tip of a knife. Brush the surface with more oil and sprinkle with salt.

👧👦 ✱ **If you are using pizza stones, pull out the rack with the hot stones. Carefully slide each calzone from the peel or baking tray to a pizza stone.** Otherwise, just slip the assembled calzone on their floured baking trays into the oven.

👧👦 ✱ Bake for about 10 minutes until golden. **Remove the calzone from the oven and transfer to the board.** Cut into portions and garnish with a few rocket leaves.

Little cups of sorrel soup

Serves   4 at home or 12 tastes in the classroom
Fresh from the garden   sorrel, garlic, eggs
This is such an elegant soup. You should warm the soup bowls so that the soup stays hot. Many people have never tasted sorrel, yet it is so easy to grow. Because of its distinctive lemony flavour, it is often served, as a purée, with fish.

Equipment

plate
kitchen paper
chopping board
knives – 1 small, 1 medium,
    1 serrated
metric measuring spoons
non-stick frying pan
egg lifter
scales
salad spinner

large saucepan (not
    aluminium)
wooden spoon
metric measuring jug
ladle
food processor
medium bowl
small plastic container
whisk

Ingredients

2 slices sourdough bread
1 tablespoon extra-virgin
    olive oil
150 g sorrel leaves
2 cloves garlic
2 tablespoons butter

1 litre Basic Chicken Stock
    (page 79)
salt
freshly ground black pepper
3 eggs

What to do

✶ Preheat the oven to 120°C. Line the plate with kitchen paper and put it in the oven to keep warm.

✶ Set out the chopping board and knives. Cut the bread into 1 cm dice. Heat the oil in the frying pan. Fry the bread in the pan over a medium heat. As the croutons are done, use the egg lifter to lift them onto the paper-lined plate, then return the plate to the oven.

✶ Weigh the sorrel. Fold each sorrel leaf along the stem line, with the rough side uppermost, then pull the stem up and along the leaf (a bit like pulling up a zip). The stem end and the central stem will come away leaving you with two pieces of leaf. Put the stems, and any yellow leaves, in the compost bucket. Rinse the good leaves and dry in the salad spinner. Tear the leaves into smaller pieces.

✶ Peel and finely slice the garlic. Heat the butter in the saucepan and sauté the garlic over a medium heat until golden, stirring with the wooden spoon. Drop in the sorrel leaves and stir so that the leaves wilt evenly. Measure out the chicken stock, then add to the saucepan and bring to a simmer. Taste for salt and pepper and simmer for 10 minutes.

✶ **Using the ladle, transfer a little soup to the food processor. Purée, then tip into the medium bowl.** Repeat with the remaining soup – this is called working in batches. When all the soup has been puréed, rinse out the saucepan and tip the soup back in. Return the soup to simmering point.

✶ Wash the medium bowl well, heat it by filling it with hot water, then pour out the water. Set out the plastic container. Separate the eggs by cracking them, one at a time, then tipping each egg into your cupped hand, which should be held over the plastic container. Slightly open your fingers and let the white slip into the container. Place the yolk in the warmed bowl and repeat with the remaining eggs. (You won't need the eggwhites for this recipe, so freeze them for another time. Remember to cover and label the container.)

✶ Whisk the yolks until creamy. **Add 2 ladlefuls of hot soup to the yolks and continue to whisk. Remove the soup from the heat.** Tip the warm egg mixture into the soup and whisk for a minute until the soup has thickened evenly. When serving, add a few crunchy croutons to each bowl.

BOTTOM DRAWER

Interesting terms/techniques   • stemming leaves
• thickening with egg yolks   • working in batches
Safety tip   When puréeing hot soup, you need to work very carefully. The steam can force the lid to come off the blender, spraying hot soup everywhere. This will make quite a mess, but, more importantly, the hot liquid could burn you quite badly. Only blend small quantities and place a thick cloth over the blender lid to protect your hand (ask for help the first time you do it).

Sweetcorn fritters with crisp sage leaves and herb yoghurt

Makes 20

Fresh from the garden sweetcorn, sage, chives, parsley, eggs

Crisp sage is delicious and different and is a popular garnish for filled pasta, such as ravioli, or thin slices of pan-fried veal.

Equipment

baking tray	plate
chopping board	kitchen paper
large knife	non-stick frying pan
fork	egg lifter
bowls – 1 small, 2 medium, 1 large	scales
	small saucepan
tea towel	whisk
small serving bowl	wooden spoon
metric measuring spoons and cups	serving plate

Ingredients

3 cobs sweetcorn	¼ cup plain (all-purpose) flour
20 large sage leaves	
10 chives	½ teaspoon salt
10 stalks parsley	1 teaspoon bicarbonate of soda (baking soda)
1 cup yoghurt	
⅓ cup extra-virgin olive oil	40 g butter
1 egg	2 cups buttermilk
275 g coarse polenta (cornmeal)	

What to do

✳ Preheat the oven to 150°C and place the baking tray in the oven to keep warm.

 ✳ Set out the chopping board and knife. Stand the corn cobs on the chopping board and, using the fork, rake over the kernels to release the milky cream within. **Cut the kernels from each cob.** Put the kernels and liquid into the small bowl (you should have 1¼–1½ cups of rather sloppy sweetcorn).

✳ Rinse the sage, chives and parsley and dry by rolling in the tea towel. Chop the chives and parsley and place in the small serving bowl. Add the yoghurt, stir to combine, then set aside.

✳ Line the plate with kitchen paper. Heat a little of the oil in the frying pan and fry the sage leaves over a medium heat until crisp. Scoop the leaves onto the paper-lined plate, then put into the oven to keep warm.

✳ Set out the 2 medium bowls. Separate the egg by cracking it, then tipping it into your cupped hand, which should be held over one of the bowls. Separate your fingers and let the white slip into the bowl, then place the yolk in the other bowl.

✳ Measure the polenta and flour, then place them in the large bowl, along with the salt and bicarbonate of soda. Melt the butter in the small saucepan over a medium heat.

✳ Add the buttermilk and melted butter to the egg yolk and whisk to combine. Make a well in the dry ingredients and pour in the buttermilk/egg yolk mixture. Mix well with the wooden spoon, then stir in the sweetcorn.

✳ Wash and dry the whisk, then whisk the eggwhite until soft peaks form. Fold the eggwhite into the batter using the spoon.

✳ Add a little more of the oil to the frying pan and place over a medium heat. Make a fritter by placing a tablespoonful of batter in the frying pan. Keep going until the pan is full, but not overcrowded. Cook for 3–4 minutes, until bubbles form, then flip over and cook on the other side. Transfer the cooked fritters to the warmed baking tray and return the tray to the oven. Repeat with the remaining mixture, adding a little extra oil to the frying pan after each batch.

✳ When all the fritters are ready, arrange on the serving plate with the bowl of herb yoghurt at the centre. Place a crisp sage leaf on the top of each fritter.

Autumn

In the cooler weather we made curries using our own potatoes and the last of the season's tomatoes. We enjoyed tasty vegetable tarts and pies. Almost every student had a turn at making and stuffing fresh pasta. And soda bread with herb butter became a great favourite. Also popular were sweet dishes made using new-season apples.

Pumpkin Gnocchi with Sage (page 181)

Menu 17

Rocket, pear and walnut salad

Fettuccine with tomato, sausage and fennel sauce

Potato cakes with chive sour cream

Apple and cinnamon muffins

Rocket, pear and walnut salad

Rinse and dry a large handful each of rocket (arugula) leaves and cos leaves (see Master Salad Recipe on page 76 for instructions). Peel, core and slice 2 pears, and place in a bowl with some lemon juice. Sauté 12 walnut halves in a frying pan with a little oil. Make a dressing of walnut oil and olive oil (half/half) and a little white-wine vinegar or verjuice. Place the leaves in a salad bowl, decorate with the walnuts and pear slices, and drizzle with the dressing.

Fettuccine with tomato, sausage and fennel sauce

Serves   6 at home or 12 tastes in the classroom

Fresh from the garden   tomatoes, fennel, red onions, garlic, parsley

To save time in the classroom, we rolled and cut pasta dough that had been made by the previous class, then prepared pasta dough for the next class.

Equipment

2 trays	frying pan with 4 cm sides
chopping board	wooden spoon
knives – 1 small, 1 large	slotted spoon
bowls – 1 medium, 1 large	very large saucepan
electric jug	grater
colander	serving bowls – 1 small,
tea towel	1 large
metric measuring spoons	

Ingredients

2 quantities Basic Pasta Dough (page 79)	1 medium bulb fennel
	1 red onion
plain (all-purpose) flour for dusting	2 cloves garlic
	15 stalks parsley
6 ripe tomatoes, or 1 × 400 g can chopped tomatoes	¼ cup extra-virgin olive oil
	2 teaspoons fennel seeds
2 Italian-style pure pork sausages, or 300 g spiced halal lamb mince	salt
	freshly ground black pepper
	small wedge parmesan

What to do

✳ Make the pasta as directed on page 79, but for this recipe, instead of using the second last setting on the pasta machine when rolling the dough (as instructed on page 79), stop after the third last setting. (Slightly thicker pasta sheets are better for making fettuccine.) To make fettuccine, pass the dough through the wider cutting blades of the pasta machine. Dust the trays with flour, lay the strands of fettuccine in a single layer on the trays and allow to dry for 10 minutes.

✳ Set out the chopping board and knives. If using fresh tomatoes, cut out the stems and cut a cross on the bottom of each tomato. Place the fresh tomatoes in the large bowl and boil the electric jug. Place the colander in the sink. **Pour boiling water over the tomatoes and leave for a minute. Tip the tomatoes and boiling water into the colander and cool with cold water.**

✳ Using your hands, peel off the tomato skins. Cut each tomato in half crossways, then squeeze gently to remove the seeds. Place the skins and seeds in the compost bucket. Roughly chop the tomato flesh and set aside in the large bowl until needed.

✳ If using sausages, slit them open and peel off and discard the skins. Break the meat into olive-sized pieces and set aside. Pull off any damaged layers of fennel and add to the compost bucket. Slice the fennel and dice into small pieces. Peel and dice the onion. Peel and slice the garlic. Rinse the parsley, dry by rolling in the tea towel, then chop.

✳ Heat half the oil in the frying pan over a high heat and add the sausage meat or the halal spiced meat, stirring with the wooden spoon. When the meat is well-browned, transfer it, using the slotted spoon, to the medium bowl, leaving all the oil in the pan. Reduce the heat to medium. Scatter the fennel seeds into the pan, stir for a few seconds, then add the onion, garlic and fennel and fry for 5 minutes. Add the chopped or canned tomatoes, along with their juice, and increase the heat so the mixture bubbles and reduces. Stir occasionally.

✳ Once the tomatoes and fennel look 'saucy', return the meat to the pan and cook for 5 minutes. Taste for salt and pepper and set aside.

✳ Fill the very large saucepan with salted water and bring to the boil. Drop in the fettuccine. Cook for 4–5 minutes (taste to check if it is al dente). Meanwhile, grate or shave about 4–6 tablespoons of parmesan and put it in the small serving bowl. Set the colander in the sink. **Tip the fettuccine and boiling water into the colander.**

✳ Return the fettuccine to the empty hot saucepan. Drizzle over the rest of the oil, then add the hot sauce and chopped parsley and mix well. Tip into the large serving bowl and serve with the parmesan.

BOTTOM DRAWER

Interesting technique   •   peeling fresh tomatoes

Potato cakes with chive sour cream

Makes   10 potato cakes

Fresh from the garden   potatoes, chives, onions

These potato cakes are very similar to 'hash browns'. On another occasion you could add a second grated vegetable to the mixing bowl after the potato gratings have been squeezed. Try one-third sweet potato, parsnip or celeriac to two-thirds potato.

Equipment

baking tray

kitchen paper

peeler

chopping board

knives – 1 small, 1 large

grater

bowls – 1 medium, 1 large

scales

small saucepan

2 tea towels

small serving bowl

metric measuring cups

wooden spoon

non-stick 24 cm frying pan

tablespoon

egg lifter

serving plate

Ingredients

5 medium potatoes

80 g butter

10 chives

½ onion

salt

freshly ground black pepper

2 teaspoons cornflour (cornstarch)

¼ cup extra-virgin olive oil

¼ cup sour cream

BOTTOM DRAWER

Interesting terms/techniques   • squeezing liquid from an ingredient using a cloth   • working in batches

Question   Why do we keep the potatoes in water?

Answer   To prevent them turning a brownish colour.

What to do

✳ Preheat the oven to 120°C. Line a baking tray with kitchen paper and place it in the oven to warm.

✳ Set out the peeler, chopping board, knives and grater. Peel the potatoes and place in a large bowl of cold water. Weigh the butter and melt it in the small saucepan. Set aside for later. Rinse the chives, dry by rolling in a tea towel, then chop and put into the small serving bowl. Peel and grate the onion and put into the medium bowl. Remove one potato at a time from the water, dry well on the tea towel used to dry the chives, and grate using the largest hole of the grater. (Your food processor may have a grating attachment, which will make this task much easier.)

✳ Add the grated potato to the grated onion. Tip the grated vegetables into the second tea towel, then squeeze the tea towel over the sink to remove the excess liquid. **An easy way to do this is to ask someone to twist the tea towel at one end, while you twist the other end in the opposite direction – this will squeeze the water out.**

✳ Wash and dry the large bowl that the potatoes were in. Pour the melted butter into this bowl, then add the grated vegetables. Season with salt and pepper. Add the cornflour and half of the chopped chives and stir all the ingredients with the wooden spoon.

✳ Grease the frying pan with a thin film of the oil and place the pan over a medium heat. Make a potato cake by spooning a few tablespoons of the mixture into the frying pan. (Each cake should be about 8 cm in diameter.) Cook for 3 minutes, then turn over, using the egg lifter, and cook for a further 3 minutes. When the potato cake is done, transfer it to the warm, paper-lined tray in the oven. Add a few drops more oil if the pan looks completely dry and continue cooking in batches until you have used all the mixture.

✳ Add the sour cream to the remaining chives and stir to combine. Arrange the potato cakes on the serving plate and place the bowl of chive sour cream in the centre.

Apple and cinnamon muffins

Makes 12

Fresh from the garden apples, eggs

While we waited for our apple trees to bear fruit, one of the volunteers kept us supplied with lovely Jonathan apples from her tree at home. She also brought in crab-apples. We used these to make a few pots of crab-apple jelly, which tasted delicious spread on muffins or toast.

 ## Equipment

metric measuring spoons and cups	sieve or sifter
	bowls – 1 medium, l large
small saucepan	grater
pastry brush	whisk
12 cupcake cases (optional)	wooden spoon
1 × 12-hole muffin tin	tablespoon
scales	wire rack

 ## Ingredients

1 tablespoon butter

220 g self-raising (self-rising) flour

½ cup castor (superfine) sugar

1 teaspoon ground cinnamon

1 eating apple

¾ cup buttermilk

1 egg

¾ cup vegetable oil

 ## What to do

✱ Preheat the oven to 180°C. If you are using cupcake cases, drop one into each of the holes in the muffin tin. Otherwise, melt the butter in the small saucepan, then use the pastry brush to grease the holes of the muffin tin.

✱ Using the scales, weigh the flour, then sift it with the sugar and cinnamon into the large bowl.

✱ Grate the apple using the largest hole of the grater (leave the peel on). Using your fingers, mix the apple evenly through the flour mixture.

✱ Place the milk, egg and oil in the medium bowl and whisk well. Make a well in the flour mixture, then pour in the milk and egg mixture. Stir lightly using the wooden spoon, but do not over-mix or the muffin mixture will become tough.

✱ Spoon the mixture into the cupcake cases or greased muffin tin, filling each hole just over two-thirds full.

 ✱ Bake for 20–25 minutes until the muffins are firm and golden brown. **Remove from the oven.** Allow the muffins to rest for a few minutes in the tin, before turning out onto the wire rack to cool.

BOTTOM DRAWER

Interesting terms/techniques • making a well in dry ingredients • testing a cake by feeling its surface

Something to think about What other flavoured muffins could you make?

Barbecued mixed vegetables

Serves   6 at home or 12 tastes in the classroom
Fresh from the garden   peppers, eggplants, red
onions, zucchini, tomatoes, garlic, rosemary, lemons
Platters of barbecued vegetables look dramatic and
are ideal party food.

Equipment

metric measuring spoons and cups	baking tray
small bowl	plate
pastry brush	2 tea towels
brown paper bag or plastic bag	medium saucepan
chopping board	sieve or colander
knives – 1 small, 1 large	kitchen paper
	large serving plate
	lemon juicer

Ingredients

½ cup extra-virgin olive oil	3 large tomatoes
2 red or yellow peppers	2 cloves garlic
1 medium eggplant (aubergine)	3 × 3 cm stalks rosemary
salt	½ lemon
1 red onion	2 teaspoons balsamic vinegar
3 medium zucchini (courgettes)	freshly ground black pepper
6 flat Swiss brown mushrooms	goat's cheese or fetta or Labna Balls (see page 156)

What to do

✳ Heat the barbecue grill to hot. Place the oil in the
small bowl. Brush the peppers all over with some of the
oil and grill until charred on all sides. Place the blackened
peppers in the brown paper bag (or plastic bag) and leave
to cool. Set out the chopping board and knives. When
the peppers are cool, rub off the blackened skin and
remove the seeds and place in the compost bucket, then
tear or cut the flesh into big pieces. Brush the pieces
with oil and transfer to the baking tray.

✳ Cut the eggplant into thickish slices. Sprinkle lightly
with salt and place on the plate. Cover with a tea towel
and put something heavy on top of the tea towel (such
as cans of tomatoes). After 30 minutes, rinse the
eggplant quickly and pat very dry using the second
tea towel. Brush both sides with oil and add to the
baking tray.

✳ Bring a saucepan of lightly salted water to the boil.
Peel the onion and cut into 6 wedges. Drop the wedges
into the saucepan and boil for 5 minutes. Place the
sieve or colander in the sink. **Tip in the water and
onion.** Dry the onion with the tea towel used to dry
the eggplant. Brush the onion with oil and add to
the baking tray.

✳ Cut the zucchini into thick slices. Brush both sides
with oil and add to the tray. Wipe the mushrooms on
both sides using the kitchen paper, then brush with oil
and add to the tray. Halve the tomatoes, brush both
sides with oil and add to the tray.

✳ Peel and finely chop the garlic. Place in the small
bowl with the remainder of the oil. Strip the needles
from the rosemary and chop finely. Add to the oil.

✳ Place all the vegetables on the barbecue grill. The
eggplant and onion will take longest and the roasted
peppers just need to be reheated. When the vegetables
are ready, transfer them to the serving plate.

✳ Add the lemon juice and balsamic vinegar to
the small bowl and mix well. Brush all the grilled
vegetables with this dressing. Season with salt and
pepper. If you like, sprinkle the vegetables with cubed
or crumbled goat's cheese, or arrange several labna
balls on top.

BOTTOM DRAWER

Interesting terms/techniques • peeling
peppers • roasting vegetables • scooping
out vegetable seeds

Leek tarts with crumbled fetta

Makes   6 individual tarts

Fresh from the garden   leeks, eggs, chives

Many of our Collingwood students had not tasted leeks before. Leeks are part of the onion family and when cooked are deliciously sweet. We used crème fraîche to make the tarts less rich (you could also use fat-reduced cream). In the classroom, we used pastry that had been prepared by the previous class. This preparation involved making, chilling, rolling and shaping the pastry, then putting it in the refrigerator. Read this recipe (and the pastry recipe) all the way through before starting, so you can work out what tasks can be done while you wait for the pastry to chill, and then bake.

Equipment

rolling pin	metric measuring spoons
6 × 12 cm loose-bottomed	and cups
flan tins	non-stick frying pan with lid
aluminium foil	wooden spoon
pastry weights (or dried	plastic container with lid
ingredient such as	whisk
chick peas)	grater
chopping board	baking tray
large knife	ladle
large bowl	scales
salad spinner	wire rack

Ingredients

1 quantity Basic Shortcrust Pastry (page 78)

plain (all-purpose) flour for dusting

2 leeks

2 tablespoons butter

4 eggs

1½ cups crème fraîche or fat-reduced cream

10 chives

1 nutmeg

salt

freshly ground black pepper

80 g fetta

What to do

✸ Make the pastry as instructed on page 78 and refrigerate for 1 hour.

 ✸ Flour the workbench. Take the pastry out of the refrigerator and divide into 6 equal pieces. **Roll one piece to a circle that is 14 cm wide, dusting with flour as needed.** Line one of the flan tins with the pastry, pressing well into the corners. Repeat this process until you have 6 flan tins of pastry. Line each tin with a double sheet of aluminium foil and tip in a quantity of pastry weights or dried chick peas. Chill in the refrigerator for at least 20 minutes or even overnight.

✸ About 15 minutes before the pastry is ready, preheat the oven to 200°C. Put the pastry shells in the oven, with the foil and weights still in them, and bake for 20 minutes. This is called baking blind.

✸ While the pastry is chilling and then baking, prepare the filling. Set out the chopping board and knife. Slice the leeks lengthways, then across into 5 mm slices. Fill the large bowl with cold water and place the leek in the bowl. Swish the leek with your fingers to make sure all the sand and dirt has been removed. Lift the leek and place in the salad spinner. Spin to dry.

✸ Melt the butter in the frying pan and tip in the leek. Cover the pan with a lid and cook over a low heat for about 15 minutes, stirring once or twice with the wooden spoon.

✳ Meanwhile, wash and dry the bowl used to rinse the leek and set out the plastic container. Separate 2 of the eggs by cracking them, one at a time, then tipping each egg into your cupped hand, which should be held over the plastic container. Slightly open your fingers and let the white slip into the container. Place the yolk in the mixing bowl. (You won't need the eggwhites for this recipe, so freeze them for another time. Remember to cover and label the container.) Place the 2 whole eggs in the bowl with the egg yolks. Add the crème fraîche or fat-reduced cream and whisk the ingredients together.

✳ Chop the chives and add to the egg/cream mixture. Grate a little nutmeg into the egg/cream mixture and season with salt and pepper. Remove the lid from the leek, increase the heat and stir to evaporate any liquid in the pan. Tip the leek into the egg/cream mixture and stir to mix evenly.

✳ **Remove the flan tins from the oven and allow to cool for a minute, before removing the foil and pastry weights.** Reduce the oven to 170°C. Transfer the baked pastry shells in their tins to the baking tray. Using the ladle, divide the leek and cream mixture between the tarts. Crumble some fetta over each tart.

✳ Bake for about 15 minutes until the filling is just set. **Remove the tarts from the oven.** Allow to cool for a moment, then push up the loose bottom of each tin and ease out the tart onto the wire rack. Grate a little nutmeg over the tarts and serve.

BOTTOM DRAWER

Interesting terms/techniques • pastry weights • baking blind
Question   1 Why do we lift the leek from the water rather than pouring it into a colander?   2 What is crème fraîche?

Answer   1 The dirt sinks to the bottom of the basin so we lift the leek away from it. If you pour the contents into a colander the dirt will re-settle in the pieces of leek.   2 Crème fraîche is made by adding a culture to cream or reduced-fat cream, which makes it taste tangy. Most crème fraîche has 18 per cent butterfat as opposed to the 35 per cent butterfat found in normal cream.

Apple strudel

Makes   8 full-sized slices or 16 tastes in the classroom
Fresh from the garden   lemons, apples

Sometimes strudels are made using pitted cherries instead of apple slices. It is intriguing working with filo pastry. Each packet contains a lot of pastry, so carefully replace the unused pastry in the wrapping and try to use it up within 2 weeks.

Equipment

metric measuring spoons
   and cups
baking tray
bowls – 1 small, 1 medium
grater
scales
medium saucepan with lid
peeler
chopping board

knives – 1 small, 1 large,
   1 serrated
wooden spoon
tea towel
aluminium foil
pastry brush
tablespoon
sugar dredger or fine sieve

Ingredients

2 tablespoons flaked almonds
⅓ cup sultanas
¼ cup castor (superfine) sugar or brown sugar
½ lemon
60 g butter
4 eating apples
3 sheets filo pastry
½ cup ground almonds
icing (confectioners') sugar for dusting
cream for serving

What to do

✳ Preheat the oven to 180°C. Spread the flaked almonds on the baking tray, place in the oven and toast until the almonds are golden. Transfer to the medium bowl and wipe down the baking tray.

✳ Add the sultanas and sugar to the toasted almonds. Grate the zest from the ½ lemon and add to the bowl. Weigh the butter and melt it in the saucepan. Pour half into the small bowl and set aside for later.

✳ Set out the peeler, chopping board and knives. Peel the apples and cut them in half from top to bottom, then into quarters and remove the core and pips. Cut each quarter crossways into thin slices and place in the saucepan with the remaining melted butter. Add 2 tablespoons of water, cover the saucepan and cook over a medium heat for 5 minutes. When done, tip the buttery apple and any juices into the bowl with the sultanas, almonds and sugar and stir well with the wooden spoon.

✳ Unwrap the packet of filo pastry. Dampen a tea towel by sprinkling it with water, then line it with aluminium foil. The lined tea towel should be rested over the roll of filo, with the foil touching the pastry, whenever you are not using it. Brush the baking tray with a little of the melted butter from the small bowl, then lay a sheet of pastry on top of the tray. Brush the pastry sheet with butter, then top with another pastry sheet. Do this once more. The tray should now hold 3 sheets of buttered pastry.

✳ Scatter the ground almonds over the pastry, avoiding the edges.
 Spoon the apple mixture down the centre of the pastry to form a shape like a log, leaving 6 cm at each end and down each side free of filling. Fold the sides and ends in and over the filling.

✳ Roll the strudel over and settle it on the baking tray seam side down. Cook for 30 minutes until golden brown. **Remove from the oven and allow to cool for 5 minutes, before cutting into thick slices using the serrated knife.** Using a sugar dredger or fine sieve, dust the strudel with icing sugar. Serve hot with cream.

Menu 19

Spicy lentil salad
with caramelised onion
and carrot

Pumpkin and
tomato gratin

Raspberry muffins

Spicy lentil salad with caramelised onion and carrot

Serves   6 at home or 12 tastes in the classroom
Fresh from the garden   onions, garlic, carrots, red onions, coriander, parsley

There are many varieties of lentils. Some are sold split, and they collapse when cooked. These are used to make soups or dhal (see Red Lentil Dhal, page 210). The dark-brown/greenish lentils used here need to soak for 1 hour before use, so we had each class prepare the lentils for the next class.

Equipment

bowls – 2 small, 1 medium,
   1 large
metric measuring spoons
   and cups
coarse strainer
chopping board
knives – 1 small, 1 large
medium saucepan
wooden spoon

peeler
vegetable-slicing gadget
   (such as a mandoline)
non-stick frying pans –
   1 small, 1 medium
mortar and pestle
tea towel
serving bowl

Ingredients

1 cup brown lentils
1 onion
2 cloves garlic
½ bunch coriander (cilantro)
   (with stems and roots)
½ cup extra-virgin olive oil
1 teaspoon sea salt
2 medium carrots

1 red onion
1 teaspoon cumin seeds
1 teaspoon coriander seeds
5 stalks parsley
freshly ground black pepper
1 tablespoon red-wine
   vinegar

What to do

✱ Fill the large bowl with cold water. Add the lentils and soak for 1 hour. Set the strainer over the medium bowl in the sink, then tip the lentils and water into the strainer. Save 1 cup of the soaking water.

✱ Set out the chopping board and knives. Peel and dice the onion. Peel and chop the garlic. Soak the coriander in a small bowl of cold water.

✱ Heat 3 tablespoons of the oil in the saucepan over a medium heat and sauté the onion until golden, stirring with the wooden spoon. Add the garlic and sauté for another minute. Add the lentils, salt and the reserved soaking water. Cook, stirring frequently, for 20 minutes, until the liquid has evaporated and the lentils are well-softened but have a little bit of a crunch. Set aside until needed.

 ✱ While the lentils are cooking, peel the carrots. **Slice the carrots into thin rounds using the vegetable slicer.**

✱ Peel the red onion, cut it in half from top to bottom, then turn it cut side down on the chopping board and slice into half rings. Put half the remaining oil into the medium frying pan and add the onion and carrot. Stir to coat with the oil. Cook over a medium heat, stirring from time to time, until the vegetables start to scorch a little around the edges and become caramelised.

✱ Heat the small frying pan over a medium heat. Toast the cumin seeds in the dry pan until they smell fragrant. Tip the seeds into the mortar. Toast the coriander seeds in the same pan until they smell fragrant. Add these seeds to the mortar. Using the pestle, work the spices to a coarse powder.

✱ Stir the caramelised vegetables and the spices into the lentils.

✱ Lift the coriander from its soaking water. Rinse the parsley. Dry the herbs by rolling in the tea towel, then chop. Stir into the lentils and taste for salt and pepper. Mix the vinegar and the rest of the oil together in the small bowl, then stir it through the lentils. Transfer the lentils to the serving bowl.

BOTTOM DRAWER

Interesting terms/techniques   • grinding in a mortar with a pestle   • toasting spices
Some things to think about   Notice the sweetness of the caramelised onions and carrots. The stems and trimmed root ends of a coriander plant have lots of flavour, not just the leaves.

Pumpkin and tomato gratin

Serves   4 at home or 12 tastes in the classroom
Fresh from the garden   pumpkin, garlic, rosemary, tomatoes
Because pumpkin can end up a bit sloppy if cooked in liquid, we steamed it so it stayed as dry as possible. Steaming is an interesting and fast way to cook many things, including fish and green vegetables.

Equipment

chopping board	metric measuring spoons
knives – 1 small, 1 large	and cups
scales	medium non-stick
wok	frying pan
bamboo steamer with lid	wooden spoon
bowls – 1 small, 2 large	pastry brush
grater	gratin dish (or other
food processor	ovenproof dish)
electric jug	heatproof board or mat
colander	

Ingredients

850–900 g pumpkin	4 ripe tomatoes, or 1 × 400 g
(750 g after peeling)	can chopped tomatoes
2 cloves garlic	2 tablespoons butter
3 × 3 cm stalks rosemary	¼ cup extra-virgin olive oil
50 g parmesan	salt
3 slices sourdough bread	freshly ground black pepper

What to do

 ✱ Set out the chopping board and knives. **Peel and seed the pumpkin.** Place the peel and seeds in the compost bucket. Using the scales, weigh the pumpkin to make sure you have 750 g.

✱ Slice the pumpkin into 1 cm slices and cut each slice into 1 cm cubes. Place the wok over a high heat and pour in enough hot water to come one-third of the way up the sides. Rest the bamboo steamer on top. Spread the pumpkin cubes in the basket, cover with the basket lid and steam for about 5 minutes until nearly tender. **Lift the basket off the wok and transfer the pumpkin to one of the large bowls.**

✱ Peel and chop the garlic and add to the pumpkin bowl. Strip the needles from the rosemary and add the needles to the bowl. Grate the parmesan and set aside in the small bowl until needed.

✱ Remove and discard the crusts from the bread. Put the bread into the bowl of the food processor, then run the motor to make breadcrumbs. Place the breadcrumbs in the bowl with the parmesan.

✱ If using fresh tomatoes, cut out the stems and cut a cross on the bottom of each tomato. Place the fresh tomatoes in the second large bowl and boil the electric jug. Place the colander in the sink. **Pour boiling water over the tomatoes and leave for a minute. Tip the tomatoes and boiling water into the colander, then cool with cold water.** Using your hands, peel off the tomato skins. Cut each tomato in half crossways, then squeeze gently to remove the seeds. Place the skins and seeds in the compost bucket. Roughly chop the tomato flesh.

✱ Preheat the oven to 200°C. Heat the butter and half the oil in the frying pan and add the chopped tomatoes (or canned tomatoes). Cook over a high heat, stirring occasionally with the wooden spoon, until the tomatoes have collapsed and look 'saucy' – about 10 minutes.

✱ Add the tomatoes to the pumpkin and mix. Add salt and pepper. Brush the inside of the gratin dish with some of the remaining oil and spoon the pumpkin/tomato mixture evenly into the dish. Scatter the gratin with the parmesan and breadcrumbs and drizzle with the rest of the oil. Bake for about 25 minutes or until the crust is golden.

 ✱ **Remove the gratin from the oven.** Place the board on the table and serve the gratin in its dish at the table.

BOTTOM DRAWER

Interesting techniques   •   peeling fresh tomatoes
•   steaming with a bamboo basket and wok
Safety tip   Peeling pumpkin can be quite dangerous because the surface is hard and slippery. Ask an adult to show you first.

Raspberry muffins

Makes 12

Fresh from the garden eggs, raspberries

We did grow lots of raspberry canes, but to be truthful most of the fruit never made it as far as the kitchen – it was picked and enjoyed in the garden.

Equipment

metric measuring spoons and cups	sieve or sifter
small saucepan	bowls – 1 medium, 1 large
pastry brush	whisk
12 cupcake cases (optional)	wooden spoon
1 × 12-hole muffin tin	tablespoon
scales	wire rack

Ingredients

1 tablespoon butter	¾ cup buttermilk
220 g self-raising (self-rising) flour	1 egg
½ cup castor (superfine) sugar	¾ cup vegetable oil
	100 g raspberries, fresh or frozen

What to do

✳ Preheat the oven to 180°C. If using cupcake cases, drop one into each of the holes of the muffin tin. Otherwise, melt the butter in the small saucepan, then use the pastry brush to grease the holes of the muffin tin.

✳ Using the scales, weigh the flour, then sift it with the sugar into the large bowl. In the medium bowl, combine the buttermilk, egg and oil and whisk to mix well. Stir the berries into the liquid mixture.

✳ Make a well in the dry ingredients, then pour in the liquid mixture. Stir lightly using the wooden spoon, but do not over-mix or the muffin mixture will become tough.

✳ Spoon the mixture into the cupcake cases or greased muffin tin, filling each hole just over two-thirds full.

✳ Bake for 20–25 minutes until the muffins are firm and golden brown. **Remove the muffins from the oven.** Allow them to rest for a few minutes in the tin, before turning out onto the wire rack to cool.

BOTTOM DRAWER

Interesting terms/techniques • making a well in dry ingredients • testing a cake by feeling its surface
Something to think about What other berries could you use to make muffins?

Linguine with pesto

Serves   4 at home or 8 tastes in the classroom
Fresh from the garden   basil, garlic

Pesto is a wonderful sauce and it keeps extremely well if packed into very clean glass jars with a film of olive oil on top to keep out any air. Cap the jars tightly and your pesto can be enjoyed for months. To save time in the classroom, we rolled and cut pasta dough that had been made by the previous class.

Equipment

2 trays
very large saucepan
chopping board
small knife
scales
grater
food processor
medium bowl

metric measuring spoons
   and cups
non-stick frying pan
tea towel
garlic crusher
spatula
colander
small ladle
large serving bowl

Ingredients

2 quantities Basic Pasta
   Dough (page 79)
plain (all-purpose) flour
   for dusting

Pesto
salt
60 g parmesan

¼ cup pine nuts
1 bunch basil (about
   1 cup well-packed
   leaves)
2 cloves garlic
¼ cup olive oil
2 tablespoons extra-virgin
   olive oil

BOTTOM DRAWER

Interesting terms/techniques
- making fresh pasta
- toasting nuts
- mayonnaise consistency

Did you know?   In Italy, pesto is almost always served with factory-made spaghetti. We used fresh egg pasta because all the children loved making it so much! Pesto also goes really well with lamb chops.

What to do

✸ Make the pasta as directed on page 79. Pass the dough through the narrow cutting blades of the pasta machine to form linguine. Dust the trays with flour, lay strands of linguine in a single layer on the trays and allow to dry for 10 minutes.

✸ Fill the very large saucepan with salted water and bring to the boil.

✸ In the meantime, make the pesto. Set out the chopping board and small knife. Weigh the parmesan and grate it. Place half the parmesan in the bowl of the food processor and set the other half aside in the medium bowl. Place 2 tablespoons of the pine nuts in the frying pan and toast over a medium heat until golden. Set aside to use as a garnish.

✸ Gently pull the basil leaves from their stems. Rinse the leaves and dry by rolling in the tea towel. Place the leaves in the bowl of the food processor and the stems in the compost bucket. Peel the garlic, crush in the garlic crusher and add to the food processor, along with the remaining pine nuts. Process until you have a rough paste. With the motor running, slowly add the two types of oil. You should have a paste that is the same consistency as mayonnaise. Using the spatula, scrape the pesto into the bowl with the remainder of the parmesan and stir to combine. Taste for salt.

✸ Drop the linguine into the boiling water. Cook for 4–5 minutes (taste to check if it is al dente). Set the colander in the sink. **Ladle 2–3 tablespoons of the cooking liquid into the bowl with the pesto and stir. Tip the linguine and boiling water into the colander.**

✸ Return the linguine to the empty hot saucepan. Tip in the pesto and mix well. Transfer the pasta to the serving bowl and scatter with the toasted pine nuts.

Roasted chicken with French tarragon

Makes   20 drumettes

Fresh from the garden   parsley, tarragon, lemons, garlic

Chicken and true French tarragon is a classic combination that is quite memorable. The tarragon has a faint aniseed flavour. Generous quantities of tarragon can also be used to flavour white-wine vinegar, which then gives a subtle flavour to salad dressings.

Equipment

scales

2 small bowls

baking dish

kitchen paper

tea towel

chopping board

large knife

lemon juicer

fork

aluminium foil

Ingredients

125 g butter, plus extra for greasing

20 chicken drumettes (actually part of the wing)

10 stalks parsley

20 sprigs French tarragon

½ lemon

2 cloves garlic

salt

freshly ground black pepper

 ## What to do

✱ Preheat the oven to 200°C. Weigh the butter and set aside in a small bowl to come to room temperature. Use a little extra butter, and a bit of kitchen paper, to grease the baking dish, then set it aside.

✱ Rinse the chicken drumettes quickly and pat very dry with kitchen paper.

✱ Rinse the parsley and tarragon and dry by rolling in the tea towel. Set out the chopping board and knife. Strip the tarragon leaves from the stems, chop the leaves and put into the second small bowl. Chop the parsley and add to the bowl. Juice the ½ lemon and add to the bowl (don't throw away the squeezed lemon half).

✱ Peel and chop the garlic and add to the bowl. Chop the butter into small pieces and add to the bowl. Mash all the ingredients together with the fork until you have a soft paste. Season with salt and pepper.

✱ Using your fingers, carefully separate the skin from the flesh of a chicken drumette, then push a little piece of herb butter into the space you have made. Pull the skin back into place and gently massage the soft butter so that it spreads a bit under the skin. Place the drumette into the baking dish.

✱ Stuff all the drumettes in this way. When finished, smear the remaining butter on the outside of the drumettes with your buttery hands, then rub the drumettes with the squeezed lemon half.

 ✱ Cover the baking dish with aluminium foil and bake for 15 minutes. **Remove the foil, carefully turn the drumettes and bake for a further 5–10 minutes. When done, remove from the oven and serve.**

Squashed flies slice

Makes   20 small slices

Fresh from the garden   eggs

Because the pastry in this recipe needs to be refrigerated before baking, we got each class to prepare the pastry for the next class.

Equipment

scales
small saucepan
pastry brush
1 Swiss-roll tin (lamington
    tin), about 20 cm × 26 cm
scissors
baking paper
rolling pin
bowls – 1 small, 1 medium

metric measuring spoons
    and cups
lemon juicer
tablespoon
fork
small knife
whisk
sugar dredger or
    coarse sieve
wire rack

Ingredients

1 quantity Basic Shortcrust
    Pastry (page 78)
60 g butter
plain (all-purpose) flour for
    dusting
½ cup currants
½ cup raisins

1½ cups sultanas
½ orange
½ teaspoon ground
    cinnamon
1 egg
2 tablespoons castor
    (superfine) sugar

What to do

✱ Make the shortcrust pastry as described on page 78. Preheat the oven to 180°C. Weigh the butter and melt it in the small saucepan. Use the pastry brush to butter the tin. Set the remaining butter aside.

✱ Cut a piece of baking paper large enough to line the tin and to provide a bit of overhang. Divide the pastry into two. Flour the workbench. Roll each piece of pastry into a rectangle large enough to fit into the tin. Place one piece of pastry in the base of the tin.

✱ In the medium bowl, mix the currants, raisins and sultanas. Add 1 tablespoon of orange juice, the cinnamon and the rest of the butter.

✱ Spread the fruit evenly over the pastry. Lay the second sheet of pastry over the fruit and press gently with your hand to get rid of any air. Press the edges very firmly together with the fork, then lightly mark the top of the pastry into squares or fingers with the small knife.

✱ In the small bowl, whisk the egg and use the pastry brush to glaze the surface of the slice. Prick each square or finger with the fork. Dust the top with castor sugar using a sugar dredger or coarse sieve.

✱ Bake for 30 minutes until well browned. **Remove from the oven.** Let the slice sit for a few minutes in the tin, then transfer to the wire rack using the baking paper. Peel the paper off the slice.

BOTTOM DRAWER

Did you know?   Raisins, currants and sultanas are all dried grapes.

Menu 21

Zucchini with mint-
flecked bocconcini

Pumpkin gnocchi
with sage

Celeriac and apple
remoulade

Simple carrot
and walnut cake

Zucchini with mint-flecked bocconcini

Thinly slice about
100 g of bocconcini (fresh
mozzarella balls) and toss
with 12 chopped mint leaves.
Make lengthways slits in
three zucchini (courgettes),
but don't slice all the way
through. Force the mint-
flecked bocconcini into the
slits. Oil three pieces of foil,
and wrap each zucchini in a
piece of foil. Bake on a tray
in a 200°C oven for about
15 minutes. Serve warm
on a serving plate.

Pumpkin gnocchi with sage

Serves   4 at home or 12 tastes in the classroom
Fresh from the garden   potatoes, pumpkin, sage
For the best gnocchi use nicola, desiree or Toolangi delight potatoes and a dry-fleshed variety pumpkin, such as butternut or Kent.

Equipment

ovenproof serving dish	baking tray
chopping board	grater
large knife	metric measuring spoons
peeler	potato ricer or
medium saucepan	Mouli food mill
scales	coarse strainer
wok	pastry scraper
bamboo steamer with lid	frying pan with 5 cm sides
bowls – 2 small, 2 medium	slotted spoon
skewer	non-stick frying pan
colander	heatproof board or mat

Ingredients

250 g potatoes	small wedge parmesan
salt	20 large sage leaves
300 g pumpkin (250g when	150 g butter
peeled and seeded)	freshly ground
160 g plain (all-purpose)	black pepper
flour, plus extra for dusting	

What to do

✳ Preheat the oven to 120°C and place the ovenproof serving dish in the oven to keep warm. Set out the chopping board, knife and peeler. Peel the potatoes, cut into chunks, then place in the medium saucepan with a little salt and enough cold water to cover generously. Place over a high heat and cook for about 15 minutes.

✳ **Peel and seed the pumpkin.** Weigh the pumpkin to make sure you have 250 g and cut into bite-sized chunks. Place the wok over a high heat and pour in enough hot water to come one-third of the way up the sides. Rest the bamboo steamer on top. Spread the pumpkin cubes in the basket, cover with the basket lid and steam for about

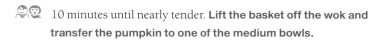

10 minutes until nearly tender. **Lift the basket off the wok and transfer the pumpkin to one of the medium bowls.**

✳ Use the skewer to check if the potatoes are tender. Place the colander in the sink. **Tip the potatoes and boiling water into the colander.** Return the potatoes to the saucepan and shake over the heat to dry out. Tip the potatoes into the second medium bowl.

✳ Place the flour in one of the small bowls. Dust the baking tray with the extra flour and set aside until needed. Grate the parmesan – you'll need 2 tablespoons. Place in the second small bowl and set aside.

✳ Flour the workbench well, and have the measured flour close by. Squash the pumpkin and potato through the largest hole of a potato ricer or through the coarsest disc of a food mill to form a loose mound on the bench. Sprinkle with a good pinch of salt. Tip most of the flour into the coarse strainer and sprinkle it over the vegetable mound. **Quickly but lightly combine the flour and vegetables, using a pastry scraper to assist.** Knead briefly until the dough is smooth, using more flour if necessary.

✳ **Cut the dough into 4 pieces and, using your fingers, roll each piece into a thin sausage about 2–3 cm wide.** Cut each sausage into pieces about 2 cm long and transfer to the floured baking tray.

✳ Fill the high-sided frying pan with water, add 1 teaspoon of salt and bring to the boil. Drop in as many gnocchi as will fit easily in one layer. Adjust the heat so the water is at a simmer. **When the gnocchi rise to the surface (about 3 minutes), lift out with the slotted spoon and slip into the warmed serving dish. Return the dish to the oven after adding each batch of gnocchi.** Scatter with the grated parmesan.

✳ Spread the sage leaves in the non-stick frying pan and add the butter. Fry until the leaves are crisp and the butter has become a medium-brown colour. Spoon the sage leaves and butter over the gnocchi in the serving dish and add some ground pepper. Place the board or mat on the table and serve the gnocchi in the ovenproof dish.

BOTTOM DRAWER

Interesting terms/techniques   • using a potato ricer or food mill   • working in batches   • steaming with a bamboo basket

Celeriac and apple remoulade

Serves   6 at home or 12 tastes in the classroom
Fresh from the garden   lemons, celeriac, apples, parsley, eggs
Celeriac remoulade is often served as part of a mixed plate of starters.

Equipment

lemon juicer	plate
metric measuring spoons and cups	2 tea towels
	plastic container with lid
bowls – 2 small, 1 medium, 1 large	food processor (with shredding attachment)
chopping board	plastic scraper
knives – 1 small, 1 large	mixing spoon
peeler	serving plate

Ingredients

1 lemon	***Mustard mayonnaise***
1 celeriac	2 eggs
1 apple	½ tablespoon
10 stalks parsley	Dijon-style mustard
¼ cup black olives (optional)	pinch of salt
	¾ cup olive oil

What to do

✳ Juice the lemon. Set aside 1 tablespoon of the juice in a small bowl and place the rest in the medium bowl and half fill with cold water.

 ✳ Set out the chopping board, knives and peeler. **Peel the celeriac thickly and cut into small chunks.** Place directly in the lemon water. Do not peel the apple, but cut it lengthways into quarters and remove the core and seeds. Place the apple pieces on the plate until needed and the core in the compost bucket. Rinse the parsley, dry by rolling in a tea towel, chop, then place in a small bowl and set aside.

BOTTOM DRAWER

Interesting terms/techniques • making mayonnaise
• separating eggs • shredding fruit and vegetables

✳ To make the mayonnaise, set out the plastic container and food processor. Separate the eggs by cracking them, one at a time, then tipping each egg into your cupped hand, which should be held over the plastic container. Slightly open your fingers and let the white slip into the container. Place the yolk in the processor. Repeat with the second egg. (You won't need the eggwhites for this recipe, so freeze them for another time. Remember to cover and label the container.)

✳ Add the mustard and salt to the egg yolks and process for 30 seconds. **With the motor running, add the oil slowly until you have a thick mayonnaise.** Scrape into the large bowl.

✳ Without washing the bowl of the food processor, attach the shredding disc. Feed the apple quarters through the disc, then tip into the bowl with the mayonnaise. Dry the celeriac pieces with a tea towel, then feed through the shredder. Add to the mayonnaise. Add the parsley and season well. Arrange on the serving plate and decorate with olives, if using.

Simple carrot and walnut cake

Makes 10 slices

Fresh from the garden carrots, eggs

Carrot is such a versatile ingredient. At Collingwood College, we used it in juice, savoury muffins, a salad, and this delicious cake.

Equipment

metric measuring spoons and cups	large knife
	grater
bowls – 1 small, 1 medium, 1 large	plate
	scales
pastry brush	whisk
loaf tin,	sieve or sifter
24 cm × 12 cm × 7 cm	wooden spoon
scissors	skewer
baking paper	wire rack
chopping board	small saucepan

Ingredients

⅔ cup vegetable oil

2–3 medium carrots

50 g walnuts

2 eggs

125 g self-raising (self-rising) flour

½ teaspoon ground cinnamon

½ teaspoon grated nutmeg

¾ cup brown sugar

Topping

2 tablespoons butter

2 tablespoons castor (superfine) sugar

2 teaspoons ground cinnamon

What to do

✱ Preheat the oven to 180°C. Place the oil in the small bowl and use the pastry brush to grease the loaf tin. Cut a piece of baking paper large enough to line the tin and to provide a bit of overhang.

✱ Set out the chopping board and knife. Grate the carrot – you'll need about 2 cups. Set aside on the plate. Roughly chop the walnuts.

✱ In the medium bowl, lightly whisk the remaining oil and the eggs together. Sift the flour, along with the cinnamon and nutmeg, into the large bowl. Add the sugar and mix lightly with the wooden spoon. Make a well in the dry ingredients, then pour in the oil/egg mixture. Combine well with the wooden spoon. Stir in the carrot and walnuts. Spoon the cake mixture into the prepared tin.

✱ Bake for 35–40 minutes. Check the cake by slipping the skewer into its middle (it should come out clean). **Remove from the oven.** Let the cake sit for a few minutes in the tin, then transfer to the wire rack using the baking paper. Discard the paper.

✱ To make the topping, melt the butter in the small saucepan, then brush the top of the cake with butter. Wash and dry one of the previously used bowls, then mix the cinnamon and sugar in it. Scatter the cinnamon sugar over the cake while it is still warm.

BOTTOM DRAWER

Interesting terms/techniques   • making a well in dry ingredients   • testing a cake with a skewer

Menu 22

Desley's mum's silverbeet,
potato and tomato curry

Flatbreads to serve
with curry

Fried green tomatoes
with yoghurt

Desley's mum's silverbeet, potato and tomato curry

Serves   6 at home or 12 tastes in the classroom
Fresh from the garden   potatoes, onions, garlic, silver beet, coriander, parsley

To save time in the classroom, we had the students prepare the potatoes for the next class. This involved peeling the potatoes, chopping them, then leaving them to soak in cold water. This was generally done while the students waited for the curry to cook.

Equipment

chopping board
knives – 1 small, 1 large
peeler
bowls – 1 small, 1 medium, 1 large
small non-stick frying pan
metric measuring spoons and cups
mortar and pestle

colander
heavy-based frying pan (or saucepan) with 6 cm sides and lid
wooden spoon
salad spinner
tea towel
serving bowl

Ingredients

6 large potatoes
1 onion
1 × 5 cm piece fresh ginger
2 cloves garlic
1 teaspoon cumin seeds
1 teaspoon coriander seeds
1 teaspoon brown mustard seeds
½ teaspoon chilli flakes
6 curry leaves

½ teaspoon ground turmeric
¼ cup olive oil
1 × 400 g can chopped tomatoes
18 silverbeet leaves
6 stems coriander (cilantro)
10 stalks parsley
salt

What to do

✳ Set out the chopping board, knives and peeler. Peel the potatoes and place the peel in the compost bucket. Chop the potatoes into 2 cm cubes, place in the large bowl and cover with water. Soak the coriander in a small bowl of water. Peel and chop the onion, ginger and garlic, and place in the medium bowl.

✳ Heat the small frying pan over a medium heat. Toast the cumin seeds in the dry pan until they smell fragrant. Tip the seeds into the mortar. Toast the coriander seeds in the same pan until they smell fragrant. Add these seeds to the mortar. Toast the mustard seeds until they start to pop, then add them to the mortar. Crush the seeds to a coarse powder using the pestle. Add the chilli flakes, crumbled curry leaves and turmeric to the crushed spices, and stir to combine.

✳ Place the colander in the sink. **Tip the potatoes and water into the colander.** Heat the oil in the heavy-based frying pan over a medium heat and tip in the onion, garlic and ginger. Fry, stirring with the wooden spoon, for a few minutes until softened. Add the crushed spices from the mortar, the potatoes, and the tin of tomatoes along with their juice. Stir with the wooden spoon to combine and add just enough water to barely cover. Cover tightly with the lid and reduce the heat to a simmer. Set the timer for 25 minutes.

✳ Meanwhile, separate the silverbeet leaves from their stems by slicing along each side of the thick central stem. Place the stems in the compost bucket. Rinse the silverbeet leaves and dry in the salad spinner. Roll the leaves into a loose bunch, then shred with the large knife. Place the shredded leaves in the bowl used to hold the onion. Lift the coriander from its soaking water. Rinse the parsley. Dry the herbs by rolling in the tea towel, chop roughly, then set aside in the small bowl.

✳ When the timer goes off, check the potatoes are tender and taste for salt. Add the silverbeet leaves, cover and cook for 10 minutes.

✳ **Transfer the hot curry to the serving bowl.** Sprinkle the chopped parsley and coriander over the top.

BOTTOM DRAWER

Interesting terms/techniques
• stemming leaves and shredding leaves   • toasting spices
Questions   1 Is there a single spice known as curry?
2 What are the countires where curry is traditionally eaten?

Answers   1 There is no single spice called curry, but there is a plant called the curry plant and its leaves are used as a flavouring in many curries.
2 Curry-eating nations include India, Sri Lanka, Pakistan, Bangladesh, Malaysia and Thailand.

Flatbreads to serve with curry

Makes 8 × 10 cm breads

This recipe is so easy you will want to make flatbreads often. Flatbreads are great served warm with a selection of dips. Try Broad-Bean Dip (page 86), Skordalia (page 87) and Hummus with Paprika Oil (page 119). The dough used to make this bread has to rest for about 30 minutes. In the classroom, each class prepared the dough ahead for the next class. At home, you could work on the other recipes in this menu while you wait.

Equipment

bowls – 1 small, 1 large
metric measuring spoons
   and cups
scales
electric mixer with dough
   hook

tea towel
baking tray
heavy-based 24 cm
   frying pan
large knife
rolling pin

Ingredients

½ teaspoon salt
½ cup lukewarm water
1 tablespoon extra-virgin olive oil
250 g plain (all-purpose) flour,
   plus extra for dusting

What to do

✻ In the small bowl, dissolve the salt in the warm water. Add the oil. Weigh the flour, then place it in the bowl of the electric mixer with the dough hook attachment fitted. With the motor running, trickle in the water and oil mixture. Run the motor for about 8 minutes until the dough looks smooth.

✻ Tip the dough into the large bowl (make sure it's very dry) and cover with the tea towel (the tea towel must be very dry also). Leave the bowl in a draught-free place for 30 minutes.

✻ Preheat the oven to 120°C and place the baking tray in the oven to keep warm.

✻ Heat the heavy-based frying pan for at least 5 minutes until very hot. Meanwhile, using the large knife, divide the dough into 8 pieces, each the size of a small egg. Flour the workbench. Flatten each piece of dough to a round and roll out thinly. As each piece is rolled, slap it into the hot dry pan and cook for 3 minutes. Flip the flatbread over and cook for a further 3 minutes. Depending on the size of the pan, you should be able to cook a few flatbreads at a time.

✻ As the flatbreads cook, they will develop a few bubbles and brown splotches. This shows they are done. Transfer the cooked flatbreads to the warm baking tray and return the tray to the oven. Continue cooking in batches until all the dough has been used. Serve alongside a curry.

BOTTOM DRAWER

Interesting terms/techniques • working in batches

Question In what way are these flatbreads different from pizza?

Answer Flatbread dough does not have yeast, which means it is quicker to prepare as it does not need to prove/rise like pizza dough.

Fried green tomatoes with yoghurt

Makes around 16 slices

Fresh from the garden green tomatoes, eggs

At the end of autumn there are usually some tomatoes that have not ripened. They are still delicious either cooked as below or made into a pickle. Polenta is made from a special variety of ground-up sweetcorn. It can be fine or coarse. The finer variety is best for this dish.

Equipment

2 baking trays	metric measuring cups
chopping board	medium non-stick
serrated knife	frying pan
plate	egg lifter for non-stick pan
2 shallow bowls	serving plate
fork	small serving bowl

Ingredients

4 large green tomatoes, or 6	½ cup olive oil
medium green tomatoes	salt
2 eggs	freshly ground black pepper
1 cup fine polenta	1 cup yoghurt
(cornmeal)	

What to do

✱ Preheat the oven to 120°C and place one of the baking trays in the oven to keep warm.

✱ Set out the chopping board and serrated knife. Cut off the top and bottom of the tomatoes and place in the compost bucket. Then cut each tomato into 3 or 4 thick horizontal slices. Stack the slices of tomato on the plate.

✱ Crack the eggs into one of the shallow bowls and whisk with the fork. Put the polenta into the second shallow bowl and place the second baking tray alongside. Using one hand only, dip slices of tomato into the egg, then into the polenta. Place the polenta-coated slices in a single layer on the nearby baking tray.

 ✱ **Heat a 1 cm layer of oil in the frying pan over a medium heat. Carefully lower a few tomato slices into the hot oil and leave undisturbed for a few minutes. Once the coating is crisp, turn carefully, using the egg lifter, and fry the other side.**

✱ Remove the cooked and crunchy slices to the warm baking tray and return it to the oven. Repeat with the remaining slices.

✱ Arrange the fried green tomatoes on the serving plate and season with salt and pepper. Spoon the yoghurt into the small serving bowl and place it on the plate.

BOTTOM DRAWER

Interesting terms/techniques • cutting tomatoes with a serrated knife • working in batches

Vietnamese vegetarian rice-paper rolls

Makes 20

Fresh from the garden carrots, spring onions, coriander, Vietnamese mint, lettuce, garlic, lemons, chillies

There are lots of steps to this recipe, so it is ideal for a group to make. Why not have a rice-paper-roll party and everyone can make their own! Read the recipe all the way through before starting. Vietnamese meals almost always have a bowl of freshly picked green leaves and herbs served at the same time as the rest of the meal. It is very important to make sure that none of the diners has an allergy to peanuts.

Equipment

metric measuring spoons
  and cups
baking tray
bowls – 2 small,
  1 medium, 2 large
scales
large saucepan
colander
3–4 tea towels
chopping board
knives – 1 small, 1 large

peeler
grater
big salad bowl
wooden spoon
salad spinner
tablespoon
lemon juicer
disposable gloves
small bowl for
  dipping sauce
serving plate

Ingredients

⅓ cup shelled peanuts
  (optional)
150 g rice vermicelli
  noodles
12 stems coriander
  (cilantro), plus extra
  for salad
2 medium carrots
2 cups bean shoots
5 spring onions (scallions)
15 Vietnamese mint
  leaves, plus extra
  for salad

10 big crisp lettuce leaves
  (iceberg is good)
25 rice-paper wrappers (a
  few will probably tear)

Dipping sauce
2 cloves garlic
1 lemon or lime
1 small red chilli
1 tablespoon sugar
¼ cup rice vinegar
¼ cup fish sauce
  (or to taste)

What to do

✳ If using peanuts, preheat the oven to 180°C. Scatter the peanuts on the baking tray and roast until golden (about 10 minutes). **Remove from the oven and set aside to cool.** Place the nuts in the small bowl then wipe down the baking tray and turn off the oven.

✳ Weigh the noodles and place them in one of the large bowls. Fill the bowl with warm water and soak the noodles for 10 minutes. Part fill the large saucepan with water and bring to the boil.

✳ Place the colander in the sink. Drain the soaking noodles in the colander, then carefully tip the noodles into the boiling water. Boil for 2 minutes. **Pour the noodles and water into the colander.** Rinse well with cold water.

✳ Tip the noodles onto a clean tea towel and pat dry. Return the noodles to the large bowl used previously for soaking.

✳ While the noodles are soaking and cooking, prepare the other ingredients. Soak the coriander in a small bowl of water. Set out the chopping board, knives, peeler and grater. Peel the carrots and grate using the largest hole of the grater, then tip the shreds into the medium bowl. Chop the roasted peanuts and add to the carrot bowl. Add most of the bean shoots to the carrot bowl and place the rest in the big salad bowl. Trim the outside layer from the spring onions, cut off the tops and ends, then slit the rest lengthways. Cut into thin strips 4 cm in length and add to the carrot bowl. Add all peelings and scraps to the compost bucket. Lift the coriander out of its soaking water. Rinse the mint. Dry the herbs by rolling in a tea towel. Add most of the mint and coriander to the carrot bowl, but place some in the salad bowl with the bean shoots. Use the wooden spoon to mix everything in the carrot bowl together.

✱ Rinse the lettuce leaves and dry in the salad spinner. Place the leaves in the salad bowl with the bean shoots and herbs. Arrange nicely and set aside to serve with the rice-paper rolls.

✱ Fill the second large bowl with warm water and place it on the workbench. Get out the rice-paper wrappers. Immerse 2 wrappers in warm water for about 30 seconds until they feel quite pliable (don't work with more than 2 at a time or they'll get soggy). Lift the wrappers from the water and spread on a dry tea towel on your workbench.

✱ Spoon a tablespoon of the carrot mixture across the wrapper (in the shape of a small log) about one-third of the way from the bottom. (Leave a little space at either end to seal the roll later.) **Fold the bottom of the wrapper over the filling and roll it over twice. Now tuck in the ends and continue to roll until you have a firm package.** Get an adult to help you with the first couple of rolls – after that, see if you can do it by yourself.

✱ Take a tea towel that is slightly damp (one of the ones used to dry the noodles or herbs) and place it on the baking tray used previously to roast the nuts. Place the spring roll seam side down on the damp cloth. Place another tea towel (again, slightly damp) over the spring roll. Keep the rolls covered like this as you work, to prevent them drying out. Keep making rolls until you have used all your filling.

✱ To make the dipping sauce, peel and finely chop the garlic and place in the small serving bowl. Juice the lemon or lime and add 2 tablespoons of juice to the bowl. Slip on the disposable gloves and cut the chilli in half lengthways. Scrape the seeds into the rubbish bin. Slice half of the chilli finely and add to the bowl (reserve the other half for another recipe). Discard the gloves. Add the sugar, rice vinegar and fish sauce to the bowl.

✱ Set out the rice-paper rolls on the serving plate with the dipping sauce and the salad nearby.

BOTTOM DRAWER

Interesting terms/techniques
- toasting nuts   • seeding chillies

Question   What other ingredients could go into these rice-paper rolls?

Answer   Peeled, cooked prawns, cut lengthways; Cold White-cooked Chinese Chicken Breast (page 150).

Simple hot and sour fish soup with broccoli

Serves   6 at home or 12 tastes in the classroom
Fresh from the garden   broccoli, garlic, spring onions, coriander, chillies

It adds to the pleasure of enjoying this soup if you serve it in Chinese rice bowls and with specially shaped Chinese soup spoons.

Equipment

chopping board	disposable gloves
knives - 1 small, 1 large	large saucepan
tweezers (or fish-bone pliers)	wooden spoon
bowls – 2 small, 2 medium	6–12 small serving bowls
metric measuring spoons and jug	serving tray/s
tea towel	ladle

Ingredients

250 g firm white fish fillets
1 head broccoli, or 6 stems broccolini
6 button mushrooms, or 3 flat mushrooms
2 cloves garlic
1 × 4 cm piece fresh ginger
2 spring onions (scallions)
6 stems coriander (cilantro)
200 g silken bean curd
1 litre Chicken Stock (page 79)

Marinade
2 teaspoons light soy sauce
2 teaspoons mirin
2 teaspoons sesame oil
1 tablespoon cornflour (cornstarch)

Bowl seasoning
1 teaspoon chilli paste, or 1 small red chilli
2 tablespoons light soy sauce
2 tablespoons Chinese red or black vinegar

BOTTOM DRAWER

Interesting terms/techniques • skinning fish
• removing pin bones • seeding chillies
Question   What is silken bean curd?

Answer   'Silken' refers to the very fine texture of the bean curd and suggests that the soy-bean liquid was strained through fine silk before being allowed to set in moulds.

What to do

✱ Set out the chopping board and knives. **Skin the fish by placing the fillets skin side down on the board. Holding the left tip of the skin very firmly in your left hand, wiggle and slide the large knife between the skin and the flesh the length of the fillet. If there are still pin bones in the fillets, remove these using tweezers that have been sterilised in boiling water.** Cut the fish fillets into bite-sized pieces and put into one of the medium bowls. Add all the *Marinade* ingredients, and mix well. Put the fish in the refrigerator for 15 minutes. Wipe down the board and knives.

✱ Cut the broccoli florets into 5 cm pieces and place in the second medium bowl. (If using broccolini cut each stem into 5 cm pieces.) Slice the mushrooms thinly and add to the broccoli bowl. Peel and finely chop the garlic and ginger and add to the broccoli bowl. Trim the outside layer from the spring onions and cut off the tops and ends. Split the rest lengthways, then cut across into thin slices and add to the broccoli bowl. Put all vegetable scraps in the compost bucket. Wash the coriander very well, dry by rolling in the tea towel, separate into sprigs, then add to the broccoli bowl. Dice the bean curd very gently and place in a small bowl.

✱ Make the bowl seasoning for the serving bowls. If using fresh chilli, slip on the disposable gloves and cut the chilli in half lengthways. Scrape the seeds into the rubbish bin and slice the chilli finely. Discard the gloves. Place the chilli or chilli paste in the second small bowl. Add the soy sauce and vinegar, mix to combine, then set aside until needed.

✱ Put the chicken stock into the large saucepan and tip the contents of the broccoli bowl into the stock and stir. Add the marinated fish and the marinade. Heat to simmering point, stirring gently with the wooden spoon. When the soup is simmering, slip in the bean curd. Lower the heat and check the fish after 3 minutes – it is cooked when the flesh flakes fairly easily when pressed with a fork.

✱ While this is happening, arrange the small serving bowls on a tray (or 2 trays if you are making 12 small serves). Place about 1 teaspoon of the bowl seasoning in each bowl. Ladle the soup into the serving bowls and serve immediately.

Peach and pistachio tarts

Makes   8 tarts

Fresh from the garden   peaches, eggs

Peaches and nectarines can either be freestone or clingstone. Try to buy freestone fruit for these tarts. Freestone fruits are easy to twist away from the stones, clingstones are not. These tarts could also be made with apricots or nectarines or even firm plums.

Equipment

chopping board
knives – 1 small, 1 large
bowls – 1 small, 1 large
electric jug
slotted spoon
plate
2 large baking trays
scales

metric measuring spoons
  and cups
food processor
fork
pastry brush
tablespoon
small saucepan
wooden spoon

Ingredients

4 ripe peaches
2 sheets all-butter pre-rolled
  puff pastry (from the
  supermarket)
1 pinch salt
2 tablespoons smooth
  apricot jam or apple jelly

Almond cream
60 g unsalted butter
¼ cup castor (superfine)
  sugar
½ cup ground almonds
1 egg
⅓ cup shelled pistachios
2–3 drops vanilla essence

What to do

✹ Preheat the oven to 200°C. Remove the butter from the refrigerator to soften. Set out the chopping board and knives. Score the peaches all the way around the natural curve of the fruit with the small knife, then put into the large bowl. (This will help the skins lift off in the next step, making it easier to divide the fruit into perfect halves.)

✹ **Boil the electric jug and tip the boiling water over the scored peaches. Leave for 1 minute. Using the slotted spoon, lift the peaches, one at a time, from the water onto the plate.** Slip off their skins and place the skins in the compost bucket. Twist the 2 halves of each peach apart, discard the stone and return to the plate until needed. Wipe down the chopping board and knives.

✹ **Cut each sheet of pastry into 4 squares and place the squares a bit apart on the 2 baking trays. Get an adult to make sure you have cut the pastry very well** – if the cuts are not clean or the edges are squeezed together, the pastry will not rise evenly. Refrigerate until needed.

✹ Now make the almond cream. Weigh the butter and place it, along with the sugar and ground almonds, in the bowl of the food processor. Process to a smooth cream. In the small bowl, lightly whisk the egg with the fork. Add half of the egg to the mixture and process briefly. Chop the pistachios and stir into the mixture together with the vanilla.

✹ Add the salt to the remaining egg and mix. Brush the egg all over the squares of puff pastry, making sure none drips down the sides.

✹ Place a tablespoon of the almond cream in the centre of each square and spread it out a bit using the back of the spoon, but leaving 2 cm of cream-free pastry around the edges. Place a peach half cut side down on top of each almond-cream-coated pastry square. The peach should cover the cream. Place the tarts in the oven for 20 minutes.

✹ Soften the jam or jelly by heating it gently in the small saucepan, stirring with a wooden spoon to prevent the jam catching.

✹ **Remove the tarts from the oven.** Brush the peach halves with the melted jam or jelly while they are still hot. Allow to cool and enjoy!

BOTTOM DRAWER

Interesting terms/techniques
• skinning fruit   • using an egg wash
Did you know?   Although puff pastry does not contain a rising agent (such as yeast), it rises to about 6 times its original thickness when heated. This is because it contains lots of layers of butter. As the butter heats it creates steam, causing the pastry to puff up.

Silverbeet and potato torte

Menu 24

Silverbeet and
potato torte

Soda bread with
herb butter

Smoky eggplant dip

Grated carrot salad
with lemon juice and
black olives

Grated carrot salad with lemon juice and black olives

Peel some carrots and
grate using the medium
hole of a grater. Dissolve a
pinch of salt in a bowl with
1 tablespoon of lemon juice.
Stir in ⅓ cup of extra-virgin
olive oil, then toss the carrot
in the dressing. Arrange in
a shallow bowl and decorate
with black olives.

Makes 12 small wedges
Fresh from the garden silver beet, potatoes,
onions, parsley, eggs

The dough used in this recipe needs to relax for an
hour after mixing, so in the classroom, we had the
students prepare ahead for the next class. This
preparation involved making the dough, kneading it,
then putting it aside for one hour. This pastry is very
easy and versatile and can be filled with all manner
of savoury combinations.

Equipment

scales
food processor
metric measuring spoons
   and cups
bowls – 1 small,
   1 medium, 2 large
2 tea towels
chopping board
knives – 1 small, 1 large,
   1 serrated
salad spinner

peeler
medium saucepan
grater
skewer
colander
wooden spoon
pastry brush
1 × 26 cm pizza tray
rolling pin
tablespoon
fork

Ingredients

Olive oil pastry
200 g plain (all-purpose)
   flour, plus extra
   for dusting
½ teaspoon salt
1½ tablespoons extra-
   virgin olive oil
½ cup cold water

Filling
15 silverbeet leaves
2 teaspoons salt
2 medium potatoes
½ onion
150 g mozzarella
10 stalks parsley
2 tablespoons
   extra-virgin olive oil
freshly ground black
   pepper
1 egg

What to do

✱ First, make the pastry. Weigh the flour and place
in the bowl of the food processor. Add the salt and
whiz for a few seconds. Combine the oil and water in
the small bowl, then, with the motor running, add to
the bowl of the food processor. Stop the machine
when the dough forms a ball.

✱ Flour the workbench. Transfer the dough to
the workbench and knead for a minute, then place
the dough in a large bowl. Cover with a dry tea towel
and leave for 1 hour.

✱ Preheat the oven to 200°C. While the dough is
resting, make the filling. Set out the chopping board
and knives. Separate the silverbeet leaves from their
stems by slicing along each side of the thick central
stem. Slice the stems finely and place in the medium
bowl. Rinse the silverbeet leaves and dry in the salad
spinner. Roll the leaves into a loose bunch, then shred
with the large knife. Put the leaves in with the stems,
add the salt and mix.

✱ Peel the potatoes. Cut the potatoes into quarters and
put into a saucepan of cold water with a pinch of salt.
Place over a high heat and cook for 15 minutes.

✱ While the potatoes are cooking, prepare the
following ingredients and place in the second large
bowl. Peel and finely chop the onion. Grate the
mozzarella. Rinse the parsley, dry by rolling in
the second tea towel, then chop finely.

✱ Check to see if the potatoes are cooked by testing
with the skewer (it should slide in easily). Set the
 colander in the sink. **Tip the cooked potatoes and
water into the colander.** When the potatoes have
cooled a little, chop them into bite-sized pieces and
place in the large bowl with the onion, mozzarella
and parsley. Mix in a tablespoon of the oil. ➤➤

✳ Put the silverbeet stems and leaves in the colander and quickly rinse with cold water. Shake to remove the water, then tip into the tea towel used previously to dry the parsley, and roll like a sausage.

Ask someone to twist the tea towel at one end, while you twist the other end in the opposite direction – this will squeeze the water out.

✳ Shake the silverbeet stems and leaves from the towel into the bowl with the potatoes and grind on some pepper. Crack the egg into the bowl and mix all the ingredients together.

✳ Place the remaining 1 tablespoon of oil in the small bowl, then brush the pizza tray with oil. Roll out two-thirds of the pastry into a large circle. Lift this pastry circle onto the oiled pizza tray. Pile the potato and silverbeet filling on top of the pastry circle, leaving a clean edge of about 5 cm all the way round.

✳ Roll out the remaining pastry to form a lid, then lay the lid over the filling. It will look a little bumpy as the pastry settles over the filling. Roll the bottom outer edge up and over the top outer edge, then pinch together to make a good seal. Prick the pastry lid with the fork, brush it with the remainder of the oil and scatter lightly with salt. Bake for 25 minutes.

✳ **Remove from the oven.** Allow to cool for 5 minutes, then use the serrated knife to cut the tart.

BOTTOM DRAWER

Interesting terms/techniques • stemming and shredding leaves • squeezing liquid from an ingredient using a cloth

Questions 1 Why is this torte cut with a serrated knife?
2 Is there a difference between a torte and a tart?

Answers 1 The pastry is quite brittle and a sawing action (with the serrated knife) is recommended to cut through the crust, rather than pushing straight down with a regular knife, which may shatter the crust.   2 A torte is covered, a tart is not.

Soda bread with herb butter

Makes   16 slices

Fresh from the garden   parsley, chives, oregano

This delicious quick bread is often associated with Ireland, where country households made it fresh each day. You could add a handful of currants or sultanas to the flour, or chopped fresh herbs, such as thyme or basil. The quicker the dough is mixed the better, as too much handling will make the finished bread tough.

Equipment

scales

bowls – 1 small, 1 large

sieve or sifter

metric measuring spoons
    and cups

fork

baking tray

pastry brush

knives – 1 large, 1 table knife

tea towel

chopping board

baking paper

wire rack

serving plate

Ingredients

250 g plain (all-purpose)
    flour, plus extra for
    dusting

200 g wholemeal plain
    (all-purpose) flour

1 teaspoon salt

1 teaspoon bicarbonate
    of soda (baking soda)

1⅓ cups buttermilk,
    plus 2 tablespoons extra

Herb butter

150 g butter

10 stalks parsley

10 chives

10 sprigs oregano

What to do

✳ Preheat the oven to 230°C. Weigh the butter needed for the herb butter, and set aside in the small bowl to come to room temperature.

✳ To make the bread dough, sift the two kinds of flour, along with the salt and bicarbonate of soda, into the large bowl. Make a well in the dry ingredients, then pour in the 1⅓ cups buttermilk. Mix quickly with the fork (or your hand) until you have a dough. Dust the workbench and the baking tray with flour. Tip the dough onto the workbench.

✳ Knead the dough briefly, then flatten to form a circle, about 3 cm high, then transfer to the floured baking tray.

✳ Brush the surface with the extra buttermilk and mark the loaf into 16 portions using the back of the table knife. Bake for 15 minutes, then reduce the heat to 200°C and bake for a further 20 minutes.

 ✳ While the loaf is baking, make the herb butter. Rinse the parsley, chives and oregano and dry by rolling in the tea towel. Pick off any leaves that are yellow or slimy and place the damaged leaves in the compost bucket. Set out the chopping board and large knife and chop the herbs finely. Work the herbs into the butter, using the fork, until evenly mixed. Place a double sheet of baking paper on the chopping board and spoon on the herb butter. **Roll the butter up tightly like a small sausage, twisting the ends to secure.** Place the roll in the refrigerator to firm up while the bread is baking.

✳ **Remove the bread from the oven.** Tap the loaf – if it sounds hollow, then it's done. Turn out onto the wire rack and allow to cool a little before cutting.

✳ Cut the herb butter into thin slices and serve alongside the bread on the serving plate.

BOTTOM DRAWER

Interesting terms/techniques   • room temperature   • making a well in dry ingredients   • making a roll of dough or butter

Tip   The soda bread could be cut into small shapes before baking, then baked for a shorter time (just 20 minutes).

Smoky eggplant dip

Makes   about 1 cup

Fresh from the garden   eggplants, garlic, basil, parsley, lemons

In the classroom, we saved time by getting the students to prepare the eggplants for the next class. This involved roasting or barbecuing them, which takes 15–25 minutes, then setting them aside. At home, you can get on with other activities while the eggplants cook. Barbecuing gives the best smoky flavour. The finished purée stores well for several days in a covered container in the refrigerator.

Equipment

skewer	lemon juicer
baking tray (if using oven)	colander
tongs	plate
chopping board	tablespoon
knives – 1 small, 2 large	metric measuring spoons
bowls – 3 small, 1 medium	serving bowl
1 tea towel	

Ingredients

3 small eggplants (aubergines)	½ lemon
1 clove garlic	2 tablespoons extra-virgin olive oil
15 basil leaves	salt
10 stalks parsley	freshly ground black pepper

What to do

✳ Preheat the oven to 200°C. Prick each eggplant 2–3 times with the skewer, place on the baking tray and bake for 25 minutes. Or for the very best flavour, cook the eggplants on a barbecue, turning with tongs as the skin blackens – this will take about 15 minutes and the skin will become quite charred. **Remove the eggplants from the oven or barbecue.** Allow to cool.

✳ Set out the chopping board and knives. While the eggplants are cooking, prepare the following ingredients and set aside in small bowls. Peel and finely chop the garlic. Rinse the basil and parsley, dry by rolling in a tea towel, then chop. Juice the lemon.

✳ If you have oven-roasted the eggplant, lift the cooled eggplant onto the chopping board. Cut each eggplant in half from top to bottom. Place the halves in the colander, then stand the colander on the plate. Press the halves with the back of the spoon to extract the moisture, then scrape the flesh from the skins and place the flesh in the medium bowl.

✳ If you have barbecued the eggplant, use a small knife to peel away the charred skin from the flesh. Place the flesh in the colander, then stand the colander on the plate. Press the flesh with the back of a spoon to extract the excess moisture, then place the flesh in the medium bowl.

✳ Place the skins in the compost bucket and wipe down the chopping board to get rid of any blackened bits of skin and any liquid. Return the eggplant flesh to the chopping board and chop to a coarse purée. **An effective but unusual technique is to use 2 knives of the same size, one in each hand, and chop.** Scoop the coarse purée back into the bowl. Add the garlic, basil and parsley and lemon juice. Stir in the olive oil and taste for salt and pepper.

✳ Place in the serving bowl and serve with warmed pita bread or normal toast.

> **BOTTOM DRAWER**
>
> **Interesting terms/techniques**   • squeezing liquid from an ingredient using a cloth   • chopping with two knives
>
> **Question**   What other flavours could you imagine in this eggplant dip?
>
> **Answer**   You could add a small quantity of leftover cooked tomato or homemade tomato sauce; sliced, sautéed onion; yoghurt; or toasted pine nuts.

Winter

We grew many cabbages, including red and green, round and pointy, along with plenty of broccoli. Our star crop, the astonishing silver beet, flourished all year and featured in many dishes. The students also all enjoyed many different thick vegetable soups and dips made from winter staples such as chick peas and dried beans.

Golden Syrup Dumplings (page 231)

Broccoli and herb frittata

Serves   6 at home or 12 tastes in the classroom
Fresh from the garden   onions, garlic, broccoli, parsley, chives, oregano, eggs
Once you know how to make a frittata you will think of many variations.

Equipment

chopping board	colander
knives – 1 small, 1 large	tea towel
bowls – 1 small,	whisk
1 medium, 1 large	large non-stick frying pan
peeler	with lid
large saucepan	kitchen paper
metric measuring spoons	egg lifter
and cups	large plate
wooden spoon	

Ingredients

½ onion	8 sprigs oregano
2 cloves garlic	4 eggs
1 large head broccoli	freshly ground
1 teaspoon salt	black pepper
12 stalks parsley	½ cup extra-virgin
10 chives	olive oil

What to do

✴ Set out the chopping board and knives. Peel the onion and cut in half from top to bottom. Place the two halves flat-side down on the chopping board and thinly slice into half-rings. Put the onion into the small bowl. Peel and slice the garlic and add to the onion. Cut the broccoli into florets, then peel the stem, with the peeler, and cut it into 5 mm thick slices. Place all vegetable scraps in the compost bucket.

BOTTOM DRAWER

Did you know?
The Spanish word for frittata is *tortilla*.

✴ Fill the saucepan with water, add the salt and bring to the boil. Carefully drop the peeled broccoli stem and florets into the saucepan and stir once with the wooden spoon. Cook for 5 minutes.

✴ Set the colander in the sink. **Tip the broccoli and boiling water into the colander.** Transfer the broccoli to the large bowl.

✴ Rinse the parsley, chives and oregano, dry by rolling in the tea towel, then chop roughly and add to the bowl with the broccoli. Break the eggs into the medium bowl, season with salt and pepper and whisk.

✴ Pour half of the oil into the frying pan and place over a medium heat. Add the onion and garlic and sauté, stirring with the wooden spoon, for 5 minutes. Tip the onion and garlic into the large bowl with the broccoli and chopped herbs. Add the whisked eggs and stir well with the wooden spoon.

✴ Use kitchen paper to wipe out the frying pan, then add the remaining oil and heat over a high heat. When the oil is hot, carefully pour the egg and vegetable mixture into the pan. The mixture should puff and frill at the edges as soon as it hits the hot frying pan. Reduce the heat to low and cook for 5 minutes or until the bottom is set and golden brown – check this by lifting the edges with the egg lifter to see underneath. The top should still be moist.

✴ **Place the plate on top of the pan and quickly flip the pan over so that the unfinished frittata is now on the plate.** Slide the frittata back into the pan with the uncooked side on the bottom. Return the pan to the heat and cook for another 5 minutes or until the bottom is golden brown. Alternatively, you could cook the top of the frittata by heating the grill to high and sliding the pan underneath for 3–4 minutes.

✴ Rinse and dry the chopping board, slide the frittata onto the chopping board, cut into neat wedges and serve straightaway.

Bubble and squeak

Serves   6 at home or 12 tastes in the classroom
Fresh from the garden   onions, cabbages, potatoes

This is a good example of how to make something really delicious from simple ingredients, including leftovers from the day before. Bubble and squeak used to be served in old-style cafes with fried eggs, much as we might see hash browns today. Although not strictly authentic, small quantities of other leftover cooked vegetables, such as carrots or pumpkin, could also be added, as could chopped parsley.

Equipment

chopping board	wooden spoon
knives – 1 small, l large	tea towel
peeler	metric measuring spoons
large saucepan	non-stick 24 cm frying pan
colander	egg lifter
medium bowl	serving plate

Ingredients

3 large potatoes
salt
1 onion
250 g cabbage (about ¼ whole cabbage)
2 tablespoons extra-virgin olive oil
freshly ground black pepper

What to do

✳ Set out the chopping board and knives. Peel the potatoes and chop each one into bite-sized pieces. Place the peel in the compost bucket and the potato in the saucepan. Cover with cold water, add a pinch of salt, then bring to the boil. Cook for 10–15 minutes or until tender.

✳ Meanwhile, peel the onion, then use the large knife to cut it in half from top to bottom. Place the onion halves flat side down on the chopping board and thinly slice into half-rings.

✳ Set the colander in the sink. **Tip the potato and boiling water into the colander.** Give the colander a good shake then transfer the potatoes to the bowl.

✳ Rinse out the saucepan, fill it with water and add a pinch of salt, then bring to the boil. Cut the cabbage into chunks, then cut away the thick stem and place it in the compost bucket. Slice each chunk of cabbage into 2 cm slices. **Carefully drop the cabbage slices into the saucepan of boiling water, stir with the wooden spoon and wait until the water returns to the boil.**

✳ Set the colander in the sink. **Tip the cabbage and boiling water into the colander**. Give the colander a good shake, then rinse the cabbage with cold water to cool it. Tip the drained cabbage into the tea towel, then squeeze the tea towel over the sink to get rid of the excess liquid. **An easy way to do this is to ask someone to twist the tea towel at one end, while you twist the other end in the opposite direction – this will squeeze the water out.**

✳ Put 1 tablespoon of the oil into the frying pan and heat over a medium heat. Add the sliced onion and fry, stirring frequently with the wooden spoon, for 6–7 minutes or until the onion is golden brown. Shake the cabbage from the tea towel into the pan and stir to combine with the onion.

✳ Add the potato and mix together. Sprinkle with salt and season with a little pepper. Continue frying over a low-to-medium heat for another 15 minutes, stirring several times with the egg lifter and turning the vegetables a bit so that most of them get a little brown.

✳ Once everything is looking golden, press down on the vegetables in the pan so that a nice golden crust forms on the bottom. Carefully tip the vegetables onto the plate and serve immediately.

BOTTOM DRAWER

Interesting technique
• squeezing liquid from an ingredient using a cloth
Tip   You could also flip the bubble and squeak onto a large dinner plate, and then return it to the pan with the top side facing down, to crisp the second side (you'll need an adult around to help with this).

Silver beet in cheesy sauce

Serves   6 at home or 12 tastes in the classroom
Fresh from the garden   silver beet
This recipe uses the stems from the silver beet, which
are often ignored, as well as the leaves.

Equipment

food processor
chopping board
large knife
salad spinner
saucepans – 1 small,
   1 medium
metric measuring spoons
   and cups
colander

tea towel
scales
grater
bowls – 1 small, 1 medium
pastry brush
ovenproof dish
wooden spoon
heatproof board or mat

Ingredients

2 slices sourdough bread
8 stems silver beet
1 teaspoon salt

Sauce
50 g cheddar
25 g blue cheese
1 cup milk

1 tablespoon butter,
   plus extra
2 tablespoons plain
   (all-purpose) flour
salt
freshly ground black pepper
1 whole nutmeg
2 tablespoons cream

What to do

✱ Remove the crusts from the bread (place crusts in the compost
bucket). Put the bread into the bowl of the food processor, then
run the motor to make coarse breadcrumbs. Set aside.

✱ Set out the chopping board and knife. Separate the silverbeet
leaves from their stems by slicing along each side of the thick central
stem. Rinse the silverbeet leaves and dry in the salad spinner. Roll the
leaves into a loose bunch, then shred with the large knife. Slice the
stems lengthways into 2–3 long strips, then slice into 5 mm pieces.

✱ Fill the medium saucepan with water, add the salt and bring to the
boil. Drop the stems into the boiling water and cook for 3 minutes,
then add the leaves and continue cooking for another 3 minutes.

 ✱ Set the colander in the sink. **Tip the silver beet and boiling water
into the colander.** Tip the drained silver beet into the tea towel, then
squeeze the tea towel over the sink to get rid of the excess liquid.

✱ Preheat the oven to 180°C. To make the sauce, weigh the cheddar
and blue cheese, then grate the cheeses into the small bowl. Place the
milk in the small saucepan and heat to scalding point, then set aside.

✱ Wipe out the medium saucepan. Melt the 1 tablespoon of butter
in the saucepan over a medium heat. Using the pastry brush, brush
the bottom and sides of the ovenproof dish with the butter.

✱ Return the saucepan of melted butter to the medium heat. When
the butter starts to froth add all the flour. Stir well with the wooden
spoon for a minute. This is called making a roux. Gradually add the
hot milk, stirring all the time to prevent lumps. Continue stirring until
the sauce comes to the boil. Drop the cheeses into the sauce, remove
from the heat, and stir until the cheeses have melted. Season the sauce
with salt, pepper and a little freshly grated nutmeg. Add the silverbeet
leaves and stems, and the cream, and stir to combine.

✱ Spoon the mixture into the buttered ovenproof dish. Scatter with
the breadcrumbs and add a few dots of the extra butter. Bake for
15 minutes or until the top is golden and bubbling.

✱ **Remove from the oven.** Place the heatproof board or mat
on the table and serve the silver beet in its ovenproof dish.

BOTTOM DRAWER

Interesting terms/techniques   •   stemming and shredding
leaves   •   making a roux   •   grating fresh nutmeg
Taste tip   White sauce (also called béchamel sauce) becomes
mornay sauce when cheese is added. You could also use
this mornay sauce to cover and bake with either pasta or cooked
broccoli or cauliflower, or spread it as a layer in your own lasagne.

French toast with caramelised pear and cinnamon sugar

Serves   6 at home or 12 tastes in the classroom
Fresh from the garden   pears, eggs

French toast makes a very special breakfast and should be cooked long enough for the bread to become very crisp around the edges.

Equipment

baking tray
chopping board
knives – 1 small, 1 serrated
peeler
melon baller (parisienne
     spoon) or teaspoon
metric measuring spoons
     and cups
medium saucepan

wooden spoon
bowls – 1 small, 1 medium
whisk
shallow rectangular dish
egg lifter
scales
frying pans – 1 small, 1 large
6–12 dessert plates

Ingredients

Caramelised pears
2 ripe pears
½ cup sugar   *110 g*
1 cup water   *225 ml*

Cinnamon sugar
1 tablespoon castor
     (superfine) sugar
1 teaspoon ground
     cinnamon

French toast
½ cup pouring cream   *120 ml*
½ cup milk   *R0ml*
2 eggs
3 drops vanilla extract
½ teaspoon ground
     cinnamon
a pinch of ground nutmeg
raisin bread or fruit loaf
80 g butter

What to do

✳ Preheat the oven to 120°C and place the baking tray in the oven to keep warm. Set out the chopping board, knives and peeler. Peel the pears, then cut in half lengthways. Use the melon baller (parisienne spoon) or teaspoon to scoop out the core and seeds, then place the core and seeds in the compost bucket. Cut the pears into bite-sized pieces.

✳ Place the sugar and water in the saucepan and bring to the boil over a medium heat, stirring constantly with the wooden spoon until the sugar completely dissolves. Drop the chopped pears into the syrup and simmer, covered, over a low heat for 10 minutes or until the pears are tender. Remove from the heat and set aside.

✳ To make the cinnamon sugar, place the sugar and cinnamon in the small bowl and stir to combine. Set aside until needed.

✳ To make the French toast, place the cream, milk, eggs, vanilla, cinnamon and nutmeg in the medium bowl and whisk until well combined. Pour the egg mixture into the shallow rectangular dish.

✳ **Use the serrated knife to cut 6 thick slices of raisin bread or fruit loaf.** Place the bread slices in the egg mixture and leave them to soak for 2–3 minutes. Turn and soak the other sides for another 2–3 minutes or until the bread is very moist.

✳ Weigh the butter and heat half in the large frying pan over a medium heat until it foams. Place as many slices of the soaked bread into the foaming butter as will easily fit into the pan. Fry for 3–4 minutes. Turn over and fry for another 3 minutes or until golden brown. Lift the bread slices onto the warmed baking tray, then return to the oven to keep warm. Heat the remaining butter in the frying pan until foaming, then repeat the procedure with the remaining slices of bread. This is called working in batches.

✳ While the French toast is in the oven, tip the chopped pears and syrup into the small frying pan and cook over a high heat, stirring with the wooden spoon until nearly all the syrup disappears.

✳ To serve, place a piece of French toast on each plate, add a spoonful of the caramelised pears, then sprinkle with cinnamon sugar.

BOTTOM DRAWER

Interesting term • working in batches
Taste tip   You can poach other firm fruits like apples, peaches, nectarines or plums in this same light syrup, then serve them with yoghurt or cream for a sweet treat, or even for breakfast with porridge or muesli.

Menu 26

Celery and walnut raita

Indian vegetable
curry from Goa

Red lentil dhal

Green coconut chutney

Celery and walnut raita

Whisk 1 cup of plain yoghurt in a bowl until smooth. Chop the leaves of 10 stems of coriander (cilantro), and add two-thirds to the yoghurt. Chop 4 celery sticks and a small handful of walnuts, and add to the yoghurt. Add salt and pepper, the juice of ½ lemon and a good pinch of ground cumin. Decorate with the remaining coriander, and serve with curry.

Indian vegetable curry from Goa

Serves 6 at home or 12 tastes in the classroom
Fresh from the garden onions, carrots, potatoes, purple potatoes, green beans, lemons
This dish was very popular. The purple potatoes were new to most students. The quantities can easily be doubled and the amount of chilli can be increased.

Equipment

chopping board
knives – 1 small, 1 large
food processor
metric measuring spoons
    and cups
bowls – 1 small, 2 large

heavy-based frying pan
    or cast-iron casserole
    with lid
wooden spoon
peeler
lemon juicer
heatproof board or mat

Ingredients

1 onion
2 carrots
2 medium potatoes
1 sweet potato
1 purple potato
12 green beans
2 tablespoons vegetable oil
½ teaspoon chilli flakes
1 teaspoon ground turmeric
1 × 400 g can chopped
    tomatoes
salt
1 lemon

Spice paste
1 onion
2 tablespoons
    coriander seeds
1 teaspoon cumin seeds
4 whole cloves
10 peppercorns
1 × 5 cm piece
    cinnamon stick
1 tablespoon vegetable oil
1 teaspoon mustard seeds
½ cup desiccated coconut
½ cup water

What to do

✳ First make the spice paste. Set out the chopping board and knives. Peel and halve the onion from top to bottom, then place the halves cut side down on the chopping board and thinly slice into half-rings. Put the onion into the bowl of the food processor.

✳ Place the coriander seeds and cumin seeds in the small bowl along with the cloves and peppercorns. Crumble in the cinnamon stick. Heat the oil in the frying pan or casserole over a low-to-medium heat. Add the spice mix and cook, stirring with the wooden spoon, for 3 minutes or until fragrant. Tip the contents of the pan into the bowl of the food processor. Add the mustard seeds, desiccated coconut and water, then run the motor to make a coarse paste.

✳ Peel and finely chop the second onion and place in the small bowl used to hold the spice mix. Peel the carrots and potatoes, then cut each vegetable into 2 cm cubes. Place the carrot and regular potato in one large bowl and the sweet potato and purple potato in the other large bowl. Trim the ends from the beans, then cut the beans into 4 cm pieces. Place all vegetable scraps in the compost bucket.

✳ Heat the oil in the frying pan over a medium heat. Add the chopped onion and stir for a few minutes or until it starts to brown. Stir in the chilli flakes and turmeric, then tip in the spice paste from the food processor and cook for 5 minutes.

✳ Tip the can of chopped tomatoes into the pan and bring to the boil over a high heat. Add the carrot and regular potato and stir to combine, then cook for 5 minutes. Add the sweet potato and purple potato, cover with the lid and cook for 10 more minutes. Add the green beans and taste for salt. Cover again, then reduce the heat to low and cook for 10 minutes or until all the vegetables are tender.

✳ If there is too much sauce, remove the lid and boil over a high heat for 3–4 minutes or until the sauce reduces. If there is not enough sauce, add a few tablespoons of water and stir to combine.

✳ Juice the lemon, then stir the juice into the curry. Place the board or mat on the table and serve the curry in its cooking pot at the table.

BOTTOM DRAWER

Interesting technique • toasting spices
Question Do you know where Goa is?
Answer Goa is a city on the south-west coast of India, fronted by the Arabian Sea. It is famous for its many beaches, tropical climate and spicy, seafood-rich cuisine.

Red lentil dhal

Makes   about 1 cup
Fresh from the garden   garlic, chillies, coriander
Dhal is a dish of dried legumes cooked to a soft purée, and served alongside curries, often with flatbread for scooping. The various types of lentils or dried peas used to make dhal have been split so they will collapse when cooked.

Equipment

bowls – 2 small, 1 large
chopping board
knives – 1 small, 1 large
disposable gloves
sieve
medium saucepan
metric measuring cups
  and jug
wooden spoon
tea towel
serving bowl
small non-stick frying pan

Ingredients

200 g split red lentils
10 stems coriander (cilantro)
2 cloves garlic
1 × 5 cm piece fresh ginger
1 long green chilli
½ teaspoon ground turmeric
salt
2 tablespoons butter
1 teaspoon black mustard seeds

What to do

✶ Tip the lentils into the large bowl, cover with water and leave to soak for 5 minutes. Soak the coriander in a small bowl of water.

✶ Meanwhile, set out the chopping board and knives. Peel and finely chop the garlic and place in a small bowl. Peel and finely chop the ginger and add to the garlic bowl. Slip on the disposable gloves and cut the chilli in half lengthways. Scrape the seeds into the rubbish bin. Slice the chilli finely and add to the bowl with the garlic and ginger. Discard the gloves. Rinse and dry the chopping board and knife.

✶ Set the sieve in the sink, then tip in the lentils and soaking water. Transfer the strained lentils to the saucepan and add 3 cups of water, the garlic, ginger and chilli, the turmeric and a pinch of salt. Bring to the boil over a high heat, then reduce the heat to low and cook the lentils, stirring from time to time, for 20–30 minutes or until the lentils are quite soft.

✶ Meanwhile, lift the coriander from its soaking water and dry by rolling in the tea towel. Chop the coriander and stir into the dhal. Tip the dhal into the serving bowl.

✶ Heat the butter and mustard seeds in the small frying pan over a medium heat for 1 minute or until the butter turns golden and the mustard seeds start to pop. Quickly spoon the butter mixture over the bowl of dhal and serve.

BOTTOM DRAWER

Did you know?   Black mustard seeds are the hottest of all seeds, and the ones used in Indian cooking. White mustard seeds are actually a brownish-yellow, and are used to make yellow mustard.
Question   Why do you cook the mustard seeds until they pop?
Answer   Because when they burst open or 'pop', they release their nutty flavour, reducing the heat of the seeds and adding flavour to the oil or butter used for the frying.

Green coconut chutney

Makes about 1 cup
Fresh from the garden coriander, mint, garlic, chillies, lemons
If red chillies are used instead of green, the coconut chutney will
be a warm pinky-red.

Equipment

small bowl   disposable gloves
tea towel   metric measuring spoons
chopping board   and cups
large knife   tablespoon
food processor   small serving bowl

Ingredients

5–6 stems coriander (cilantro)
10 mint leaves
1 × 5 cm piece fresh ginger
2 cloves garlic
½ long green chilli
½ cup desiccated coconut
1 teaspoon salt
1 teaspoon ground cumin
1 tablespoon lemon juice or lime juice

What to do

✱ Soak the coriander in a small bowl of water. Rinse the mint leaves.
Lift the coriander from its soaking water. Dry the mint and coriander
by rolling in the tea towel. Set out the chopping board and knife.
Chop the herbs and place in the bowl of the food processor.

✱ Peel and chop the garlic and ginger and add to the bowl of the
food processor. Slip on the disposable gloves and cut the chilli in half
lengthways. Scrape the seeds into the rubbish bin. Slice half of the
chilli and add to the bowl of the food processor. Discard the gloves.

✱ Add the desiccated coconut, salt and cumin, then run the motor
to make a paste. Spoon the chutney into the serving bowl and taste,
then stir in the lemon or lime juice and more salt if needed. Serve
alongside a curry.

BOTTOM DRAWER

Did you know? Chutney is originally an Indian word, as the
Indians were the first to make chutney, or *chatni* as they call it.
Question Can you think of other uses for this fresh chutney?
Answer This spicy, refreshing chutney is also delicious served with
barbecued fish or grilled lamb, as well as when used in its more traditional
place as an accompaniment for rice and curries.

Menu 27

Minestrone with
parmesan

Spanakotiropitakia

Banana and pear
smoothies

Minestrone with parmesan

Serves 8 at home or 16 tastes in the classroom
Fresh from the garden onions, garlic, carrots, celery, cabbages, green beans, zucchini

In the classroom, we cooked beans for the class ahead, so each class started this dish with soaked, cooked beans. For a cheat's version use drained, rinsed, canned red kidney beans – you will need 2 × 400 g cans. The chicken stock was also prepared ahead of time.
If it's available, Tuscan kale is the best cabbage to use for this recipe.

Equipment

bowls – 1 medium, 1 large
colander
saucepans – 1 large,
   1 stockpot
chopping board
knives – 1 small, 1 large
peeler

metric measuring spoons
   and cups
wooden spoon
grater
small serving bowl
ladle
8–16 soup bowls

Ingredients

200 g dried borlotti beans,
   soaked overnight
2 onions
3 cloves garlic
2 large carrots
2 sticks celery
¼ cup extra-virgin olive oil,
   plus extra to serve
1 tablespoon butter
1 × 400 g can chopped
   tomatoes

2 litres Chicken Stock (page
   79) or water
1 bay leaf
4 cabbage leaves
150 g green beans
2 zucchini (courgettes)
salt
freshly ground
   black pepper
160 g parmesan

What to do

✳ Place the beans in the large bowl, cover with water and soak overnight.

✳ Set the colander in the sink. Tip the borlotti beans and soaking water into the colander and rinse with cold running water. Rinse and dry the bowl. Place the beans in the large saucepan, then add enough cold water to cover the beans with 8 cm of water. Bring to the boil, cover, then reduce the heat and simmer for at least 1 hour or until the beans are tender. Remove the saucepan from the heat and leave the cooked beans to cool in the cooking water.

✳ Meanwhile, set out the chopping board and knives. Peel and dice the onions and place in the medium bowl. Peel and finely chop the garlic and add to the onion. Peel and dice the carrots, then place in the bowl used previously for soaking beans. Slice the celery and add to the carrot. Put all vegetable scraps in the compost bucket.

 ✳ Set the colander in the sink. **Tip the borlotti beans and cooking water into the colander.**

✳ Heat the oil and butter in the stockpot over a medium-to-high heat and, when the butter foams, tip in the onion and garlic. Stir with the wooden spoon for 2 minutes, then add the carrot and celery, and stir well. Add the drained borlotti beans, chopped tomatoes, chicken stock (or water) and bay leaf, cover with the lid and bring to the boil. Reduce the heat and simmer for 30 minutes.

✳ Meanwhile, cut away the central stalks from the cabbage, then shred the cabbage leaves and place in the previously used large bowl. Trim the ends of the green beans, then chop the beans into 2 cm pieces and add to the cabbage. Cut the zucchini into 1 cm dice and add to the cabbage. Place all vegetable scraps in the compost bucket.

✳ Lift the lid of the stockpot and tip in the cabbage, beans and zucchini. Give the soup a big stir, then replace the lid and cook for another 10 minutes. Taste the soup and add salt and pepper. Shave the parmesan and place in the small serving bowl.

✳ To serve, ladle the soup into the serving bowls, top each bowl with a bit of parmesan and drizzle with olive oil.

Spanakotiropitakia

Makes 15 triangles

Fresh from the garden silver beet, spring onions, mint, parsley, onions, eggs

My Greek friend says that 'spanakotiropitakia' is the name for pastries made with both spinach and cheese, like these.

Equipment

chopping board	colander
knives – 1 small, 1 large	tablespoon
salad spinner	fork
bowls – 1 medium, 1 large	grater
tea towel	aluminium foil
scales	pastry brush
small saucepan	2 baking trays
metric measuring spoons	baking paper
small frying pan	serving plate
wooden spoon	

Ingredients

8 stems silver beet	1 egg
2 spring onions (scallions)	100 g fetta
10 mint leaves	100 g ricotta
6 stalks parsley	50 g pecorino or parmesan
60 g butter	1 whole nutmeg
1 small onion	salt
1 tablespoon extra-virgin olive oil	freshly ground black pepper
	5 sheets filo pastry

What to do

✳ Preheat the oven to 180°C. Set out the chopping board and knives. Separate the silverbeet leaves from their stems by slicing along each side of the stem. Rinse the leaves and dry in the salad spinner. Roll the leaves into a loose bunch, then shred with the large knife. Slice the stems lengthways into 2 or 3 pieces, then cut into thin slices. Put the leaves and stems into the medium bowl.

✳ Trim the outside layer from the spring onions and cut off the tops and ends, then slice the rest. Rinse the mint and parsley, dry by rolling in the tea towel and chop. Add the herbs and onions to the silver beet.

✳ Melt the butter in the small saucepan and set aside. Peel and chop the onion. Heat the oil in the frying pan over a high heat and gently sauté the onion, stirring with the wooden spoon, for 2–3 minutes or until well-softened. Add the silver beet and herbs, stir to mix well, then cook for 5 minutes or until there is no liquid in the bottom of the pan. Set the colander in the sink. **Tip the silver beet and onion into the colander and press with the back of the tablespoon.** Leave to drain for 5–6 minutes.

✳ Meanwhile, break the egg into the large bowl and mix with the fork. Crumble in the fetta and ricotta. Grate the pecorino or parmesan and add to the egg bowl, along with the cooled silverbeet mixture. Stir, then grate in some nutmeg and add salt and pepper.

✳ Unwrap the packet of filo pastry. Take the damp tea towel (used previously to dry the herbs) and line it with aluminium foil. The lined tea towel should be rested over the roll of filo, with the foil side touching the pastry sheets, whenever you are not using the pastry.

✳ Place 1 sheet of filo pastry on the workbench with the shortest side facing you. **Using a sharp knife, cut the pastry lengthways into 3 even-sized long strips. Brush with melted butter. Place a heaped teaspoonful of filling in the top right-hand corner of the first strip. Fold the pastry over the filling to form a triangle shape, then keep folding over to enclose the filling and form a neat triangle.**

✳ Repeat this process with the remaining strips of pastry and filling. You should now have 15 cheese-and-silverbeet triangles. Brush the outside of each triangle with melted butter. Return the unused portion of filo to the box and refrigerate or freeze.

✳ Line the baking trays with sheets of baking paper, then divide the triangles between trays. Bake for 20 minutes or until golden brown.

✳ **Remove the triangles from the oven.** Place on the serving plate and serve warm or at room temperature.

BOTTOM DRAWER

Interesting terms/techniques • grating fresh nutmeg
• stemming and shredding leaves

Banana and pear smoothies

Makes 3–4 drinks

Fresh from the garden pears, lemons, oranges

A smoothie is the perfect speedy breakfast. Vary the fruit or the fruit juice as you like. At Collingwood, we made smoothies at other times with our garden-grown cantaloupes and strawberries. Soy milk can be substituted for yoghurt if you prefer.

Equipment

chopping board
knives – 1 small, 1 large
peeler
melon baller (parisienne
   spoon) or teaspoon
baking tray

lemon juicer
metric measuring spoons
   and cups
blender
jug to serve

Ingredients

2 ripe pears
1 lemon
1 orange
2 ripe bananas
1 cup plain yoghurt
1 teaspoon ground cinnamon

What to do

✱ Set out the chopping board, knives and peeler. Peel the pears, then cut in half lengthways. Use the melon baller (parisienne spoon) or teaspoon to scoop out the core and seeds, and place the core and seeds in the compost bucket.

✱ Cut the pear halves into chunks, then lay them in a single layer on the baking tray. Place in the freezer for at least 20 minutes.

✱ Juice the lemon and orange. Peel and chop the bananas. Place the bananas, pear, lemon juice, orange juice, yoghurt and cinnamon in the jug of the blender and blend until smooth. If the smoothie is too thick, add a little milk or extra orange juice.

✱ Pour into the serving jug and serve at the table.

Cauliflower and broccoli salad

Serves 6 at home or 12 tastes in the classroom

Fresh from the garden broccoli, cauliflowers, lemons, chives, parsley

Many of the students told us that this was the first time they had enjoyed broccoli. When cooked with plenty of water and no lid, broccoli cooks very quickly and remains bright green and a little firm, which is how it tastes best.

Equipment

large saucepan	lemon juicer
metric measuring spoons	kitchen paper
chopping board	tea towel
knives – 1 small, 1 large	colander
peeler	slotted spoon
bowls – 1 small, 2 medium	

Ingredients

1 teaspoon salt
1 large head broccoli
¼ cauliflower
½ lemon
10 button mushrooms
6 chives
10 stalks parsley
2 tablespoons extra-virgin olive oil
freshly ground black pepper

BOTTOM DRAWER

Did you know? Broccoli and cauliflower belong to the cabbage family, and have quite a similar structure – heads that are made up of clusters of flowers, and which sit at the end of short, fat stalks. Many recipes call for broccoli and cauliflower to be divided into 'florets', as is done here.

What to do

✷ Fill the saucepan with plenty of water, add the salt and bring to the boil.

✷ Meanwhile, set out the chopping board and knives. Trim the broccoli and the cauliflower florets into very small bite-sized pieces. Peel the broccoli stalk and cut into 3 mm thick slices. Place the broccoli in one medium bowl, and the cauliflower in the other.

✷ Juice the lemon. Wipe the tops of the button mushrooms with a damp piece of kitchen paper. Slice the mushrooms finely and put into the small bowl. Drizzle with the lemon juice. Rinse the chives and parsley leaves and dry by rolling in the tea towel. Chop the parsley and chives, add to the mushroom bowl and stir to mix.

✷ Drop the broccoli into the boiling water and boil, uncovered, for 3 minutes. Place the colander in the sink. **Using the slotted spoon, scoop the broccoli from the water and place in the colander.** Give the colander a really good shake, then return the broccoli to its bowl. Drizzle the broccoli with half of the oil.

✷ Once the water is boiling strongly again, drop in the cauliflower and boil, uncovered, for 3 minutes. Place the colander in the sink. **Tip the water and cauliflower into the colander.** Give the colander a really good shake, then tip the cauliflower into the broccoli bowl. Add the mushroom mixture and salt and pepper and drizzle with the rest of the oil. Mix gently but very well so that the salad is a pretty mix of green and white with the mushroom slices evenly distributed.

Silver beet braised with pine nuts and currants

Serves 6 at home or 12 tastes in the classroom
Fresh from the garden silver beet, onions, garlic
This combination of flavours is very Sicilian. Serve this dish
on its own or, for a change, toss it through spaghetti and serve
with pan-fried sardines.

Equipment

ovenproof serving dish
salad spinner
chopping board
knives – 1 small, 1 large
bowls – 1 small, 2 medium
plate

kitchen paper
metric measuring spoons
    and cups
large frying pan with lid
wooden spoon
slotted spoon

Ingredients

12 stems silver beet
1 onion
2 cloves garlic
⅓ cup extra-virgin olive oil
⅓ cup pine nuts
⅓ cup currants
salt
freshly ground black pepper

BOTTOM DRAWER

Interesting techniques • stemming and shredding leaves
• toasting nuts
Did you know? Pine nuts are not really nuts; they are the
edible seeds of certain pine trees, known as stone pines,
and are contained in their pine cones.

What to do

✱ Preheat the oven to 120°C and place the ovenproof dish
in the oven to keep warm.

✱ Rinse the silverbeet leaves and dry very gently in the salad spinner.
Set out the chopping board and knives. Separate the silverbeet leaves
from their stems by slicing along each side of the thick central stem.
Roll the leaves into a loose bunch, shred with the large knife, then
place in one of the medium bowls. Cut the stems lengthways into
3 long pieces, then cut widthways into thin slices and place in the
other medium bowl.

✱ Peel and finely chop the onion and place in the small bowl.
Peel and finely chop the garlic and place in the onion bowl. Put all
vegetable scraps into the compost bucket.

✱ Line the plate with kitchen paper. Place 1 tablespoon of the oil
in the frying pan over a medium heat, then add the pine nuts and fry,
stirring with the wooden spoon, for a couple of minutes until golden.
Scoop the pine nuts from the pan using the slotted spoon and
transfer to the paper-lined plate.

✱ Heat another tablespoon of the oil in the frying pan over a
medium-to-high heat and cook the onion and garlic for 2–3 minutes,
stirring with the wooden spoon. Add the silverbeet stems and turn to
coat with the oil. Reduce the heat to low, cover with the lid and cook
for 5 minutes.

✱ Remove the lid, add the rest of the oil, then increase the heat to
high and add the silverbeet leaves. Stir to mix well, then cover and
cook for another 2–3 minutes. Add the pine nuts and currants and
cook uncovered, stirring to prevent sticking, for 3 minutes or until
the silverbeet leaves and stems are tender. Taste for salt and pepper.

✱ To serve, remove the ovenproof dish from the oven and tip
the silver beet into the dish.

Barbecued bananas with butterscotch sauce

Serves   6 at home or 12 tastes in the classroom

This very simple dessert amazed the students because of the way the banana skins blackened so quickly as the bananas cooked, but inside their skins, the bananas baked beautifully.

Equipment

barbecue or chargrill pan	wooden spoon
electric jug	small jug
metric measuring spoons and cups	chopping board
	small knife
small saucepan	tongs
metal spoon	6–12 dessert plates

Ingredients

¾ cup sugar

2½ tablespoons unsalted butter

¾ cup brown sugar

few drops pure vanilla extract

⅓ cup cream

6 bananas

What to do

 ✳ Heat the barbecue or chargrill pan to very hot. **Boil the electric jug, then measure out ¼ cup water.** Place the sugar in the small saucepan over a medium heat and stir with the metal spoon.

Allow the sugar to melt, then to turn a golden caramel colour, which will take about 5 minutes. **Carefully pour the hot water over the sugar, standing back from the stove as the caramel will sizzle and boil up.** Stir with the wooden spoon until you have a smooth syrup.

✳ Add the butter and brown sugar and stir until the brown sugar has completely dissolved. Add the vanilla extract and cream and stir to combine. Pour the sauce into the jug and set aside until needed.

✳ Set out the chopping board and knife. Cut a slit down the side of each banana skin (try not to dig into the flesh). Place the bananas on the hot barbecue or chargrill plate and cook for 6 minutes. Use the tongs to turn the bananas over and cook the other side for 6 minutes. During cooking, the bananas' skins will become completely black and their flesh will soften and become very hot.

✳ To serve, lift the bananas onto the serving plates, then gently peel back their skins and pour over a little butterscotch sauce.

> **BOTTOM DRAWER**
>
> **Tip**   For a banana sundae with a twist, serve the barbecued bananas and butterscotch sauce with scoops of vanilla ice cream and sprinkled with chopped pecans or almonds (if no one has nut allergies).
>
> **Did you know?**   While butterscotch contains butter, it has nothing to do with Scotland. To 'scotch' means to score or cut something. When butterscotch lollies were originally made, the caramel was poured out to cool, then cut or scotched so it would be easier to break into pieces later.

Menu 29

Vietnamese chicken
and cabbage salad

Stir-fried broccoli with
Chinese sausage and
oyster sauce

Baby beetroot and
blood-orange salad

Vietnamese chicken and cabbage salad

Serves   6 at home or 12 tastes in the classroom
Fresh from the garden   spring onions, garlic, chillies, limes, carrots, daikon, cabbages, mint, coriander
This delicious salad can be made up to an hour before you wish to eat it and kept refrigerated, but if made too far in advance the cabbage and daikon will lose their crunchy texture. On another day you could use prawns or poached fish instead of chicken.

Equipment

chopping board
knives – 1 small, 1 large
medium saucepan with lid
ladle
tongs
plate
plastic film
bowls – 1 small, 1 large
disposable gloves
lemon juicer

metric measuring spoons
   and cups
peeler
food processor with
   shredding disc or
   vegetable-slicing gadget
tea towel
large metal spoon
6–12 serving bowls

Ingredients

Poached chicken fillets
2 spring onions (scallions)
1 × 2 cm piece fresh ginger
2 skinless chicken breast
   fillets

Dressing
3 cloves garlic
1 long red chilli
¼ cup lime juice
1 tablespoon rice vinegar

⅓ cup fish sauce
¼ cup vegetable oil
2 tablespoons sugar

Cabbage salad
1 carrot
1 daikon (Chinese radish)
½ cabbage
1 small red onion
20 mint leaves
12 stems coriander (cilantro)

What to do

✱ Set out the chopping board and knives. Trim the outside layer from the spring onions and cut off the tops and ends, then cut the rest into 4 pieces. Peel and slice the ginger. Fill the saucepan with water, add the spring onions and ginger, then bring to a simmering point over

 a high heat. **Carefully slip the chicken breasts into the saucepan and allow the water to return to a simmering point, then use the ladle to skim off and discard any froth that rises to the top.** Cover
 with the lid, reduce the heat and simmer for 10 minutes. **Remove the saucepan from the heat and leave the chicken to cool in the liquid for 5 minutes.** Do not lift the lid during this time. Use the tongs to transfer the chicken breasts to the plate. Cover with plastic film and refrigerate until needed.

 ✱ Now make the dressing. Peel the garlic. **Place the cloves on the chopping board and flatten with the side of the large knife.** Finely chop the garlic and place in the large bowl.

✱ Slip on the disposable gloves and slit the chilli in half lengthways. Scrape the seeds into the rubbish bin. Slice the chilli as finely as you can and place in the garlic bowl. Discard the gloves. Wash and dry the chopping board and knife. Juice the lime. Add the lime juice, rice vinegar, fish sauce, oil and sugar to the garlic bowl, and stir.

✱ Make the cabbage salad. Soak the coriander in a small bowl of
 water. Peel the carrot and daikon. **Using the food processor or the vegetable-slicing gadget, shred the carrot and daikon** and add to the dressing bowl. Cut away the thick stalk from the cabbage, then cut the cabbage into 2 or 3 pieces. Using the large knife, shred the cabbage and add to the dressing bowl. Peel the red onion and cut it in half lengthways, then place the flat sides on the chopping board and slice each half into fine rings. Add to the dressing bowl. Place all vegetable scraps in the compost bucket.

✱ **Using your fingers, shred the cooked chicken breasts.** Add the chicken to the bowl with the dressing and vegetables.

✱ Lift the coriander from its soaking water. Rinse the mint. Dry the herbs by rolling in the tea towel. Set aside 6–12 leaves to use as a garnish, then roughly chop the rest and add to the bowl.

✱ Use a large spoon to mix all the ingredients together, then spoon into serving bowls and top with the reserved coriander or mint.

BOTTOM DRAWER

Tip   The dressing for the cabbage can be used on cabbage alone.
Did you know?   Daikon is a large Asian radish with juicy, crisp white flesh.

Stir-fried broccoli with Chinese sausage and oyster sauce

Serves 4 at home or 8–10 tastes in the classroom

Fresh from the garden broccoli, garlic

Chinese sausages are sold in Asian supermarkets, several to a packet, and are dried. They are very aromatic and are often used in the manner described in this recipe – steamed in order to make them plump, then sliced and stir-fried with other ingredients. They are very good in fried rice.

Equipment

wok	kitchen paper
1 × 16 cm bamboo steamer basket with lid	metric measuring spoons and cups
chopping board	wok sang or
knives – 1 small, 1 large	large slotted spoon
peeler	serving plate
bowls – 1 small, 1 large	

Ingredients

1 Chinese sausage (lap cheong)

500 g broccoli, or assortment of broccoli, Chinese broccoli (gai laan) and broccolini

2 cloves garlic

1 × 2 cm piece fresh ginger

2 tablespoons vegetable oil

1 teaspoon sugar

¼ cup water

few drops sesame oil

¼ cup oyster sauce

What to do

✳ Place the wok over a high heat and pour in enough hot water to come one-third of the way up the sides. Rest the bamboo steamer on top, and put the Chinese sausage into the steamer.

✳ Meanwhile, set out the chopping board and knives. Cut the broccoli florets off the stems, then peel the stems and cut into 1 cm rounds. Place the florets and stems in the large bowl. If using Chinese broccoli, trim off any yellow leaves and 1 cm from the base of the stems, then cut the remaining stems and leaves into 6 cm lengths and add to the bowl. If using broccolini, trim 1 cm from the base of each stem, then cut the broccolini into 6 cm lengths and add to the bowl. Place any scraps in the compost bucket.

✳ Peel the garlic. **Place the cloves on the chopping board and flatten with the side of the large knife.** Finely chop the garlic and place it in the small bowl. Peel and slice the ginger and add to the garlic. Wash and dry the chopping board.

✳ **Remove the wok from the heat and the basket from the wok.** Take the sausage out of the steamer basket and cut it diagonally into thin slices. **Tip out the hot water from the wok.** Wipe the wok dry with kitchen paper.

✳ Place the dry wok over a high heat and add the vegetable oil. When the oil is hot, tip in the garlic, ginger and sliced sausage. Use the wok sang or slotted spoon to toss the ingredients for 30 seconds, then scatter in the sugar. Add all the broccoli to the wok and toss with the wok sang until the broccoli is shiny.

✳ Tip the ¼ cup water into the wok, then quickly stir and cover with the lid. Reduce the heat to medium and cook for about 3 minutes. Remove the lid and add the sesame oil.

✳ Scoop the broccoli and sausage onto the serving plate, then drizzle with the oyster sauce and serve immediately.

BOTTOM DRAWER

Interesting terms and techniques • steaming with a bamboo basket and wok • flattening garlic with a knife • stir-frying

Something to think about Have you tasted the three different varieties of broccoli before? Do they taste very different?

Question What is broccolini?

Answer Broccolini is actually a cross between normal broccoli and Chinese broccoli (called gai laan). All parts are edible.

Baby beetroot and blood-orange salad

Serves 6 at home or 12 tastes in the classroom

Fresh from the garden beetroots, rocket, red onions, chives

Blood oranges have a short season so look out for them. I think they taste like orange with a touch of cherry. Balsamic vinegar is a highly specialised product that comes from Northern Italy. It is made by maturing vinegar in wooden barrels, often for several years.

Equipment

medium saucepan	kitchen paper
chopping board	colander
knives – 1 small, 1 large	disposable gloves
skewer	bowls – 2 small, 1 medium
salad spinner	metric measuring spoons
2 tea towels	shallow serving bowl

Ingredients

salt	3 blood oranges
15 small beetroots	2 tablespoons extra-virgin
1 handful rocket (arugula)	olive oil
leaves	1 teaspoon balsamic vinegar
½ small red onion	freshly ground black pepper
10 chives	

What to do

✱ Fill the saucepan with water, add a pinch of salt and bring to the boil. Wash the beetroots very well. Set out the chopping board and knives. Trim away any leaves. (If the leaves are very young and fresh they can be added to this salad along with the rocket leaves.) Put any damaged leaves in the compost bucket. **Carefully place the beetroots in the saucepan of boiling water.** Cook for 15 minutes or until the beetroots are tender (test this by slipping in the skewer).

✱ Rinse the rocket leaves (and beetroot leaves, if using), and dry them very gently in the salad spinner. Lay out a dry tea towel and line it with a long piece of kitchen paper. Spread the dried leaves over the paper and roll the whole lot up like a log. Keep the rolled parcel of leaves in the refrigerator until needed.

✱ Set the colander in the sink. **Tip the beetroot and boiling water into the colander.** Slip on the disposable gloves and rub off the beetroot skins, then place the skins in the compost bucket. Cut each beetroot in half and drop the halves into the medium bowl. Discard the gloves.

✱ Peel the red onion and cut it in half lengthways. Place one half flat on the chopping board and slice into fine rings, then add to the bowl with the beetroot. Rinse the chives, dry by rolling in a tea towel, chop finely, then add to the beetroot bowl.

✱ **Carve the skin from each orange.** Holding an orange in one hand, over the beetroot bowl to catch the juice, slip the knife down one side of a single segment and then down the other side of the segment, cutting the flesh away from the membrane. Drop the segment into the bowl and continue until all the segments are in the bowl. Squeeze the juice from the remaining blood orange 'skeleton' in your hand into a small bowl and set aside. Repeat with the remaining oranges.

✱ Place the oil in the second small bowl. Add 2 tablespoons of the reserved blood-orange juice and the balsamic vinegar. Stir to combine, then taste and season with salt and pepper. Pour the dressing over the oranges and beetroots and gently toss to combine.

✱ Place the rocket leaves (and beetroot leaves, if using) on the bottom of the shallow serving bowl, then spoon over the baby beetroot and blood-orange salad and serve immediately.

BOTTOM DRAWER

Interesting terms/techniques • testing with a skewer • making a parcel of leaves • segmenting citrus fruit

Question How are blood oranges different to other oranges?

Answer Thought to have originated in Sicily, blood oranges have more or less ruby-coloured skin and flesh. There are several varieties and some are much more highly coloured than others. The flesh is sweeter than that of other more common orange varieties.

Menu 30

Speedy croutons
for soup or salad

Jerusalem
artichoke soup

Cheese and herb bread
in terracotta pots

Roasted winter
vegetables with
rosemary and garlic

Golden syrup dumplings

Speedy croutons
for soup or salad

Butter thick slices of bread
on both sides. Place a non-
stick frying pan over a
medium-to-high heat and
fry the bread slices until
golden on the underside
(about 3 minutes). Flip the
bread with an egg lifter and
brown the other side.
Transfer the fried bread to
a chopping board and, using
a serrated knife, cut the fried
bread into 1 cm cubes. Place
on a baking tray and keep
warm in an oven preheated
to 120°C until ready to
serve. (For a change, rub
the fried bread lightly with
a peeled and sliced clove of
garlic before cutting the
bread into cubes.)

Jerusalem artichoke soup

Serves 6 at home or 12 tastes in the classroom
Fresh from the garden lemons, Jerusalem artichokes, potatoes, onions, garlic, celery, chives
Despite their name, Jerusalem artichokes do not come from Jerusalem, nor are they related to globe artichokes. They are a root vegetable related to sunflowers.

Equipment

bowls – 1 medium, 1 large	metric measuring cups
lemon juicer	and jug
chopping board	skewer
large knife	ladle
peeler	food processor or blender
colander	coarse strainer
2 tea towels	spatula
large saucepan	6–12 soup bowls
wooden spoon	

Ingredients

1 lemon	1.5 litres Chicken Stock
750 g Jerusalem artichokes	(page 79)
2 medium potatoes	salt
1 large onion	freshly ground black pepper
2 cloves garlic	15 chives
2 sticks celery	⅓ cup cream or sour cream
80 g butter	croutons to serve (page 226)

What to do

✱ Fill the large bowl with water. Juice the lemon and add the lemon juice to the water. Set out the chopping board and knife. Peel the Jerusalem artichokes, cut into walnut-sized chunks, then drop into the bowl of acidulated (lemon) water. Peel the potatoes, cut into chunks, then drop into the bowl of acidulated water.

✱ Peel the onion and cut it in half lengthways, then place the flat sides on the chopping board and slice into rings. Peel and slice the garlic. Slice the celery. Place the onion, garlic and celery in the medium bowl.

✱ Set the colander in the sink. Tip the artichoke and potato into the colander. Wipe out the large bowl and set aside. Place a tea towel on the workbench. Shake the colander to remove excess water, then tip the vegetables onto the tea towel and dry well.

✱ Weigh the butter, then melt in the large saucepan over a high heat. When the butter foams, tip in the onion, garlic and celery. Stir with the wooden spoon to coat the vegetables in melted butter. Add the drained artichoke and potato and stir for 1–2 minutes.

✱ Pour the chicken stock into the saucepan and bring to a simmer. Reduce the heat to low and simmer for about 10 minutes or until all the vegetables are tender when pierced with a fine skewer.

 ✱ **Working in batches, ladle the soup into the bowl of a food processor or the jug of a blender – don't add too much at once.** Process to a smooth purée. Set the coarse strainer over the now-clean large bowl, then tip the soup through the strainer into the bowl. Use the spatula or the wooden spoon to help push the soup through the strainer and to break up any lumps. Repeat this process with the remaining soup. Rinse out the saucepan and put the soup back in.

✱ Reheat the soup over a low-to-medium heat until it reaches a simmering point, stirring in a little water or stock if the soup is too thick. Season to taste with salt and pepper. While the soup is heating, rinse the chives, dry by rolling in a tea towel, then chop finely.

✱ Ladle the soup into bowls, sprinkle each bowl with chives, then top with a dollop of cream or sour cream and croutons.

BOTTOM DRAWER

Interesting terms/techniques • acidulated water • testing with a skewer • working in batches • pushing through a sieve
Safety tip When puréeing hot soup you need to work very carefully. The steam can force the lid to come off the blender, spraying hot soup everywhere. This will make a mess, but, more importantly, the hot liquid could burn you quite badly. Only blend small quantities and place a thick cloth over the blender lid to protect your hand (ask for help the first time you do it).

Cheese and herb bread in terracotta pots

Makes   6 small flowerpot loaves
Fresh from the garden   parsley, chives, eggs

These little breads look wonderful when served in their terracotta pots. If you can't find the right sized pots (usually available from plant nurseries), use little loaf tins or a large-hole muffin tin. To save time, we had the children prepare the dough ahead for the next class.

Equipment

2 tea towels
chopping board
large knife
small plastic container
bowls – 2 small, 1 large
scales
grater
electric mixer with
   dough hook

metric measuring jug
   and spoons
whisk
pastry brush
6 terracotta flowerpots, or
   loaf tins 13 cm × 7 cm ×
   5 cm, or a large-hole
   muffin tin
2 baking trays

Ingredients

20 stalks parsley
20 chives
1 egg
50 g cheddar or mozzarella
50 g fetta
200 g unbleached plain (all-
   purpose) flour, plus extra
   for dusting

50 g wholemeal plain
   (all-purpose) flour
1 teaspoon salt
1 teaspoon instant yeast
1½ tablespoons extra-virgin
   olive oil
150 ml lukewarm water

What to do

✳ Rinse the parsley and chives and dry by rolling in a tea towel. Set out the chopping board and knife, then coarsely chop the herbs.

✳ Set out the plastic container and one of the small bowls. Separate the egg by cracking it, then tipping it into your cupped hand, which should be held over the plastic container. Slightly open your fingers and let the white slip into the container. Place the yolk in the small bowl and set aside. (You won't need the eggwhite, so freeze it for another time. Remember to cover and label the container.)

✳ Weigh the cheddar or mozzarella and grate into the second small bowl. Weigh the fetta, then crumble with your fingers into the bowl.

✳ Put the combined flours into the bowl of the electric mixer with the dough hook attached. Add the salt, chopped herbs and yeast.

✳ Add 2 teaspoons of oil and the lukewarm water to the small bowl with the egg yolk and whisk until lightly combined. With the motor running, tip the water mixture into the flour mixture and knead for about 4 minutes. With the motor still running, tip the cheeses into the bowl and continue kneading until the mixture looks smooth.

✳ Brush the inside of the large bowl and the flowerpots (or tins) with the remaining oil. Tip the dough into the large bowl and cover it with a dry tea towel. Leave the dough in a draught-free place to prove for at least 1 hour or until the dough has doubled in size.

✳ Flour the workbench, then carefully transfer the dough to the bench. Use the knife to cut the dough into 6 even pieces. Roll each piece into a ball, then place one in each of the oiled flowerpots.

✳ Preheat the oven to 220°C. Divide the flowerpots evenly between the 2 baking trays, then cover with the dry tea towel used previously, and leave in a draught-free place to prove for 15 minutes.

✳ Put the baking trays with the flower pots into the hot oven and bake for 15 minutes or until the tops of the loaves are golden.

 ✳ **Remove the baking trays and flower pots from the oven and leave them to cool for 15 minutes.** Serve the breads in the flowerpots.

BOTTOM DRAWER

Interesting terms/techniques   • kneading dough
• proving dough   • separating eggs
Question   Why do we place the flowerpots onto baking trays?

Answer   It is easier (and safer) to lift out the flowerpots when they are on trays, rather than taking out each flowerpot individually.

Roasted winter vegetables with rosemary and garlic

Serves   6 at home or 12 tastes in the classroom
Fresh from the garden   rosemary, garlic, carrots, parsnips, potatoes, onions, celeriac, pumpkin

These roasted vegetables are delicious just as they are, but they are also great when combined with a lamb roast. You could add a seasoned lamb rump roast to each baking tray at the same time as the vegetables. If you like your lamb rosy-pink in the middle, add the meat 15 minutes after the vegetables have started to cook.

Equipment

large bowl	wooden spoon
metric measuring cups	2 large non-stick baking
chopping board	dishes
large knife	egg lifter
peeler	serving plate

Ingredients

5 small stalks rosemary	1 onion
¼ cup extra-virgin olive oil	1 celeriac
3 cloves garlic	350 g pumpkin (250 g after
2 medium carrots	peeling)
2 parsnips	freshly ground black pepper
3 large potatoes	salt

What to do

✳ Preheat the oven to 200°C. Place the rosemary stalks in the large bowl with the oil. Set out the chopping board and knife. Peel the garlic. **Place the cloves on the chopping board and flatten with the side of the large knife.** Put the crushed garlic into the bowl with the rosemary and oil.

✳ As you prepare the following ingredients, add them to the rosemary bowl. Peel the carrots and cut them on an angle into 1 cm slices. Peel the parsnips and cut them on an angle into 1 cm slices. Peel the potatoes, halve them lengthways and cut each half into 4 wedges. Peel the onion, halve it lengthways and cut each half into 3 wedges. Peel the celeriac thickly and cut into 2 cm slices, then cut each slice into 2 cm cubes.

✳ **Peel and seed the pumpkin.** Cut the pumpkin into 2 cm slices, then cut each slice into 2 cm cubes and add to the vegetable bowl. Put all the vegetable scraps into the compost bucket.

✳ Use the wooden spoon or your washed and dried hands to turn all the vegetables, making sure they are all coated with the oil mixture. Season with pepper.

✳ Divide the vegetables evenly between the 2 baking dishes. Transfer to the oven and roast for 20 minutes. **Remove the baking dishes from the oven and use the egg lifter to carefully turn all the vegetables so that they brown and cook evenly.** Return the baking dishes to the oven and roast for another 20 minutes.

✳ **When the vegetables are cooked and golden, remove the baking trays from the oven.** Arrange the vegetables on the serving plate, sprinkle with salt and serve immediately.

BOTTOM DRAWER

Interesting technique   • flattening garlic with a knife
Safety tip   Peeling pumpkin can be quite dangerous because the surface is hard and slippery. Ask an adult to show you how to do it safely.
Question   What other vegetables could be used?
Answer   You could also try roasting wedges of sweet potato, beetroot, Jerusalem artichokes and red peppers, or halved roma tomatoes or halved heads of garlic.

Golden syrup dumplings

Serves   6 at home or 12 tastes in the classroom
Fresh from the garden   lemons, eggs

This old-fashioned recipe has proved popular with a new generation.
The dumplings are poached in the syrup, so it is most important that
the frying pan you select is deep and has a lid – the dumplings swell
to at least double their uncooked size.

Equipment

ovenproof serving dish
lemon juicer
frying pan (at least 4 cm
    deep), with lid
scales
metric measuring jug,
    spoons and cups

wooden spoon
bowls – 3 small, 1 large
whisk
sieve or sifter
dinner plate
slotted spoon
small jug

Ingredients

Syrup
½ lemon
2 cups water
175 g brown sugar
¼ cup golden syrup
2 tablespoons butter

Dumplings
2 tablespoons butter
2 eggs
2½ tablespoons milk
1 tablespoon plain
    (all-purpose) flour
225 g self-raising
    (self-rising) flour
pouring cream to serve

BOTTOM DRAWER

Interesting terms/techniques   • rubbing in butter
• making a well in dry ingredients   • working in batches
Questions   1 What is golden syrup?   2 Why do we keep a lid
on the pan when the dumplings are cooking?

Answer   1 Characterised by its rich golden colour and honey-like
consistency, golden syrup is a by-product of the process where sugar cane
is turned into sugar.   2 The dumplings in this recipe are cooked by
poaching, so the pan needs to be covered with a lid to create the steam
inside the pan.

What to do

✳ Preheat the oven to 120°C. Rub the ovenproof dish with a tiny
piece of butter and place in the oven to keep warm.

✳ To make the syrup, juice the lemon half, then pour the juice into
the frying pan or saucepan. Weigh/measure the water, brown sugar,
golden syrup and butter and add to the pan. Stir with the wooden
spoon over a low heat until the butter has melted and the brown
sugar has completely dissolved. Increase the heat to medium and
bring the syrup to the boil, then immediately remove the pan from
the heat and set aside until needed.

✳ To make the dumplings, place the butter in a small bowl and allow
it to come to room temperature. Meanwhile, place the eggs and milk
in a second small bowl and whisk until well combined. Put the plain
flour into the third small bowl and place on your workbench.

✳ Sift the self-raising flour into the large bowl. Using your fingertips,
rub in the softened butter. Make a well in the centre of the flour
mixture, then tip in the whisked-egg mixture. Use the wooden
spoon to gently stir until all the ingredients are combined.

✳ Dip your fingers into the plain flour in the small bowl (this helps
stop the dough from sticking to your hands). Working in batches,
pull out a walnut-sized piece of dough and use your floured fingers
to roll it into a small dumpling. Place it on the dinner plate, then
repeat the process with the remaining dough.

✳ Place the pan containing the syrup on the stove and bring to a
simmering point, stirring with the wooden spoon to heat it evenly.
Carefully put the dumplings into the simmering syrup, quickly cover
with the lid and cook over a medium heat for 10 minutes without
lifting the lid.

 ✳ Lift the lid to check the dumplings are cooked – they should look
well-risen and fluffy. **Use the slotted spoon to carefully lift the
dumplings out of the syrup and put them in the warm serving
dish. Pour the syrup over the dumplings.**

✳ Serve the dumplings with a jug of pouring cream on the side.

Menu 31

Red and green cabbage coleslaw with warm bacon

Cauliflower fritters with mint yoghurt

White-bean dip with pita bread

Honey cakes

Red and green cabbage coleslaw with warm bacon

Cut 2 or 3 rashers of bacon into strips and cook gently in a non-stick frying pan until crisp. Set aside until ready to serve. Shred a wedge of green crinkly cabbage and a wedge of red cabbage as finely as you can (or grate on a coarse grater), and mix together in a bowl. Make a dressing with 3 parts extra-virgin olive oil, 1 part fresh lemon juice and some chopped parsley, and mix through the cabbage. Season with salt and pepper and, at the last minute, add the warm bacon.

Cauliflower fritters with mint yoghurt

Makes   12 fritters

Fresh from the garden   cauliflower, eggs, mint

Fry the fritters immediately, otherwise the cauliflower will become very wet and the fritters will be less successful.

Equipment

large ovenproof dish	knives – 1 small, 1 large
kitchen paper	grater
frying pans – 1 small,	2 tea towels
1 medium	whisk
metric measuring spoons	baking tray
and cups	tablespoon
wooden spoon	plastic film
mortar and pestle	slotted spoon
bowls – 1 small, 1 large	serving bowl and plate
chopping board	

Ingredients

2 teaspoons cumin seeds	⅓ cup chickpea flour
2 teaspoons coriander seeds	500 g cauliflower
1 teaspoon salt	1 egg
1 teaspoon ground turmeric	½ cup plain yoghurt
1 teaspoon ground ginger	15 mint leaves
½ teaspoon cayenne pepper	¼ cup vegetable oil

What to do

✳ Preheat the oven to 120°C. Line the ovenproof dish with kitchen paper and place it in the oven to keep warm.

✳ Heat the small frying pan over a medium heat. Toast the cumin seeds in the dry pan, stirring with the wooden spoon, until they smell fragrant. Tip the seeds into the mortar. Toast the coriander seeds in the same pan until they smell fragrant. Add these seeds to the mortar. With the pestle, work the spices to a coarse powder. Tip the spice powder into the large bowl. Add the salt, turmeric, ginger, cayenne pepper and chickpea flour.

✳ Set out the chopping board and knives. Using the small knife, cut the cauliflower (including the stem) into big pieces. Grate the pieces using the coarsest hole of the grater. Place a clean tea towel on the workbench, then tip the grated cauliflower into it and squeeze the towel over the sink to extract any excess liquid. Tip the squeezed cauliflower into the large bowl with the spices.

✳ Crack the egg into the small bowl, then whisk and tip into the bowl with the cauliflower. Stir all the ingredients with the wooden spoon until they are well combined.

✳ Using your hands, squeeze the mixture into small balls the size of a walnut – there should be enough mixture to make 12 balls. Place the balls on the baking tray.

✳ Wash and dry the small bowl used for the egg, and put the yoghurt into it. Rinse the mint leaves and dry by rolling in a tea towel. Coarsely chop the mint and add to the yoghurt. Stir using the tablespoon. Cover with plastic film and refrigerate.

✳ Put about 1½ tablespoons of the oil into the medium frying pan and place over a high heat. When the oil is hot, remove the warmed dish from the oven and place it on the stove next to the frying pan.

✳ Working in batches, carefully put half the fritters into the hot oil and fry them, turning them with a slotted spoon, until they are golden brown all over. Don't crowd the pan. Lift out the fritters with the slotted spoon and place them in the warm dish, then return the dish to the oven.

✳ Add the remaining oil to the frying pan and repeat the process with the rest of the fritters. Remove the fritters from the oven and transfer them to the large plate.

✳ Serve the fritters immediately, with the bowl of mint yoghurt.

> **BOTTOM DRAWER**
>
> **Did you know?**   Chickpea flour is sometimes called 'besan flour' in Indian and Middle Eastern shops.

White-bean dip with pita bread

Makes   about 2 cups
Fresh from the garden   garlic, rosemary, lemons

As the beans need to soak overnight, in the classroom we had each class prepare the beans for the class ahead. At home, you will need to start the recipe the day before and allow plenty of time for the beans to cook.

Equipment

scales
bowls – 1 small, 1 large
large sieve
medium saucepan
metric measuring spoons
   and cups
chopping board
large knife

lemon juicer
wooden spoon
ladle
food processor
baking tray
large non-stick frying pan
serving bowl

Ingredients

175 g dried cannellini beans
1 tablespoon tomato paste
2 cloves garlic
1 × 4 cm stalk rosemary
½ lemon
pita bread (1 per person)

¼ cup extra-virgin olive oil
¼ cup Chicken Stock
   (page 79)
salt
freshly ground black pepper

What to do

✱ Weigh the cannellini beans, then place in the large bowl and cover with cold water. Leave to soak overnight.

✱ The next day, set the large sieve in the sink, then tip the cannellini beans and soaking water into the sieve. Rinse the beans with running water, then tip into the medium saucepan. Add enough cold water to cover the beans by 8 cm. Place the saucepan over a high heat and bring to the boil, then reduce the heat to low and simmer for 1 hour.

Add the tomato paste and continue to cook until the beans are completely tender – another 10 minutes or so.

✱ Meanwhile, set out the chopping board and knife. Peel and finely chop the garlic and place in the small bowl. Using your fingers, strip the needles from the rosemary. Finely chop the needles and put in the garlic bowl. Juice the ½ lemon and set aside. Place the scraps in the compost bucket.

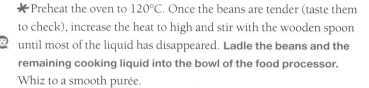 ✱ Preheat the oven to 120°C. Once the beans are tender (taste them to check), increase the heat to high and stir with the wooden spoon until most of the liquid has disappeared. **Ladle the beans and the remaining cooking liquid into the bowl of the food processor.** Whiz to a smooth purée.

✱ Place the pita bread on the baking tray and put in the oven to warm.

✱ Heat 1 tablespoon of the oil in the frying pan over a medium heat, then add the garlic and rosemary and fry for 30 seconds. Carefully tip the bean purée into the frying pan, along with the chicken stock, and stir with the wooden spoon until you have a smooth paste. Stir in the lemon juice and the remaining oil. Taste for salt and pepper.

✱ Remove the warm pita bread from the oven. Spoon the dip into the serving bowl and serve it with the warmed pita bread alongside.

Honey cakes

Makes 15 mini-muffin sized cakes
Fresh from the garden eggs
These little cakes are often baked in special shell-shaped tins and are then known by their French name, madeleines.

Equipment

sieve or sifter

metric measuring spoons
 and cups

medium bowl

scales

small saucepan

wooden spoon

food processor

spatula

2 × 12-hole mini-muffin tins

pastry brush

small strainer

dessertspoon

wire rack

Ingredients

⅔ cup plain (all-purpose)
 flour, plus extra for
 dusting

1 teaspoon baking powder

90 g butter, plus
 2 tablespoons extra for
 greasing

1 tablespoon honey

2 eggs

⅓ cup castor (superfine)
 sugar

1 tablespoon brown sugar

a tiny pinch of salt

1 drop pure vanilla extract

pure icing (confectioners')
 sugar, to serve

What to do

✳ Sift the flour and baking powder together into the medium bowl. Weigh the butter and put the 90 g into the small saucepan along with the honey. Heat over a medium heat until the butter melts, stirring with the wooden spoon to combine. Remove from the heat and set aside.

✳ Break the eggs into the bowl of the food processor, then add the sugars, salt and vanilla extract. Tip in the butter and honey mixture and process to combine. Wash and dry the medium bowl.

✳ Add the flour mixture to the food processor and mix to a smooth batter. Scrape the batter into the medium bowl and leave to rest for 20 minutes.

✳ Meanwhile, preheat the oven to 180°C. Wash and dry the small saucepan and use it to melt the remaining 2 tablespoons of butter over a medium heat. Brush the mini-muffin tins with the melted butter. Place the extra flour in the small strainer and scatter the flour over the muffin tins, then turn the trays upside down and tap sharply to remove excess flour. (This is called dusting.) Spoon the batter evenly into the greased muffin tin, filling each hole about two-thirds full.

✳ Bake for 10 minutes or until the cakes are pale golden and just firm to the touch. **Remove from the oven**. Allow to cool for 1 minute in the tin, then turn the tin upside-down and bang the bottom of the tray to remove the cakes. Transfer the cakes to the wire rack to cool completely.

✳ When the cakes are cool, put a little icing sugar in the sieve, then dust the cakes with icing sugar and serve.

BOTTOM DRAWER

Did you know? Pure vanilla extract is very different from vanilla essence – it is thicker and more syrupy than vanilla essence, which only imitates the taste of true vanilla.

Grated raw vegetable salad

Select firm vegetables that grate well and are good to eat raw, such as beetroots, carrots and celeriac. Peel and grate each vegetable separately. Dissolve a pinch of salt in 1 tablespoon of lemon juice in a medium bowl. Stir in ⅓ cup of extra-virgin olive oil, then toss the vegetables in the dressing. Arrange the vegetables in a shallow bowl and decorate with chopped herbs, including parsley, coriander or mint. This salad would be great in an open pita bread with some freshly made falafel.

Falafel

Makes 20 falafel

Fresh from the garden garlic, parsley, coriander, mint, lemons

Thanks to the multicultural character of Australia, falafel have become a readily available and favourite snack food for people from many different backgrounds. As the chick peas need to soak overnight, in the classroom we had the students prepare the chick peas for classes on the following day.

Equipment

bowls – 3 medium, 1 large	chopping board
colander	large knife
ovenproof dish	grater
kitchen paper	tea towel
frying pans – 1 small, 1 large	tablespoon
	food processor
metric measuring spoons and cups	baking tray
	slotted spoon
wooden spoon	serving plate
mortar and pestle	

Ingredients

225 g chick peas
2 tablespoons cumin seeds
1 tablespoon coriander seeds
¼ red onion
2 cloves garlic
20 stalks parsley
15 stems coriander (cilantro)
20 mint leaves
1 teaspoon baking powder
1 teaspoon salt
freshly ground black pepper
¼ teaspoon cayenne pepper
½ cup vegetable oil
1–2 lemons

What to do

✳ Place the chick peas in the large bowl, cover with cold water and leave to soak overnight.

✳ The next day, set the colander in the sink. Tip the chick peas and soaking water into the colander. Rinse with cold, running water, then drain and give the colander a good shake. Wash and dry the large bowl and return the chick peas to the bowl.

✳ Preheat the oven to 120°C. Line the base of the ovenproof dish with kitchen paper and place in the oven to keep warm. Soak the coriander in a bowl of water.

✳ Heat the small frying pan over a medium heat. Toast the cumin seeds in the dry pan until they smell fragrant. Tip the seeds into the mortar. Toast the coriander seeds in the same pan until they smell fragrant. Add these seeds to the mortar. Using the pestle, work the spices to a coarse powder. Tip the spice powder into the chickpea bowl.

✳ Set out the chopping board and knife. Peel and grate the onion and add to the chick peas. Peel and chop the garlic and add to the chick peas. Rinse the parsley and mint. Lift the coriander from its soaking water. Dry the herbs by rolling in the tea towel, then roughly chop and add to the chick peas. Add the baking powder, salt, pepper and cayenne pepper and stir to mix well.

✳ Working in batches, spoon a little mixture into the bowl of the food processor, then process until the mixture combines and looks bright green with little white flecks – it should not be a paste. Tip each batch into the second medium bowl as it's done.

✳ When all the mixture has been processed, use your hands to form the mixture into little patties, about 4 cm wide, squeezing them very firmly. Place each patty on the baking tray as you make it. You should have 20 falafel. ➤➤

✳ Pour half the oil into the large frying pan. **Heat over a high heat until hot.** Remove the warmed dish from the oven and place it next to the frying pan. **Working in batches, and being mindful not to overcrowd the pan, carefully put some falafel into the hot oil and fry them, turning with the slotted spoon, until they are a deep golden brown all over. Lift out with the slotted spoon and place in the warm dish, then return the dish to the oven. Add the remaining oil to the frying pan and repeat the process with the remaining falafel.**

✳ When all the falafel are cooked, place on the serving plate with some lemon wedges alongside.

Interesting terms/techniques • soaking dried beans • toasting spices • grinding with a mortar and pestle • working in batches

Tip   Falafel (page 236) are great as a filling for open pita breads, along with some salad or sliced tomatoes, cucumbers and lettuce. They are also good with Hummus with Paprika Oil (page 119).

Did you know?   The Egyptian version of falafel (sometimes called *ta'amia*) is made with dried broad beans instead of chick peas.

Potato and leek soup

Serves   6 at home or 12 tastes in the classroom
Fresh from the garden   leeks, potatoes, garlic, onions, celery, thyme, bay leaves, parsley, chives
Leeks are a member of the onion family. Their special sweetness helps make this a wonderful-tasting soup.

Equipment

bowls – 1 small, 2 medium, 1 large
chopping board
large knife
salad spinner
peeler
large saucepan with lid
wooden spoon

metric measuring jug
tea towel
tongs
ladle
food processor or blender
coarse strainer
spatula
6 soup bowls

Ingredients

1 large leek
2 large potatoes
2 cloves garlic
1 small onion
1 stick celery
2 tablespoons butter
1 sprig thyme

1 bay leaf
1.5 litres water
12 stalks parsley
8 chives
salt
freshly ground black pepper

What to do

✳ Half fill one medium bowl with cold water. Set out the chopping board and knife. Trim off the base and most of the dark-green part of the leek and place in the compost bucket. Cut the rest into fine rings and place in the bowl of water. Swish with your fingers to release any dirt. Lift the leek into the salad spinner and spin gently. Wash and dry the medium bowl and return the leek to the bowl.

✳ Half fill the second medium bowl with water. Peel the potatoes, cut into 1 cm cubes and drop into the bowl of water.

✳ Peel and slice the garlic and onion and add to the leek bowl. Slice the celery and add to the leek bowl. Tip the potato and water into the colander, then shake the colander to drain well.

✳ Melt the butter in the saucepan over a medium-to-high heat. When the butter sizzles, tip in the leek, garlic, onion, celery and potato. Stir with the wooden spoon to combine, then reduce the heat to low, cover with the lid and cook for 5 minutes or until the leek starts to soften. Remove the lid and add the thyme and bay leaf. Pour in enough of the water to cover the vegetables. Bring to the boil over a high heat, then cook with the lid ajar for 20 minutes or until all vegetables are very soft.

✳ Meanwhile, rinse the parsley and chives and dry by rolling in the tea towel. Chop the herbs, then put into the small bowl and set aside.

 ✳ Turn off the heat under the soup. **Using the tongs, remove and discard the thyme and bay leaf. Working in batches, ladle the soup into the bowl of a food processor or the jug of a blender – don't add too much at once.** Process to a smooth purée. Set the coarse strainer over the large bowl, then tip the soup through the strainer into the bowl. Use the spatula or the wooden spoon to push the soup through the strainer and to break up any lumps. Repeat this process with the remaining soup. When all the soup has been puréed and strained, rinse out the saucepan and return the soup to the saucepan.

✳ Reheat the soup over a low-to-medium heat until it reaches a simmering point. Season to taste with salt and pepper. Ladle the hot soup into the serving bowls, then sprinkle a pinch of chopped herbs in each bowl and serve immediately.

BOTTOM DRAWER

Interesting terms/techniques   • puréeing
• straining through a sieve   • working in batches
Safety tip   When puréeing hot soup you need to work very carefully. The steam can force the lid to come off the blender, spraying hot soup everywhere. This will make a mess, but, more importantly, the hot liquid could burn you quite badly. Only blend small quantities and place a thick cloth over the blender lid to protect your hand (ask for help the first time you do it).

Orange and cardamom cakes with cream cheese icing

Makes 10

Fresh from the garden oranges, eggs

The grated orange zest gives a lovely flavour to these little cakes.

Equipment

scales

metric measuring spoons
  and cups

small saucepan

pastry brush

10 cupcake cases (optional)

1 × 12-hole muffin tin

scissors

chopping board

large knife

food processor

lemon juicer

bowls – 2 medium, 1 large

grater

whisk

sieve or sifter

2 dessertspoons

skewer

wire rack

spatula

serving plate

Ingredients

125 g butter

¾ cup castor (superfine)
  sugar

2 large oranges

2 eggs

125 g self-raising (self-
  rising) flour

2 teaspoons ground
  cardamom

Cream cheese icing

60 g pure icing
  (confectioners') sugar

60 g cream cheese

30 g butter

What to do

✳ Preheat the oven to 190°C. If using cupcake cases, drop one into each of the holes in the muffin tin. Otherwise, weigh the butter, then melt 1 tablespoon in the small saucepan and use the pastry brush to grease the holes of the muffin tin.

✳ Set out the chopping board and knife. Cut the remainder of the butter into small cubes and place in the bowl of the food processor. Add the sugar and run the motor for 1 minute.

✳ Juice the oranges and place the juice in a medium bowl. Grate the zest from the oranges and add the zest to the bowl. Crack the eggs into the same bowl, then lightly whisk to combine. Sift the flour and ground cardamom into the second medium bowl.

✳ With the food processor running, and working quickly, add about one-third of the egg and juice mixture, then add about one-third of the sifted flour. Immediately add another one-third of the egg mixture and another one-third of the flour, then the remaining egg mixture and flour and process until smooth and creamy.

✳ Spoon the batter evenly into 10 holes of the greased muffin tin, filling each hole about two-thirds full. Bake for 15 minutes or until cooked. **To test the cakes, remove from the oven and insert a skewer.** If the skewer comes out clean, the cakes are done.

✳ While the cakes are cooking, make the icing. Wash and dry the bowl of the food processor and place the sieve over the top. Tip the icing sugar into the sieve and use a spoon to push the icing sugar through. Cut the cream cheese into small cubes, then tip into the food processor, along with the butter, and process until smooth and creamy.

 ✳ **Remove the cakes from the oven.** Allow them to cool for 1 minute in the tin, then turn the tin upside-down and bang the bottom of the tray to release the cakes. Place right side up on the wire rack to cool completely. When the cakes are cool, use the spatula to spread a little icing on top of each cake and serve.

Acknowledgements

This book is dedicated to the students of Collingwood College.

The successful creation of the Kitchen Garden at Collingwood College has been due to the combined efforts of numerous extraordinary people, many of whom are introduced in the text. As well as acknowledging individuals, it is important to record that the Kitchen Garden exists because of the support that both it and, in more recent times, the Stephanie Alexander Kitchen Garden Foundation has had from government bodies, generous philanthropists and corporate supporters. For a full list of sponsors, benefactors and friends, go to the Kitchen Garden Foundation website (see below).

Many people involved in the program have contributed to this book. We thank Peta Christensen, Liz Moore and Heidi Sanghvi for practical garden material and Peta Heine for assistance with recipe organisation. We also thank Collingwood College staff, who handed on written and anecdotal material collected from the students. We thank the volunteers who have turned up, rain or shine, to work with eager students in both the garden and kitchen.

Our visionary publisher and friend Julie Gibbs offered us the opportunity to tell our story and we are truly grateful. We extend our thanks to those at Penguin who have worked to make this ground-breaking project the beautiful book it is. Editor Ingrid Ohlsson has dealt incredibly calmly with a mix of prose and practical information that posed many editorial challenges, supported by the expert eye and organisational skills of Susan McLeish, as well as Fay Donlevy (indexing), Kathleen Gandy (additional editing) and Anouska Jones (proofreading). Tony Palmer gave us a design that is both beautiful and easy for children to use. Simon Griffiths' food photography is delicious and accessible and very true to the food prepared every week in the Kitchen Garden class-room, while his photographs of the kitchen and garden at Collingwood have captured the essence of the program, as have the photographs supplied by Karen Yann, Peta Christensen, Liz Moore and Kirsty Argyle.

We would also like to thank Zoi Condos of Sweet Source in Carlton, Desley's Mum and Antonio Carluccio for allowing us to reproduce their recipes.

Selected contacts

Stephanie Alexander Kitchen Garden Foundation
In response to the overwhelming interest shown by other schools in the Collingwood College pilot project, the Stephanie Alexander Kitchen Garden Foundation Limited was incorporated in early 2004, with a charter to investigate ways of setting up similar programs in other Australian schools. We are a charitable organisation that relies totally on the generosity, shared vision and commitment of schools, foundations, government, business and individuals. Donations are fully tax deductible and can be made online via our website.

Garden shed
Several schools have expressed interest in the garden shed. Contact architect Freda Thornton for design specifications and a materials list.

Garden teachers
The garden teachers in the Kitchen Garden program came from Cultivating Community, a not-for-profit community-based organisation that works on a variety of urban agriculture and community gardening projects in Melbourne. Consisting of both volunteers and paid workers, the group is playing a major role networking schools with edible gardens at a national level, and through the organisation of an annual conference. For details of projects in other states, contact Cultivating Community (see below).

Contact details

Stephanie Alexander Kitchen Garden Foundation
PO Box 104, Abbotsford, Vic 3067; (03) 8415 1993
info@kitchengardenfoundation.org.au
www.kitchengardenfoundation.org.au

Simon & Freda Thornton Architects
(03) 9489 8082
emailsimonthornton@smartchat.net.au

Cultivating Community
(03) 9415 6580
info@cultivatingcommunity.org.au
www.cultivatingcommunity.org.au

General index

Recipe index